Pop Music, Culture and Identity

Series Editors

Steve Clark
Graduate School Humanities and Sociology
University of Tokyo
Bunkyo-ku, TokyoJapan

Tristanne Connolly
Department of English
St. Jerome's University
Waterloo, OntarioCanada

Jason Whittaker
School of English & Journalism
University of Lincoln
Lincoln, LincolnshireUK

Aims of the Series

Pop music lasts. A form all too often assumed to be transient, commercial and mass-cultural has proved itself durable, tenacious and continually evolving. As such, it has become a crucial component in defining various forms of identity (individual and collective) as influenced by nation, class, gender and historical period. Pop Music, Culture and Identity investigates how this enhanced status shapes the iconography of celebrity, provides an ever-expanding archive for generational memory and accelerates the impact of new technologies on performing, packaging and global marketing. The series gives particular emphasis to interdisciplinary approaches that go beyond musicology and seeks to validate the informed testimony of the fan alongside academic methodologies.

More information about this series at
http://www.springer.com/series/14537

Rosemary Lucy Hill

Gender, Metal and the Media

Women Fans and the Gendered Experience of Music

palgrave
macmillan

Rosemary Lucy Hill
School of Sociology and Social Policy
University of Leeds
Leeds, UK

Pop Music, Culture and Identity
ISBN 978-1-137-55440-6   ISBN 978-1-137-55441-3   (eBook)
DOI 10.1057/978-1-137-55441-3

Library of Congress Control Number: 2016958134

Cover image © Old Visuals / Alamy Stock Photo
Cover design by Jenny Vong

Printed on acid-free paper

This Palgrave Macmillan imprint is published by Springer Nature
The registered company is Macmillan Publishers Ltd. London
The registered company is: The Campus, 4 Crinan Street, London, N1 9XW, United Kingdom

ACKNOWLEDGEMENTS

This book has been ten years in the researching and writing, and many people have supported me over that time. Special thanks go to my partner, Oliver Gardiner, and to my family, without whose care, encouragement and financial assistance this book would never have been possible. Special thanks to Ann Kaloski-Naylor, who supervised the research and whose love and dedication to feminist scholarship inspired me to write a much better book than I thought possible. And thanks to Stevi Jackson, Gabriele Griffin, Harriet Badger and everyone present at the Centre for Women's Studies during the time I was based there. Thanks to numerous fellow scholars, including colleagues at the University of Leeds and members of the International Society for the Study of Metal Music, who have commented on drafts and improved my understanding of how the experience of music is gendered.

Finally, an almighty thank you all to the wonderful women who spoke to me about their love of music and enabled the research and this book to be possible.

CONTENTS

LIST OF FIGURES

CHAPTER 1

Gender, Metal and the Media: An Introduction

Music is a gendered experience. Rock is assumed to be transcendent of the everyday world, with universal, timeless themes that appeal to everyone (Kruse 2002). Yet, even as rock critics have peddled this myth, they have underpinned their ideology with the sexist claim that women are incapable of understanding the music as an art form. In this context, what 'universal' actually means is 'relevant to men'. However, understandings of how people engage with rock music are implicitly gendered. As Green (1997) and Kruse (2002) make clear, music does not exist outside of the social: it is shaped by our lived experiences and heard in our social contexts. Gender is a crucial part of that shaping, yet gender is typically only seen as relevant to women; men's experiences are seen as general and universal (Wittig 1992). These sexist beliefs mean that understandings of musical engagement are skewed towards men's experiences, with women's added in for a bit of spice in order to cover the 'gender aspect'. This book takes the position that *all* musical experiences are shaped by gender and that the differing social positions of women and men greatly determine those experiences. Sexism creates different climates for men and women in which they seek to enjoy music. And it is a crucial factor in both women's and men's participation in hard rock and metal culture.

Hard rock and metal looks masculine. It is full of glaring, massive, warrior-like men in black. Metal songs are about war, gore and rape. Women are sidelined in this male-dominated and hypermasculine genre. Rarely performing as musicians, they appear in music videos, song lyrics

© The Editor(s) (if applicable) and The Author(s) 2016
R.L. Hill, *Gender, Metal and the Media*, Pop Music, Culture and Identity, DOI 10.1057/978-1-137-55441-3_1

and popular representations as groupies, girlfriends and gorgons. Here's Seb Hunter describing the metal attitude towards women:

> Ask a male Heavy Metal fan if he believes there's a place within its walls for women, and more often than not he'll scrunch up his face and reply, "Yes. On her knees with my cock in her mouth". (Hunter 2004, 238)

Hunter is describing a particular version of metal (late 80's/early 90's glam) and his interpretation of that scene (though not necessarily his own views). However, academic research in media, sociology and cultural studies has come to roughly the same conclusion. Metal uses women to create a fantasy world for men (Walser 1993) and uses violently misogynistic imagery in artwork and lyrics (Kahn-Harris 2007; Overell 2010; Vasan 2011; Griffin 2012). Amongst this sexism and the ubiquitously male band line-ups there would seem to be no place for women in the genre.

But, even if extremely underrepresented amongst musicians, women do participate in hard rock and metal, predominantly as fans: around one-third of metal fans are estimated to be women (Purcell 2003). Recent research shows that their experiences are different to those of men in the genre. They are subject to a barrage of questions from male fans to prove the authenticity of their fandom (Nordström and Herz 2013), sidelined by male fans at rock and metal events (Kahn-Harris 2007) and feel they must tolerate male metal fans' sexist attitudes towards their femininity; some choose to wear masculine dress rather than allowing themselves to appear sexually available (Vasan 2010, 2011).

Why then, would women choose to be involved in hard rock and metal?

This paradoxical conundrum has personal import for me: I love hard rock and metal, but I am also a feminist. How can I square these two important parts of my identity? What role is there for me in metal, as a fan, as an aspiring musician, as a woman committed to bettering the lives of women?

Growing up, my brother and I were rock fans, but it seemed easier for him. His friends shared his taste in music, he never had to qualify whether he *really* liked Metallica, and he never felt excluded by the rock magazines we read. Those magazines rarely felt as if they were speaking to me: women existed outside the pages of the magazines as punchlines of jokes that aimed to unify the audience as heterosexual, male readers engaged in a battle of the sexes. They assumed that women either did not like the music or were involved in the culture because they were attracted to the musicians. I felt this injustice deeply and worked hard to represent my fandom as one that was as good as any male fan's. I spoke of my fandom in terms of the music itself, and although I felt attracted to some of the musicians, I denied having these feelings. And then I saw that the way to *really* show that I was an authentic fan was to become a rock musician, which I did. Becoming a musician meant stepping out of the role of fan, and that also felt like I was leaving my femininity behind. However, in practice, aiming for the higher-status role of musician meant that my femininity was not forgotten. Instead, I had to work even harder to diminish any girlishness and to be 'one of the guys'. At least I was not a groupie, I thought to myself.

For me, growing up also meant growing feminist sensibilities. And there rock was a stumbling block, for much of the music I loved was made by men—women were conspicuously absent—and many of the singers sang unpleasant things about women. How could I accept this? Was it, as Norma Coates wonders, 'false consciousness' (Coates 1997, 51)? No, it was not as simple as that. I loved the music, and I could not entirely hear my own subjugation in it. Summing up and dismissing the genre as misogynist left out the way in which the music made me feel powerful. In fact, like Ellen Willis (2014), I felt that the music gave me strength to *fight* sexism when I encountered it. How could this understanding of rock 'n' roll be reconciled with assessments that see it as sexist? And didn't these perspectives reduce all rock music to a single monolithic sound and fail to consider the differences between bands' attitudes and politics, their images, their lyrics and music?

These questions, which have not been asked before by metal scholars, are crucially important in understanding how male dominance is reproduced in music cultures and the media's role in this. It is also vital for understanding how musical experience is never not gendered; in fact, the way we experience music through the media, through our social and public interactions and through our private listenings is shaped by gendered expectations, assumptions and roles. Although not all of our experiences are gendered all of the time (and music can sometimes give women spaces in which to temporarily forget gender), the overall experience of hard rock and metal is different for women and men.

In this book I ask these questions to come to grips with the conundrum of what hard rock and metal means for women fans—its sexisms and contradictions, its pleasures and ambiguities, its highs and its lows. I rise to Sue Wise's (1984) challenge for feminist music scholars. Wise describes her experience of loving Elvis. For her, he was a friend, a teddy bear, rather than the macho god of the mainstream (patriarchal) media. But feminist readings of Elvis took on this image of The King as a macho, sexist god, and this reading made no sense to her—it contradicted her own experience. Wise's challenge is that feminists need to both contest male knowledge about rock music and examine how feminist orthodoxy has taken on male knowledges without rethinking them. This challenge opens up new areas for reinterpreting music, fandom and the media. Addressing these areas brings new light to a dark corner in which female fans of hard rock and metal have been dismissed, having been accused of being cahoots with patriarchy. Furthermore, knowledge about rock music has been left in the hands of male writers who are both invested in retaining the status quo and unaware that being a fan is different for women.

Here are some of the assumptions about women and hard rock and metal that were reinforced at the 2009 Heavy Metal and Gender International Congress in Cologne:

1. if women are not involved in making hard rock and metal music as musicians it is because they choose not to be, rather than that there are structural problems hindering them;
2. metal is asexual because men are involved for the sake of the music, not to meet women—this ignores that metal masculinity can be attractive for some fans, men and women alike. Women and men as desiring subjects are excluded from the discussion;
3. metal is inclusive, and so women can be participants as long as they love the music, are prepared to wear the uniform (jeans, black T-shirt), refrain from desiring metal men, and adopt the same value system. In real terms this sounds very much like an assertion that women can participate in metal as long as they are prepared to be more like men.

These orthodoxies are congratulatory of the genre's open and inclusive attitude—an attitude also prevalent in non-academic discourse about hard rock and metal—even as they reinforce heterosexual masculinity as the norm. Moreover, anyone looking at hard rock and metal magazines and festival line-ups can see that the genre's musicians are nearly all white men; the genre is obviously not inclusive. It may offer strength and a sense of community to those who feel excluded from more mainstream groups, but the rules of hard rock and metal are inflexible. It remains an exclusive 'club', and the rules are written by white, straight men. It precludes the involvement of women, homosexual men and black people.

Increasingly, attention is being paid to women's experiences, and questions about metal's Western whiteness are beginning to be asked. Exciting work is being done on race and gender (e.g., Lucas et al. 2011; Dawes 2012; Spracklen 2015), queerness (Clifford-Napoleone 2015b), masculinities (Overell 2010, 2012; Kartheus 2015) and women's experiences (Vasan 2011; Riches 2011, 2014, 2015; Nordström and Herz 2013) in the hard rock and metal context. The music media remains one area that needs further investigation (but see Brill 2008; Spracklen 2010; Hagen 2014). The media have a part to play in creating a sense of metal community and in reproducing the community's gendered notions which exclude women from full participation (Hill 2014a). Furthermore, the music media's representation of women fans as groupies—adoring and defending of, and ever-available to musicians—is not only a misrepresentation (because most women fans are not groupies), it is damaging. For women it deprives them of role models in their musical aspirations, and it limits the ability to express their fandom. It also places them in danger of sexual exploitation. Understanding how women feel about and reflect upon this representation, and how they negotiate its impact, is therefore vitally important.

One important question to ask is, what is so wrong with being attracted to musicians anyway? Kant's (2010 [1790]) emphasis on disinterestedness as a crucial element of the aesthetic experience of beauty underpins dominant values in hard rock and metal culture, as it does in all rock's claims to be 'art' (Regev 1994). Kant's theory has been critiqued as blind to socially learned responses to culture and reifying of a particular middle and upper class experience (Bourdieu 2010). It is also dismissive of sexual and somatic responses. The diminution of this sort of musical appreciation results in a smaller and less nuanced understanding of our fandoms. Susan Fast's (1999) work on Led Zeppelin is informative on this point. Just as Wise counters typical understandings of Elvis by reflecting on her feelings about The King, so Fast challenges most readings of Led Zeppelin. She examines her own passion for their music alongside a large number of survey responses from fans, close readings of the band's visual imagery, and analysis of the music in order to parry journalistic accounts, and Frith and McRobbie's (1990 [1978]) conceptualisation of the band as 'simply' masculine. The conclusions Fast draws are staggering because they complicate notions of what the band and their music mean for the fans. She problematises those ideas about listening and musical engagement that are narrowly defined by gender. Rather than challenging suggestions that women fans do not pay serious attention to the music, Fast engages closely with the different kinds of relationships that women and men fans have with the object of their fandom. It signals that there is something wrong with the model of 'real' fans as *only* interested in the music. That model is based on an idea of what it means to be a music lover that is embedded in the mind/body, rational/emotional, man/woman dichotomies. It ignores other kinds of experience of women's fandom, such as the sensual and erotic—but these are crucial elements of music fandom.

My key argument in this book is that gender and sexism shape our engagements with music and that hard rock and metal is not just for men. The musical genre and its culture have much to offer fans and is much more diverse than it is has been characterised. To assume that it only appeals to men is to rely upon narrow definitions of what it means to be feminine or masculine, to be a woman or a man. This assumption plays into the undervaluing of women's fandom—reducing women fans to heterosexually desiring bodies whose cultural interests are unsophisticated and unimportant (Radway 1984; Baym 1999). This is exactly how women fans are characterised in the hard rock and metal media, and this presents a significant barrier to women's musical aspirations. The assumption that hard rock and metal is only for men also ignores the different ways in which people make meaning in the media they encounter—this means men as well as women. Drawing on Stuart Hall's work on how we engage with the media (1973) and the impact of representations (1997), I argue that women fans carefully negotiate the representation of women fans that they encounter in the media in order to forge their own identities as metal fans. And they choose music and listen in ways that enable them to 'flourish' (Hesmondhalgh 2013) without feeling oppressed by 'repressive representations' (Whiteley 2000) in the music. Note that whilst much of the writing about hard rock and metal concentrates on the public aspects of music fandom (attending concerts and festivals, for instance), in this book I am much more interested in private experiences of fandom: listening to music at home, in the car, on headphones and so on.

Gender

Gender is a complex term with a range of different uses, some that are very politically loaded and some that are less so, or are perceived to be neutral. But the use of the term 'gender' is never truly neutral. Even in a simple survey to determine shopping habits, the use of 'gender' has profound implications both for those completing the questionnaire and those using the data. 'Gender' on the questionnaire is used to divide the respondents, to group them and to market to them as a distinct group. Gender therefore makes a division and has an impact on how we see ourselves, how we are perceived by others, the institutional and structural boundaries placed upon us, and how we are able to live our lives. In this study, gender is an important concept which is used to understand what the impact of these kinds of division are. In this book, 'gender' refers to the socially constructed distinction between the groups 'women' and 'men'—gender as a concept, the idea of the divide itself. When I refer to gendered experiences I mean experiences that are shaped by the belief in the differences between women and men. I am not examining gender performances, as a Butlerian approach might; rather, I am interested in how gender works to structure our social lives and to naturalise hierarchy between apparently distinct groups ('women', 'men'). This definition of gender—as a division rather than as two distinct things (feminine and masculine)—is drawn from the work of Christine Delphy (1993), amongst others, and is fundamental to the book. Therefore, it requires a bit more explanation.

Feminists such as Ann Oakley (1972) have conclusively shown that the relationship between biological sex (whether one is female or male) and gender, as its social expression (whether one is feminine or masculine), is not natural. Gendered traits do not automatically follow from sex traits; rather, they are learned or culturally ascribed and are 'independent of sex' (Delphy 1993, 3). But because the relationship between sex and its social expression has been overstated, traits which are thought to mark differences between women and men have also been exaggerated and confused. Biologists have shown that sex is defined by several indicators—there is no single indicator, which would be needed for a binary distinction—and most of these are variable, that is, not found only in one sex or the other. In spite of this, for the most part people are still represented in ways that say they are distinctly in one group or the other; sex is believed to be an undeniable fact. Delphy points out, though, that because sex is variable and has several indicators, deciding which aspects specify sex—and how much of that aspect—is a social act. For example, the distinction between those who can bear children and those who cannot does not divide humans into two clear groups (there are many more people who cannot bear children than there are men: age, infirmity, fertility all play a role). The most logical way to understand the foundation of the difference between men and women is therefore as a social division, one created by people in order to create a division and hierarchy. Sex is consequently socially determined and acts as a sign, a marker of a social division which creates two groups. 'Sex' is therefore a social rather than biological category. Thus 'women' is a social group, with no biological basis (as is 'men'). Similarly, Butler (1993) argues (perhaps more famously) that sex is socially determined rather than biologically given. Where for Butler sex comes into being only through its continual performance, for Delphy gender is a construct that functions to ensure hierarchy. The emphasis is placed on social structure and it is political. I find Delphy's 'gender' more convincing because it is inextricably linked with the oppression of women and therefore allows structural inequalities to be addressed (Jackson 1998). She argues that the division created by gender is only reproduced in order to repeat the division. Imagining a world without gender is therefore a key role of feminism. In this, feminism shares something with metal: imagining the future world in different ways is a recurrent theme in the genre. But perhaps that's where the similarity ends.

It is this version of gender that underpins the book, one which does not believe in essential differences between women and men. The differences that I discuss are socially constructed, taught to us or shaped by our experiences as we perceive ourselves and are perceived to be different from the other group. Therefore, the differences in the media's representations of women and of men that I discuss in Chapter 3 are fundamentally problematic. They serve to reproduce gender and, because gender is designed to create and support hierarchy, they thereby create, support and maintain men's dominance over women: women and men are not different-but-equal.

I argue in Chapter 4 that women's erotic and sexual responses are important kinds of musical engagement—as are men's. That is not to assert that particular bodies produce particular sexual responses (that is, sexuality does not follow from biology). I do not here explore sexuality in detail, but I do draw on the ideas of Jackson and Scott (2010) whose work on sexuality takes it not as a presocial fact, but rather explores its social function and social expression. For further reading on metal and sexuality see Fast (1999) and Clifford-Napoleone (2015b).

EXPERIENCE

The women I spoke to when researching this book self-identified as women. Considering women's experiences is a feminist method that, in this case, uses the Marxist theory of the 'view from below', allowing different standpoints to draw attention to the ways in which oppressive ideas are normalised. For Nancy Hartsock this means employing a specifically feminist standpoint in order to 'understand patriarchal institutions and ideologies as perverse inversions of more humane social relations' (1983, 284). However, the category of experience is problematic and it is crucial to ask, whose experience counts (hooks 1984)? There is a risk of collapsing women into a unified category, eliding differences between women (not least those of race, sexuality and class) (Scott 2008). Plus, not all women are feminists, and so examining women's experiences does not necessarily offer a direct route to critiques of patriarchy. Acknowledging different standpoints is therefore essential for valuing women's experiences and challenging knowledge about women (Hill Collins 1990; Smith 2008). Marginalised groups—such as women in hard rock and metal culture—can bring new perspectives to institutions and structures that affect social lives and that are taken for granted. For this reason, experience remains an important concept with which to examine orthodoxies about hard rock, metal and women fans. It is a useful tool with which to assess theory that claims to be universal (Stanley and Wise 1993). Wise's use of her own experience as an Elvis fan is a case in point, as it enables her to challenge dominant *and* feminist constructions of rock music.

In this book I use 'experience' to refer to the way in which the women I interviewed described to me things that happened in their lives. In relating what had happened to them and reflecting upon those incidents, the incidents became experiences—things that had happened that were then theorised from each particular woman's viewpoint. Experiences are therefore shaped by our gendered, classed and raced positions, as well as other positions. The experiences were also mediated by memory, emotions, later incidents and by the context of the telling. As Liz Stanley argues, we make sense of ourselves and incidents in our past, putting together events and using 'fictive devices' (1992, 62) to construct a necessarily partial self tied together by limited memory. Events, emotions and people are 'linked only in such accounts and not in life as it was lived' (1992, 62). Not all of the women's experiences are constructed via memories; some women used hypothetical situations to discuss their fandom, which were imaginative fictions drawing on their experiences and their knowledge about hard rock and metal bands and culture. In the process of making sense of their experiences, imagination played an important role in my interviewees' answers. Of course, the use of fictive devices and imagination in reconstructing events and experiences 'does not mean that the past and its mythologies are not "real"' (Stanley 1992, 86). The way in which the selves are imagined and the experiences put together is a real process, and the experiences the women related, rethought, reconstructed and reimagined have real meaning in the world.

I spoke to 19 women living in cities in England during 2008–2011. All were white and but one were British (she was Finnish). The whiteness of my sample was not a conscious decision, although it is regrettable, but came about through the snowballing method: I was introduced to white women or white women responded to my advert. It is generally accepted by British metal scholars that visible fans of metal in Britain are predominantly white, although little work has been done to ascertain this. It must be assumed that the conclusion has been reached from metal scholars' observations at concerts and festivals. It should be noted that in other parts of the world metal fandom is not the preserve of white people: hard rock and metal has appeal around the globe (Wallach et al. 2011). Whiteness in my interviewees' responses is an invisible, unacknowledged privilege, and none mentioned issues of race and fandom. This is distinct from Dawes' (2012) work in which race is a vital analytical category and one which is discussed at length by interviewees. Notably her participants are in the main black; this distinction highlights the assumption that whiteness is the norm, or is even perceived as an essential quality of metal in the UK. Metal and race remains an area that is in need of greater attention.

Participants' ages ranged from 19 to 69, clustering around late 20s and early 30s. Therefore, this study takes into account the viewpoints of young women, older women and those in between. This is not research across the life course, and I reflect upon interviewees' ages only where it is salient to the analysis. It also marks a difference between much published work on hard rock and metal fans, which looks at the experiences of young people. However, hard rock and metal is not just young men's music. It is genre which holds onto fans into adulthood and old age. The prospect of old people's homes for aged metallers is therefore not just a joke made by one of my interviewees: it has a distinct possibility of becoming reality.

My interviewees described themselves as working or middle class. Class is a controversial area in metal studies. Weinstein argues that it is a working class genre (Weinstein 2000 [1991]), and others have suggested that whatever the class make-up of the genres' bands and fans in the post-2000s, it remains symbolically working class (Brown 2009; Riches 2011). Conversely, it has been argued that for all its working-class roots, in many ways metal is a very middle class genre. Drawing on Walser's argument of the necessity of high musical standards in metal (Walser 1993), I argue that to be a successful musician requires significant musical training and equipment, and the kinds of intense practice and musicianship that are required for classical music. This suggests access to funds that are more likely to be available in middle class families. Published discussions of metal and class have drawn on the known class backgrounds of the musicians, but there is little quantitative data on the class backgrounds of fans. In her study of the death metal subculture, Purcell found that 'the majority of respondents were middle class' (Purcell 2003, 108), but her respondents were a mixture of fans and musicians (and fan-musicians). There is then, no published evidence of the class make-up of fans, and no consensus amongst metal scholars either. There is therefore no reason to assume a working class audience for the genre in the UK, and my data bears this out. Those interviewees who declared a class identity were fairly evenly split; four described themselves as working class and five middle class. Others described their identity in more ambiguous terms that reflected upon their family backgrounds and their childhoods, as well as weighing up their current circumstances. Four described themselves as working/middle class and one claimed the identity of 'ex-working class'. One interviewee said she did not know her class, another that she had none, and three did not answer the question. No interviewees claimed an upper- or under-class identity.

My interviewees had various occupations. Eight were professionals (teacher, lecturer, charity manager, laboratory manager, bank mediator, accountant and market analyst); four were students (three undergraduates, one MA); two were unemployed having just completed their studies (one GCSEs, one PhD); three were administrators; one worked in the service industry; one was retired. From this can be seen that generally there was a high level of education amongst my interviewees. Sally, who managed a domestic abuse charity, was in the process of completing her third degree! In some ways this high level of education and the number of professional occupations is symptomatic of the snowballing method of introductions to interviewees, but if this is a trend more general it is suggestive of hard rock and metal as appealing to listeners with higher educations. More information about my interviewees is available in the Appendix.

METAL

I delineate the genre of hard rock and metal very roughly by emphasising those bands who feature in *Kerrang!* magazine. This definition will not suit all readers, but *Kerrang!* with its solid history and reputation as a key publication for the genre is a useful benchmark. The magazine was first published in 1981 as a platform for the new heavy metal bands that were then being excluded from other rock magazines. It was at one time considered the 'headbanger's Bible' (Brown 2007, 644) and, despite recent challenges to its reputation, it retains its status as a key part of the metal media. Over the years since *Kerrang!*'s was first publicised, the music of heavy metal has split into numerous subgenres, so that what 'counts' as metal has changed. Punk influences have led to the inclusion of political and emotional themes, while pop influences make for more light-hearted, melody-driven music. Other subgenres have developed, such as death and black metal, which have a denser and more intense soundscape with harsh, bestial vocals. *Kerrang!* gives column inches to bands from across this spectrum, but its inclusion of more melodic subgenres like emo and pop punk has led to questioning of its original undisputed status as the magazine of heavy metal. Therefore, focussing on bands who appear in the magazine is not a straightforward measure of the hard rock and metal genre. Metal's boundaries are frequently squabbled over by fans, and the status of bands and magazines hotly disputed. These disputes signify that there are no clear borders, and the arguments are in themselves an integral feature of the genre. I do not enter into genre arguments, but within the debate there is much at stake: gendered, raced, classed, religious and national aspects need careful consideration, some of which I have discussed elsewhere (Hill 2011). *Kerrang!* offers a good practical solution to the difficult matter of defining the boundaries of the hard rock and metal genre. In seeking participants for interviews I asked for women who either self-defined as metal fans or liked bands featured in *Kerrang!*. In using *Kerrang!* in this way I acknowledge that the magazine presents a particular viewpoint of what hard rock and metal is, who its fans and musicians are, and the values and traditions of the culture are. These concepts have gendered notions embedded within that bear examination, which I address in Chapter 3.

My purpose is to explore how fans relate to their favourite music across the hard rock and metal genre, to elicit stories of passionate engagement from a range of subgenres. Typically in studies of metal fans, research has focussed on particular subgenres in order to make generalisations. However, all of my interviewees liked bands from a range of subgenres and described the feeling of, on occasion, needing to supress some of these preferences in order to fit in. Aime, for example, minimised her affection for My Chemical Romance when in the company of her newer friends who preferred Avenged Sevenfold, a heavier band. The broad genre-umbrella of hard rock and metal brings together people with common ideas about music, and this is more apparent when looking at the broad genre than only looking at fans of specific subgenres. In particular, the assertion that hard rock and metal music is different to (and better than) pop music was common amongst my interviewees, no matter which subgenre they preferred. This is not to deny the differences between subgenres, but rather to address the fact that whilst there is research on particular subgenres there are no contemporary studies of the broad genre. *Kerrang!* itself covers artists across subgenres and caters for fans of this broad community, even if its coverage is not even or equally extensive.

The women I spoke to liked music from the following genres: progressive rock, post-hardcore, metalcore, alternative rock, pop punk, emo, alternative metal, nu metal, post-metal, instrumental rock, ambient, stoner metal, sludge metal, Neue Deutsche Härte, doom, melodic hardcore, death metal, black metal, thrash metal, speed metal, blues rock, black metal and folk rock. There is some crossover between these subgenres, and being a fan of one band from one subgenre does not mean liking all bands of that subgenre or that bands in other subgenres are disliked (Bennett 1999). Furthermore, a preference for a band at one end of the hard rock and metal spectrum (if that spectrum is defined by the level of heaviness in the sound) may lead to an exploration of increasingly heavy bands, as it did for my interviewee Sally, who described progressing from Skid Row (glam metal) to Metallica (thrash metal) and to increasingly 'hard' bands. Thinking about hard rock and metal as a spectrum means that strict genre boundaries are jettisoned and that the flow of a band's oeuvre between subgenres (for instance My Chemical Romance moving between emo and Queen-like pomp rock, or Enslaved moving from black metal to prog metal) can be acknowledged. As far as fans go, un-pigeonholing musical taste means that fans may enjoy music outside of the genre altogether yet still hold some degree of identity or allegiance with the hard rock and metal community.

All of my interviewees were familiar with *Kerrang!* magazine, although not all were current readers. Not all declared themselves 'heavy metal fans'. This may have been due to a number of reasons. For example, fans may express personal preferences for a range of bands, meaning that an assertion of fandom of a single genre did not seem to apply to them. Others made distinctions between the bands appearing in *Kerrang!* and the bands they thought of as heavy metal. A final reason for not declaring herself a heavy metal fan is that being a 'fan' implies a particular level of engagement: wearing the right clothes, going to concerts, purchasing music and merchandise, knowing a good deal about the music and its production. That is, being a fan may be perceived to be contingent on the amount of subcultural capital (Thornton 1995) one possesses.

As Thornton shows, and as I discuss further in Chapter 3, subcultural capital is linked to authenticity in a way that makes it a great deal more difficult for women to acquire.

THE MEDIA

The mass media mediate communications between people and may take the form of newspapers, magazines, television, radio, social networking sites, music and computer games, amongst other communicative phenomena. The media are not homogenous: there are many different industries, institutions, and technologies at work, with various political and cultural positions, national and regional perspectives, all of which determine the form the medium takes and the content it provides, that is, how they mediate the communications we make between us. This means that media have a powerful controlling role as gatekeepers, determining what we see, read, hear and know.

Examining the media is important because the representations they emit matter: cultural meanings are 'not only "in the head"' (Hall 1997, 3) but have a role to play in constructing how we think, speak and act. Media representations that, for example, depict unequal relationships between women and men as normal or natural, or that continually portray women as less competent, contribute to understandings of women and men which then shapes behaviour, policy, and so on. The media can therefore reproduce dominant ideologies of gender. Examining representations enables understanding of how they are linked to 'patterns of inequality, domination and oppression' (Gill 2007, 7), particularly with regards to the mass media. Here, I discuss one particular case study: the UK print magazine *Kerrang!*. *Kerrang!* is part of the mass media, but it tries hard to not look like it and maintains some independent credibility (Chapter 3). In Chapter 2 I theorise how the magazine enables hard rock and metal fans, musicians and other industry workers (those reading the magazine, those writing, designing and providing photos for it, the musicians who are the subject matter, and others who work in the industry such as promoters, A&R staff, publishers, and so on) to imagine one another without necessarily meeting—they form an imaginary community that believes itself to be equal and open. In looking at the magazine, I am specifically interested in the ways in which it portrays women fans and how this is part of the ideology of hard rock and metal. In order to investigate these representations I employ a semiotic, ideological critique. This is a methodology that pays close attention to the visual and textual elements of the magazine and builds up a picture of how ideological messages are communicated.

By using a specifically feminist standpoint, ideological critique enables the delineation of how oppressive ideas are normalised and how sexism works in the media (Gill 2011). Following the method laid out in Barthes' *Mythologies* (2009 [1957]), I use semiotic myth reading to identify the ideological message of the text and to articulate how that message contributes to sustaining the ideology. Myth reading can be used to bring together a number of similar texts and to pay close attention to their meanings. Where it lacks in its grasp of polysemy, it is strong in its capacity to read powerful subtle messages and how they are presented as natural or common sense. The interaction of music, the industry and ideology has a key role to play in establishing the genre (Frith 1996), so examining these messages also helps to understand the media's part in the reproduction of hard rock and metal as a genre.

Myth works by communicating a message in such a way that it appears obvious or common sense: particular ideas are transmitted under the guise of communicating facts (Barthes 2009 [1957], 149). So, for instance, in the logo of the UK Conservative Party the image of a tree (Fig. 1.1), its canopy coloured like the Union flag, appears alongside the word 'Conservatives'. The logo connotes Britishness through its Union flag, and Englishness in the romanticised 'old English oak tree'. Building on this, the myth communicated by the logo is that the Conservatives are a political party who value the unification of the Kingdom, tradition and pastoral Englishness. Myth communicates ideology through immediacy: it 'points out and it notifies, it makes us understand something and imposes it on us' (2009 [1957], 140). Barthes' system for reading the meanings of images and texts thereby pays attention to the accretion of the small meanings of individual elements into larger myths.

Fig. 1.1   UK Conservative Party logo (*Source*: Conservative Party)

There are some problems with myth reading. The question of how much an author means to participate in myth making is not considered in *Mythologies* and is complicated by Barthes' later work 'Death of the Author' (1977). Furthermore, myth reading pays little attention to the reader, the context of reading or the differences between readers (Bignell 2002). Myth reading therefore only tells a partial story about women and hard rock and metal, but it is nevertheless an important approach for understanding the ideology of the genre.

The media case study I draw on here is the letters pages of *Kerrang!* magazine at the start of the twenty-first century. Although references to fans appear throughout the magazine, this is where they are most consistently represented, and, most importantly, where they are purportedly given a voice and the ability to represent themselves. I interrogate the text of fans' letters (topic, tone and style), the images and photographs (gender and role of the subject, clothing, hair and make-up, posture, gesture and facial expression, locations of the photo shoots and props in use) and the designs of the pages, and extrapolate the myths that *Kerrang!* presents about fans of hard rock and metal, musicians and other 'community' members. The examples I use here are representative and the most pertinent to understanding *Kerrang!*'s dominant representation of women fans. But they are not the only representations, and there are letters and photographs that do not fit with the dominant representation of women fans, as I have written about elsewhere (Hill 2011).

Because myth reading only considers the textual message, exploring the readings of media texts is vital to understanding their impact. In his encoding/decoding model, Stuart Hall (1973) highlights the importance of two elements in engagements with media products: the *encoding* of meaning as the media product is produced, and the *decoding* of meaning as it is used or consumed. The encoding of texts takes place within the sociocultural milieu of producers, whereas decoding happens within the sociocultural milieu of audiences. Audiences may share the same milieu as the producers and decode the message encoded in the text by producers in a straightforward manner—this is known as the *preferred reading*. They may have different 'frameworks of knowledge', socioeconomic relations, 'technical infrastructures' or relationships to producers (Hall 1973, 130) and therefore decode a different, unintended message. Such readings may be *negotiated* (the dominant message is understood and accepted at an abstract level, but not entirely) or *oppositional* (the intended message is understood, but an 'alternative framework of reference' (Hall 1973, 138) is used to make meaning). Following Bourdieu (2010), Hall suggests that how media products are decoded depends on the educational and class background of the viewer, amongst other factors. Using Hall's model to assess my interviewees' engagement with one particular myth—that all women fans are groupies—shows that although particular media representations may be ubiquitous, they are not necessarily read in the preferred way: negotiation and opposition is more usual.

FANS

Since the 1990s, fans have come under increasing academic scrutiny, and interpretations of what it means to be a fan, fans' relationships with the fan object and fans' role in society have all changed in that time. The figure of the fan is mixed up with ideas around audience, popular culture, mass media, consumerism, capitalism, resistance and production, amongst other things. Very early understandings of what it means to be engaged with popular culture come from the Frankfurt School, for whom being engaged with popular culture, especially pop music, was to be a pliant, passive victim of the ideological state apparatus of mass media; thus the risk of proletarian revolt was reduced. Moreover, the mass media audience were not viewed as being genuinely interested in the culture they claimed to love. Adorno was particularly scathing of pop music and pop music fans, arguing that,

> Everything is so completely identical that preference in fact depends merely on biographical details or on the situation in which things were heard (Adorno 2002, 289)

In this argument, fans of mass culture are cultural dupes whose fandom prevents them from seeing their 'real' situation as subordinated and exploited.

On the other side of this is the treatment of fans as hysterical stalkers, absolutely obsessed with their idols and potentially with murderous intent (Mark Chapman, killer of John Lennon, being a typical example). But as Joli Jenson (1992) argues, whilst the Mark Chapman kind of fan was studied in depth, those involved in more 'normal, everyday' forms of fandom were overlooked. The result was that little was known about the 'variety of ways that people make meaning in everyday ways' (Jenson 1992, 25), giving a skewed understanding of what it is to be a fan. Furthermore 'the characterization of fandom as pathology is based in, supports, and justifies elitist and disrespectful beliefs about our common life' (Jenson 1992, 10). Since Lisa A. Lewis' (1992) groundbreaking collection of essays, in which Jenson's chapter appears, a big shift in thinking about fandom has occurred. The work of the essayists in the collection, together with important work on television science fiction fans by Camille Bacon-Smith (1992) and Henry Jenkins (1992), re-evaluated the fan for postmodern times and concluded that fans are not abnormal (hurray!); in fact 'we are all fans of something. We respect, admire, desire. We distinguish and form commitments' (Lewis 1992, 1). Far from being passive dupes, Bacon-Smith and Jenkins show that fans can be very active not only as they make meaning in the object of their fandom but in their ability to rework texts (such as fanfic) and to intervene in the decision making of producers (for example, fans of *Arrested Development* sending bananas to network executives in an effort to prevent its cancellation).

Until very recently most fan studies were conducted on fans of television programmes, especially science fiction. A few studies of popular music fans as music fans (rather than as members of subcultures or scenes) existed, and these were typically based around a particular artist (see, for example, Fiske 1989 on Madonna fans, Cavicchi 1998 on Bruce Springsteen fans, Vroomen 2004 on Kate Bush fans). Mark Duffett's edited collection (2014) brought together many studies of music fans and has moved away from challenging media portrayals of fans to focus on practices. Nevertheless, the debate remains shaped by the mass culture treatment of fandom as consolation or as hiding character flaws.

'Fandom is both personal and collective', Duffett (2014, 7) argues, and the coming together of these two elements is key to understanding metal fandom. Work in metal studies that has drawn on scene and subculture has prioritised the collective to the almost total neglect of the personal, echoing much other work on fandom (Sandvoss and Kearns 2014). Angela McRobbie's (1991) concept of 'bedroom culture' addresses this more personal element of fandom, but emphasis is on pop music, practices and consumption. Similarly Rob Walser's definition of a metal fan brings music to the fore but retains the importance of public and consumption activities—going to concerts and buying records. But this isn't all that fandom is about: twenty-first century musical engagement does not require listeners to purchase albums, but even before this massive consumer shift, 'record collector' was not synonymous with fan. Rather than consumption practices, I argue that it is the passionate response to the music that makes a fan.

Duffett (2013) discusses a range of different definitions of fandom. He does not plump for one single definition but rather determines that fandom should be an umbrella term that covers a range of practices and elements. This includes consumption, thinking of fandom as a pastime, identity creation, the practices of fandom, performance of fandom, and fandom as an essence of existence. What Duffett does not discuss is gender. This is particularly relevant in the discussion of identity in which he draws on Sandvoss (2005), who argues that not all fans would determine their identity as a fan as based on emotional intensity. In that sense Sandvoss describes fandom as sometimes being about knowledge acquisition. However, this is unconvincing because who is using this language of knowledge acquisition matters. When emotional attachments are so derided in our culture, to think that those who create fan identities based on knowledge acquisition do not have an emotional relationship with the fan object is inadequate. The question must be asked, why might they deny or downplay their emotional engagement? *Pace* Sandvoss, who argues that to think *only* about the emotional engagement with the fan object is limited, I argue that considering emotions is the most important part of thinking about fandom.

Therefore, I define music fans as individuals who love music, who have strong emotional reactions to it and for whom music is very important in their everyday lives. Often the passion is centred upon a particular musical genre and/or band. This is true of rock fans, and they often enjoy music from across the breadth of the genre, although usually focussing on bands within one or two subgenres. Being a fan is about more than regularly listening to songs or albums by a band; being a fan is more than being a consumer. A fan has an intense response to the music, an emotional attachment to it and, in some cases, to the idea of the artist (which may or may not focus on the musicians themselves). A fan may or may not attend performances by the object of their fandom or bands that they wish to hear, and factors such as location and cost of performances, mortality of the musicians and peer pressure will all play a part in this. My definition, which I have created based on my reflections on my interviewees' descriptions of their fandom and my own experience of being a fan, takes into account activities and emotions which are hidden in research using subcultural theory and the concept of scene, and neglected in fan studies that emphasise the collective and fan practices. However, because fandom is not only personal but also a shared, collective experience, understanding how the two interact is an important aspect of understanding the fan experience.

OUTLINE OF THE BOOK

In the following chapter, Hard Rock and Metal as an Imaginary Community, I explore the ways in which the terminology and frameworks that have been used to examine hard rock and metal fans highlight particular aspects of fandom but ignore others, to the detriment of understanding the gendered experience of music. I argue that the dominant framework for investigating the experiences of hard rock and metal fans—subculture—is inadequate because it does not give enough room to consider women's experiences, including pleasure in the music. I propose a new way to think about fandom that draws on the feelings of togetherness that fans report, and that is created in *Kerrang!* magazine. Drawing on Anderson's theory of imagined community (1991), and feminist writings on community (Weiss and Friedman 1995), I outline the concept of 'imaginary community'. I argue that this is a better reflection of the way in which fans report a sense of community and a concept which can open up the ideology of the community to an examination of the ways in which particular ideas, traditions or 'myths' are deployed to create a sense of cohesion in spite of inequalities and unacknowledged privileges.

In Chapter 3: The Media and the Imaginary Community, I investigate how *Kerrang!* creates an imaginary community of hard rock and metal fans, with particular reference to how women fans are represented. I extrapolate four myths that are forged in the letters pages, two that are presented by the magazine as being common sense values of the community (equality and authenticity) and two that are less obvious: the groupie and the warrior, which determine how women and men are portrayed. These myths work together to depict the imaginary community as ideologically invested in maintaining the masculinity of the genre at the expense of femininity. I argue that the representation of women in the imaginary community renders them as adjuncts to the real members of the community—the men—with damaging consequences.

Engaging with that representation, in Chapter 4 I scrutinise the impact of the myth on the women fans I interviewed. From the fans' responses to questions about the groupie stereotype—for instance, whether they would like to meet their favourite band—I tease out the different ways in which my interviewees respond to the figure of the groupie in their own fan lives. There was a good deal of discomfort in the interview discussion around groupies, and all women found ways to negotiate the stereotype without accepting the title. Some women spoke out against groupie behaviour, positing that it was an inferior kind of fandom. Others attacked the representation of women as groupies or the underlying sexism that generated the vilified figure. Still others sought to redefine what 'groupie' meant. In some women's words I saw the impact of the myth in their defence of their own sexual and fannish reputations, or in their seeking out of bands that avoided the positioning of women as sexual objects in hard rock and metal. I also examine the ways in which women *did* express desire for musicians and the complicated ways in which they negotiated the meanings of their sexual interest. I argue that the myth of the groupie exerts pressure on women fans by impacting upon their ability to express their fandom and their sexuality. The problem of the groupie myth is not just about the expectations it places upon women but also in the ways in which it prevents discussion of more sensual and embodied experiences of musical pleasure.

In Chapter 5, I examine women's accounts of their experiences of musical pleasure. I analyse how my interviewees described heavy metal and also what they liked about their favourite bands. Some women defined the genre with language that reflected the myth of the warrior, particularly when it came to considering guitars. Others used language that can be associated with the myth of authenticity as they heralded the importance of 'real' instruments, high quality musicianship and meaningful lyrics. They did so in distinction to pop music, relying therefore on a rock/pop conceptual divide. I then draw on the work of feminist writers on rock music to argue that considering hard rock and metal as a masculine genre neglects important aspects of women's fandom. I turn back to my interviewees' words to analyse how some of their descriptions diverge from those dominant myths and complicate readings of hard rock and metal as masculine music.

Chapter 6 considers the allegations that hard rock and metal is sexist. Examining the interviews with women fans, I explore the different ways in which women fans describe their experiences at hard rock and metal events. Their somewhat surprising—given the historical allegations of the genre's sexism and much of the academic work on the genre—responses show that in their experiences hard rock and metal is *less* sexist than the 'mainstream'. Using research on sexism in a range of fields I argue that understanding what counts as sexism is complex and requires critical work by fans when sexism is normalised. What is important when it comes to hard rock and metal is to listen to what fans say about the context of their experiences within their broader lives. The genre provides moments for women fans in which they may feel that gender does not matter—a feeling of genderlessness. Ultimately, however, the feeling of liberation only comes through assimilation into the culture, which ignores women as much as possible (Walser's (1993) world without women). Nevertheless that temporary feeling is a valuable one.

In the concluding chapter I argue that close examination of the specific experiences of women in their engagements with the hard rock and metal media, the music, and other fans at musical events, reveals how the experience of music is shaped by assumptions about women and assumptions about how music should be listened to. Musical pleasure does not exist on some universal, transcendental plane. It is informed and shaped by the socio-cultural circumstances of the listener. It is vital to acknowledge how these circumstances make for differing experiences, and this is an important first step for countering the sexisms that women face. Finally, I provide a short plan for how hard rock and metal may use science fiction imagery to truly become an oppositional genre and imagine a genderless future, as figures across the genre grapple with the 'metalgate' controversy.

REFERENCES

Adorno, Theodor W. 2002. *Essays on Music: Theodor W. Adorno; Selected, with Introduction, Commentary, and Notes by Richard Leppert; New Translations by Susan H. Gillespie*. London: University of California Press.

Anderson, Benedict. 1991. *Imagined Communities: Reflections on the Origin and Spread of Nationalism*. Rev. and extended ed. London: Verso.

Bacon-Smith, Camille. 1992. *Enterprising Women: Television Fandom and the Creation of Popular Myth*. Philadelphia: University of Pennsylvania Press.

Barthes, Roland. 1977. *Image, Music, Text*. Translated by Stephen Heath. London: HarperCollins.

———. (1957) 2009. *Mythologies*. Translated by Annette Lavers. London: Vintage.

Baym, Nancy K. 1999. *Tune in, Log on: Soaps, Fandom, and On-line Community*. Thousand Oaks, CA: Sage Publications.

Bennett, Andy. 1999. Subcultures or Neo-Tribes? Rethinking the Relationship Between Youth, Style and Musical Taste. *Sociology* 33(3): 599–617.

Bignell, Jonathan. 2002. *Media Semiotics: An Introduction*. 2nd ed. Manchester: Manchester University Press.

Bourdieu, Pierre. 2010. *Distinction: A Social Critique of the Judgement of Taste*. London: Routledge.

Brill, Dunja. 2008. *Goth Culture: Gender, Sexuality and Style*. Oxford: Berg.

Brown, Andy R. 2007. Everything Louder Than Everything Else. *Journalism Studies* 8(4): 642–655.

Brown, Andy R 2009. 'Girls Like Metal, Too!': Female Reader's Engagement with the Masculinist Ethos of the Tabloid Metal Magazine. *Heavy Metal and Gender International Congress*, Cologne University of Music and Dance, 10 October.

Butler, Judith. 1993. *Bodies that Matter: On the Discursive Limits of Sex*. Farnham: Routledge.

Cavicchi, Daniel. 1998. *Tramps Like Us: Music & Meaning Among Springsteen Fans*. New York: Oxford University Press.

Clifford-Napoleone, Amber. 2015b. *Queerness in Heavy Metal Music: Metal Bent*. Abingdon: Routledge.

Coates, Norma. 1997. (R)evolution Now? Rock and the Political Potential of Gender. In *Sexing the Groove: Popular Music and Gender*, ed. Sheila Whiteley, 50–64. Abingdon: Routledge.

Dawes, Laina. 2012. *What Are You Doing Here? A Black Woman's Life and Liberation in Heavy Metal*. Brooklyn: Bazillion Points.

Delphy, Christine. 1993. Rethinking Sex and Gender. *Women's Studies International Forum* 16(1): 1–9.

Duffett, Mark. 2013. *Understanding Fandom: An Introduction to the Study of Media Fan Culture*. New York and London: Bloomsbury.

———. 2014. *Popular Music Fandom: Identities, Roles and Practices*. London: Routledge.

Fast, Susan. 1999. Rethinking Issues of Gender and Sexuality in Led Zeppelin: A Woman's View of Pleasure and Power in Hard Rock. *American Music* 17(3): 245–299.

Fiske, John. 1989. *Reading the Popular*. London: Routledge.

Frith, Simon. 1996. Music and Identity. In *Questions of Cultural Identity*, eds. Stuart Hall, and Paul Du Gay, 108–127. London: Sage.

Frith, Simon, and Angela McRobbie. (1978) 1990. Rock and Sexuality. In *On Record: Rock, Pop, and the Written Word*, eds. Simon Frith and Andrew Goodwin, 371–389. London: Routledge.

Gill, Rosalind. 2007. *Gender and the Media*. Cambridge: Polity.

———. 2011. Sexism Reloaded, or, It's Time to Get Angry Again! *Feminist Media Studies* 11(1): 61–71.

Green, Lucy. 1997. *Music, Gender, Education*. Cambridge: Cambridge University Press.

Griffin, Naomi. 2012. Gendered Performance Performing Gender in the DIY Punk and Hardcore Music Scene. *Journal of International Women's Studies* 13(2): 66–81.

Hagen, Ross. 2014. 'Kvlt-er Than Thou': Power, Suspicion and Nostalgia Within Black Metal Fandom. In *The Ashgate Research Companion to Fan Cultures*, eds. Linda Duits, Koos Zwaan, and Stijn Reijinders, 223–236. Farnham: Ashgate.

Hall, Stuart. 1973. *Encoding and Decoding in the Television Discourse Birmingham Centre for Contemporary Cultural Studies*. Birmingham: The University of Birmingham.

——, ed. 1997. *Representation: Cultural Representations and Signifying Practices*. Milton Keynes: The Open University.

Hartsock, Nancy C.M. 1983. The Feminist Standpoint: Developing the Ground for a Specifically Feminist Historical Materialism. In *Discovering Reality: Feminist Perspectives on Epistemology, Metaphysics, Methodology and Philosophy of Science*, eds. Sandra Harding, and Merrill B. Hintikka, 283–310. Hingham, MA: D. Reidel.

Hesmondhalgh, David. 2013. *Why Music Matters*. Chichester: Wiley-Blackwell.

Hill Collins, Patricia. 1990. *Black Feminist Thought: Knowledge, Consciousness, and the Politics of Empowerment*. London: Routledge.

Hill, Rosemary Lucy. 2011. Is Emo Metal? Gendered Boundaries and New Horizons in the Metal Community. *Journal for Cultural Research* 15(3): 297–313.

——. 2014a. Reconceptualising Hard Rock and Metal Fans as a Group: Imaginary Community. *International Journal of Community Music* 7(2): 173–188.

hooks, bell. 1984. *Feminist Theory: From Margin to Center*. Cambridge, MA: South End Press.

Hunter, Seb. 2004. *Hell Bent for Leather: Confessions of a Heavy Metal Addict*. London: Harper Perennial, 2005.

Jackson, Stevi. 1998. Theorising Gender and Sexuality. In *Contemporary Feminist Theories*, eds. Stevi Jackson, and Jackie Jones, 131–146. Edinburgh: Edinburgh University Press.

Jackson, Stevi, and Sue Scott. 2010. *Theorizing Sexuality*. Maidenhead: McGraw-Hill International.

Jenkins, Henry. 1992. *Textual Poachers: Television Fans and Participatory Culture*. New York: Routledge.

Jenson, Joli. 1992. Fandom as Pathology: The Consequences of Characterization. In *The Adoring Audience: Fan Culture and Popular Media*, ed. Lisa A. Lewis, 9–29. London: Routledge.

Kahn-Harris, Keith. 2007. *Extreme Metal: Music and Culture on the Edge*. Oxford: Berg.

Kant, Immanuel. (1790) 2010. Critique of the Power of Judgement. In *The Norton Anthology of Theory and Criticism*, eds. Vincent B. Leitch and George Lynn Cross, 411–449. New York: W. W. Norton & Company.

Kartheus, Wiebke. 2015. The 'Other' as Projection Screen: Authenticating Heroic Masculinity in War-themed Heavy Metal Music Videos. *Metal Music Studies* 1(3): 319–340.

Kruse, Holly. 2002. Abandoning the Absolute: Transcendence and Gender in Popular Music Discourse. In *Pop Music and the Press*, ed. Steve Jones, 134–155. Philedelphia: Temple University Press.

Lewis, Lisa A. 1992. *The Adoring Audience: Fan Culture and Popular Media*. London: Routledge.

Lucas, Caroline, Mark Deeks, and Karl Spracklen. 2011. Grim Up North: Northern England, Northern Europe and Black Metal. *Journal for Cultural Research* 15(3): 279–295.

McRobbie, Angela. 1991. *Feminism and Youth Culture: From 'Jackie' to 'Just Seventeen'*. London: Macmillan.

Nordström, Susanna, and Marcus Herz. 2013. 'It's a Matter of Eating or Being Eaten.' Gender Positioning and Difference Making in the Heavy Metal Subculture. *European Journal of Cultural Studies* 16(4): 453–467.

Oakley, Ann. 1972. *Sex, Gender and Society*. London: Temple Smith. Original edition.

Overell, Rosemary. 2010. Brutal Belonging in Melbourne's Grindcore Scene. *Studies in Symbolic Interaction* 35: 79–99.

———. 2012. '[I] Hate Girls and Emo[tion]s: Negotiating Masculinity in Grindcore Music. *Popular Music History* 6(1): 198–223.

Purcell, Natalie J. 2003. *Death Metal Music: The Passion and Politics of a Subculture*. London: McFarland.

Radway, Janice A. 1984. *Reading the Romance: Women, Patriarchy, and Popular Literature*. Chapel Hill: University of North Carolina Press.

Regev, Motti. 1994. Producing Artistic Value. *The Sociological Quarterly* 35(1): 85–102.

Riches, Gabrielle. 2011. Embracing the Chaos: Mosh Pits, Extreme Metal Music and Liminality. *Journal for Cultural Research* 15(3): 315–332.

———. 2014. "Throwing the Divide to the Wind": Rethinking Extreme Metal's Masculinity Through Female Metal Fans' Embodied Experiences in Moshpit Practices. *IASPM UK & Ireland Conference*, Cork, Ireland, 12–14 September.

———. 2015. Re-conceptualizing Women's Marginalization in Heavy Metal: A Feminist Post-structuralist Perspective. *Metal Music Studies* 1(2): 263–270.

Sandvoss, Cornel. 2005. *Fans: The Mirror of Consumption*. Cambridge: Polity.

Sandvoss, Cornel, and Laura Kearns. 2014. From Interpretive Communities to Interpretative Fairs: Ordinary Fandom, Textual Selection and Digital Media. In *The Ashgate Research Companion to Fan Cultures*, eds. Linda Duits, Koos Zwaan, and Stijn Reijinders, 91–106. Farnham: Ashgate.

Scott, Joan W. 2008. 'Experience': Becoming Visible. In *Just Methods: An Interdisciplinary Feminist Reader*, ed. Alison M. Jaggar, 272–281. Boulder, CO: Paradigm Publishers.

Smith, Dorothy E. 2008. Women's Perspective as a Radical Critique of Sociology. In *Just Methods: An Interdisciplinary Feminist Reader*, ed. Alison M. Jaggar, 39–43. Boulder, CO: Paradigm Publishers.

Spracklen, Karl. 2010. Gorgoroth's Gaahl's Gay! Power, Gender and the Communicative Discourse of the Black Metal Scene. In *Heavy Fundametalisms: Music, Metal and Politics*, eds. Rosemary Lucy Hill, and Karl Spracklen, 89–102. Oxford: ID Press.

———. 2015. 'To Holmgard ... and Beyond': Folk Metal Fantasies and Hegemonic White Masculinities. *Metal Music Studies* 1(3): 359–377.

Stanley, Liz. 1992. *The Auto/Biographical I: The Theory and Practice of Feminist Auto/Biography*. Manchester: Manchester University Press.

Stanley, Liz, and Sue Wise. 1993. *Breaking Out Again: Feminist Ontology and Epistemology*. 2nd ed. London: Routledge.

Thornton, Sarah. 1995. *Club Cultures: Music, Media and Subcultural Capital*. Cambridge: Polity.

Vasan, Sonia. 2010. 'Den Mothers and Band Whores': Gender, Sex and Power in the Death Metal Scene. In *Heavy Fundametalisms: Music, Metal and Politics*, eds. Rosemary Lucy Hill, and Karl Spracklen, 69–78. Oxford: Inter-Disciplinary Press.

———. 2011. The Price of Rebellion: Gender Boundaries in the Death Metal Scene. *Journal for Cultural Research* 15(3): 333–349.

Vroomen, Laura. 2004. Kate Bush: Teen Pop and Older Female Fans. In *Music Scenes: Local, Translocal and Virtual*, eds. Andy Bennett, and Richard A. Peterson, 238–253. Nashville: Vanderbilt University Press.

Wallach, Jeremy, Harris M. Berger, and Paul D. Greene. 2011. *Metal Rules the Globe: Heavy Metal Music around the World*. Durham, NC: Duke University Press.

Walser, Robert. 1993. *Running with the Devil: Power, Gender, and Madness in Heavy Metal Music*. Hannover, NH: University Press of New England.

Weinstein, Deena. (1991) 2000. *Heavy Metal: The Music and Its Culture*. Rev. ed. Boulder, CO: Da Capo Press.

Weiss, Penny A., and M. Friedman. 1995. *Feminism and Community*. Philedelphia: Temple University Press.

Whiteley, Sheila. 2000. *Women and Popular Music: Sexuality, Identity, and Subjectivity*. New York: Routledge.

Willis, Ellen. 2014. Beginning to See the Light. *(Village Voice, 1977)*. In *The Essential Ellen Willis, ed. Aronowitz Nona Willis, 51–58*. Minneapolis: University of Minnesota Press.

Wise, Sue. 1984. Sexing Elvis. In *On Record: Rock, Pop, & the Written Word*, eds. Simon Frith, and Andrew Goodwin, 390–398. London: Routledge.

Wittig, Monique. 1992. *The Straight Mind and Other Essays*. Boston: Beacon Press.

CHAPTER 2

Hard Rock and Metal as an Imaginary Community

INTRODUCTION

When, in the late 1980s and early 1990s academics started studying metal, metal was an extremely popular genre. Visually, the mainstream media cashed in with MTV's *Beavis and Butthead* cartoon (Judge and Kaplan 1993–1997, 2011), *Wayne's World* (Spheeris 1992) and the *Bill & Ted* films (Herek 1989; Hewitt 1991). Each tells stories about young men for whom heavy metal is a vital component of their identity, so that metal forms not only the soundtrack to the films and cartoon, but the backbone of much of the humour too: in-jokes for metal fans. What they also have in common is their portrayal of American adolescence: bungling boys who struggle with authority and whose friendships with each other are more important than their relationships with women, but who are empowered and given purpose in their lives through their love of rock 'n' roll. They exemplify Arnett's depiction:

> Heavy metal music plays an important part in the lives of the boys who like it. It is not just a musical preference to them, but an intense avocation that shapes their view of the world, their spending habits, their moods, their friendships, their notions of who and what is admirable, and their hopes for what they might become. (Arnett 1991, 92)

In other words, heavy metal is not just a music preference; it is a way of life. Note, though, that this is male adolescence. No similar films portrayed

© The Editor(s) (if applicable) and The Author(s) 2016
R.L. Hill, *Gender, Metal and the Media*, Pop Music, Culture and Identity, DOI 10.1057/978-1-137-55441-3_2

young women's love of metal, and aside from Cassandra, the musician who is the love interest in *Wayne's World*, women are very marginal in these portrayals.

It was not that women were not fans of metal, however—they were, although in fewer numbers and certainly less visible. But women fans were ignored or portrayed not as fans but as groupies—more interested in musicians than music. Seb Hunter's characterisation of male metal fans' attitudes towards women at the time (cited in the introduction) sums up the demeaning way in which women were perceived. Sadly, the academic work of the time similarly undervalued women's involvement, treating metal as something boys were interested in and could possibly be damaged by. Women, when research did consider them of interest, were either the potential victims of male metal fans' misogynistic attitudes (see for example Lawrence and Joyner 1991; Hansen and Hansen 1991) or treated stereotypically (Arnett 1991; Weinstein 2000 [1991]; Walser 1993).

More recently however, feminist scholars have begun to challenge the boy-focussed view of metal and to assert that women have a place within the understandings of the genre (Riches 2011, 2014, 2015; Patterson 2011; Griffin 2012; Dawes 2012; Overell 2014; Kitteringham 2014). These studies have implications for understanding women's cultural participation, especially in male-dominated arenas, for media representations of women fans, and for metal as a music and a culture. But these new studies sit alongside the older books, whose significance persists as they continue to be consulted and their problematic elements reproduced uncritically (e.g., Gruzelier 2007). This book forms part of the new wave of feminist metal media studies and therefore takes as crucial the need to examine the gendered assumptions in the older books, starting with the question, where are the women?

WHERE ARE THE WOMEN HARD ROCK AND METAL FANS?

Studying popular music fans as fans is only just gaining currency (Duffett 2014). What is exciting about this work is that it prioritises people's relationship with the music and musicians they love. Fans of artists as diverse as the Grateful Dead (Smith and Inglis 2013), Lady Gaga (Bennett 2014) and John Coltrane (Whyton 2013) have received attention. However, hard rock and metal fans are still typically studied within sociological frameworks of subculture and scene (see, amongst others, Gross 1990; Weinstein 2000 [1991]; Purcell 2003; Sinclair 2014; Vasan 2011). This means that they are studied as part of a group of other fans, and their social interactions rather than their fannish experiences are highlighted. That sounds like it might be beneficial for thinking about the experiences of women fans, but historically such frameworks have omitted women from the picture (see for example work on mods and rockers [Cohen 1972]; skinheads [Clarke 1976]; punk [Hebdige 1979]; and goth [Hodkinson 2002]). One striking exception is Lauraine Leblanc's (1999) study of punk women where she redefines resistance to focus on gendered norms rather than the parent culture. Yet, despite the centrality of music in drawing people together into these subcultures, the fannish passion for music is not a focus of the research. These researchers have honed in on the sensational aspect of young people's extroverted fandom, on clothing, on how people group together, and how the subculture is 'resistant' to the parent culture. As Hesmondhalgh rightly postulates, subcultural theory was never about music (2005); yet subcultural theory remains the dominant framework for studies of hard rock and metal music fans.

For studying women, subcultural theory and scene are not only problematic because they have omitted women in the past. As Leblanc's book shows, subcultural theory needs quite a lot of modification to take into account the specific experiences of women. In 1978, Angela McRobbie and Jenny Garber (McRobbie 1991) were already critiquing the concept of subcultural theory both for ignoring or trivialising the roles that women fans play within subcultures and for the focus on external activities. They argued that Willis (1978), Fyvel (1963) and others made no attempt to question the gendered positions of their informants (typically young men) so that the researchers' biases informed their research, reinforcing stereotypes of girls and focussing on their appearance. In short, McRobbie and Garber contend that these studies do not consider women to be *serious* members of subcultures. But the omission is not only a result of the sexism of researchers. They assert that it is difficult to judge whether women really were absent from subcultures because these accounts emphasise 'male membership, male focal concerns and masculine values' (McRobbie 1991, 4). Considering the 1950s teddy boy subculture, the authors posit that girls were less visible members because financial dependency and concerns about sexual reputations kept them off the streets and out of the cafés. Yet, argue McRobbie and Garber, women *did* participate in subcultures but were more likely to be found in their homes listening to music, reading magazines, wearing subcultural fashions, trying out make-up and hairstyles and socialising in their bedrooms. These behaviours are different from those (acknowledged) behaviours of male subculturalists, but because they take place in the home they reduce women's visibility as subcultural members. At a basic level then, subcultural theory privileges men's activities to the exclusion of other kinds of musical engagement— and this is a problem for understandings of women's fandom and also for better understandings of men's fandom.

The concept of scene also has been widely utilised for examinations of hard rock and metal fans. For example, Keith Kahn-Harris (2007) uses the concept to explore the ways in which extreme metal is experienced around the world; Karl Spracklen (2010) employs the term to group together black metal fans online. The concept of scene focuses on activities that coalesce around public music venues and considers the relationships between those working in the production of music on a local level and, to some extent, fans. Sara Cohen's (1997) critique of the male dominance and sexism which limited women's participation in the Liverpool indie music scene of the 1990s complements McRobbie and Garber's argument about the invisibility and marginalisation of women's participation in music. Like subcultural theory, the concept of scene retains the focus on public or visible engagement with music. This is problematic because scenes are often male dominated as men have greater access than women to money and time to devote to participating in a scene. Women face sexism and sexual harassment from male scene members and also may have childcare commitments. They may also fear for their safety as they need to attend music venues in empty town centres late at night (Cohen 1997). Should women wish to become musicians there are further practical and prejudice problems for them to overcome (as described by, amongst others, Bayton 1998; Clawson 1999; Reddington 2011). The problems restricting women's participation in Liverpool's indie scene that Cohen highlights are in some ways caused by larger societal structures that limit women's behaviour and allow men to assert dominance and participate in activities that subjugate women. In describing these difficulties Cohen is critical of the male dominance of the scene itself, but because scenes are primarily masculine areas, women's non-scenic activity is excluded. The concept of scene therefore excludes women in the same way as subcultural theory.

Because subculture and scene rely upon public expressions of fandom, and since men are able to move more freely outside the home, the two concepts privilege male fandom, leaving other means of expressing fandom unconsidered. McRobbie and Garber (1991) argue that modes of being fans that are undertaken in private houses are more available to women, but the emphasis in research on music fans that uses subcultural theory or scene does not take this into account. Such work therefore structurally ignores ways of being a fan that are more open to women. Indeed, Deena Weinstein's very influential book about hard rock and metal, *Heavy Metal: The Music and the Culture* (2000 [1991]), is a key example. Weinstein acknowledges that she is describing only a portion of metal fans—young, white working class men in the USA—and she has little to say about women fans. She tacitly acknowledges McRobbie and Garber's work, commenting that women fans enact their fandom in their bedrooms, but she does not go any further. *Heavy Metal*'s subcultural framework has set the tone for much later work on hard rock and metal.

For my interviewees most music listening took place at home, in cars or on headphones: that is, in intimate spaces. Not all participants emphasised bedrooms (all but one no longer lived their parental homes and so the significance of bedrooms had shifted for them), but it is clear that private activities are integral to a passionate engagement with music. The frameworks of subcultural theory and scene tell a very narrow story about fandom, but because they remain dominant they prioritise fans' outdoor/public activity and the fans who are best able to participate in this way. Within metal studies the effects of this are striking and have important consequences for the understanding of metal.

CHARACTERISING HARD ROCK AND METAL FANDOM AS A MASCULINE PASTIME AND OCCUPATION

Three very influential studies of metal by Deena Weinstein, Rob Walser and Nathalie Purcell were written in response to a particular moment in the history of hard rock and metal in the United States. Their aim is to defend metal from its detractors who made very serious allegations. In the mid-1980s there was a moral panic that centred on heavy metal music. This culminated in senate hearings at which the campaign group the Parents Music Resource Center (PMRC) gave evidence of allegedly dangerous lyrics in popular songs, especially those by heavy metal bands. They offered a frightening list of dangers: provoking suicide, violence, drug-taking, madness, self-harming and Satanism (more detail on the senate hearings can be found in Weinstein 2000). The moral panic spurred a number of studies in the field of psychology which assumed that heavy metal was damaging

(Rosenbaum and Prinsky 1991; Hansen and Hansen 1991; Lawrence and Joyner 1991; Mitchell et al. 2001). Weinstein (2000) and Purcell (2003) use subcultural theory to provide a more sympathetic viewpoint and do not begin by looking for the ways in which metal damages its listeners. Perhaps because they position themselves as defenders of hard rock and metal against serious accusations, the studies avoid discussing problematic issues in metal such as sexism.

Walser (1993) criticises Weinstein for omitting women's responses to metal, but I consider her book a woman's response to metal: her love of the genre is apparent throughout, even if she does not reflect on it. In fact Weinstein's discussion of gender in metal is rather brief. When women fans do appear they are at concerts: if they wear black T-shirts and jeans they are accepted as equals by men, but if they wear heels and mini-skirts they are 'denounced as sluts' (Weinstein 1991, 105) or subject to harassment. Weinstein implies that sexism does not exist in the metal community as long as women are prepared to conform to the 'masculine code'. She does not problematise the culture's attitude towards femininity, nor is there any analysis of what it is like to be a female fan of a genre that values the masculine and disdains the feminine. To read *Heavy Metal* is to read about male fans at concerts so that the few women who participate are either 'one of the guys' or positioned by their sexual attractiveness and availability. In this Weinstein replicates the problems that McRobbie and Garber highlight in the studies of Willis, Fyvel and others, by presuming a male participant and by positioning herself alongside those male participants.

Natalie Purcell's book, *Death Metal Music: The Passion and Politics of a Subculture* (2003), does not explicitly state that her research focuses on men (unlike Weinstein) and she does include some data from female interviewees. Yet she neglects the specificity of women's experiences as metal fans (and, horror of horrors, she uses 'man' as a generic term). For instance, in the discussion of pornographic imagery in the music, pornography is equated with gore in horror films, without explanation. She posits that pornography makes the human body grotesque but does not consider the differences between male and female bodies in pornography. Nor is there much discussion of violence against women in the music. These problems stem from the defensive position that Purcell takes up: in her desire to reposition the subgenre as a positive cultural force, she ignores the problems that women encounter in the subculture. However, there is a hint of such analysis in her epilogue. Here she reflects on her research experiences and suggestively states that 'placing trust in the wrong persons and taking risks based on idealistic assumptions about other human beings landed me in more trouble than I care to discuss' (Purcell 2003, 193). How disappointing not to hear more of these troubles! If she had incorporated her experiences into the book this would have given a different picture of fandom. As it is, Purcell positions her own experiences as just one of those things that could occur in any 'group, scene, or culture' (Purcell 2003, 193). Whilst this may be the case, a male fan experience is assumed as the norm, with women's experiences being sidelined, even in the face of the author's own experiences.

Whilst the women writing about metal (Weinstein and Purcell) in the context of a response to metal's vilifiers do not consider the specificity of women's participation in metal, Walser (1993) and Kahn-Harris (2007) do make an attempt to grasp what it means for women to enjoy hard rock and metal. However, like Weinstein and Purcell they too presume a model of a male fan. Walser's book, *Running With the Devil*, is one of the few non-psychological studies of hard rock and metal that does not use subcultural theory. Nevertheless, he replicates the assumption of a male fan as 'normal' and women fans as an exception. The book looks in depth at the cultural meanings of metal, with particular attention to misogyny and madness. Despite Walser's criticism that Weinstein does not investigate the perspectives of female fans, neither does he. He attributes 1987's increase of women metal fans to Bon Jovi's *Slippery When Wet* album containing more romantic themes than previous heavy metal albums! In this dismissive view he makes no attempt to think about the complex reasons people have for enjoying a particular kind of music, and he accepts patronising accounts of women that position love and romance as the zenith of female interest.

Kahn-Harris (2007) uses the framework of scene, spotlighting the previously little-studied subgenres of death metal, black metal, power metal and goth metal. He argues that in general women are marginalised within the extreme metal scene, although in the power metal and goth metal scenes women are more numerous because the music is 'more melodic' (Kahn-Harris 2007, 71). Kahn-Harris provides some nuanced discussion of the causes of women's marginalisation, yet underlying this analysis is an undisclosed assumption that men are the 'normal' fans and women fans are adjuncts. Women are marginalised partly through their socialisation as feminine (habitus guides what feels 'natural', and for women this does not include sounds of powerful metal because power is associated with masculinity), partly through their treatment at musical events (they see few women in the scene, they are excluded in social interactions and sexism is condoned by other scene members), and partly through the music and imagery of the genre (many pornographic images, song lyrics about sexual violence). Kahn-Harris thus creates a sense of the extreme metal scene as hostile to women, which goes some way to explaining why women are not involved in the scene in greater numbers. Yet, in theorising women's place in extreme metal, Kahn-Harris himself theorises women as exceptional cases, thus contributing to the marginalisation he exposes. The position of full scene member is available to men, as the archetype is drawn up with the male participant in mind. 'Real' fans are men not only in Kahn-Harris' description of metal events, but in his theory too. As Clifford-Napoleone (2015b) and Riches (2015) both argue metal is more than just a boys' club. To characterise it as such misses out on the rich experience of metal for all its fans, purposefully ignoring the ways in which metal can be an empowering and transgressive space for women (Riches 2015).

However, increasingly it is being recognised that the manifestation of gender and gender politics is an important area of study for hard rock and metal. 2009 saw an international congress on Metal and Gender in Cologne, and subsequent metal conferences have all featured papers on the topic. The main focus of these studies tends to be women, which highlights how women have been left out of previous studies where the male experience is the norm (but also worryingly reinforces the idea that only women are gendered). Some of these studies look at experiences of sexism, such as Susanna Nordström and Marcus Herz (2013) and Sonia Vasan (2011); others at sexuality, for example Amber Clifford-Napoleone (2015b); still others at pleasure, for example Gabrielle Riches (2011, 2014) and Jamie Patterson (2011, 2016); at the intersection of sexism and racism Laina Dawes (2012); and at fans becoming musicians, for example Berkers and Schaap (2015).

The growing amount of research on gender and the number of women researching the topic (Hickam and Wallach 2011) shows how interesting the topic is—and how much there is still to learn. *Pace* Phillipov (2012), the 'problem of gender' (Phillipov 2012, 63) is not limiting; it is a vital area of study that opens up myriad avenues for investigation. Indeed, to *not* consider gender in regards to hard rock and metal is limiting (Clifford-Napoleone 2015b). However, getting a balance between defending the genre from sexism and considering its barriers for women's participation is a task which is not easily dealt with.

Where Walser and Kahn-Harris attempt to describe women's place in the metal world, but assume a male subject, Sonia Vasan (2011) places the woman fan at the heart of her research on the experiences of women death metal fans in Texas. Employing subcultural theory and scene, she focuses on the public space of the gig, shining a light on misogyny in death metal. At concerts, women fans, she argues, must negotiate the sexism they face in lyrics, artwork and onstage 'banter'. They do this with a technique of 'cost reduction' in which they ignore sexism or downplay its significance. This reasoning leads her to focus upon fan practices that are most problematic for the women she interviews, and therefore she is unable to consider other facets of their fandom. It is clear that Vasan is bewildered by women's enjoyment of death metal: for her the sexism trumps any potential pleasure. Similarly, Nordström and Herz (2013), drawing on interviews with women fans and musicians, argue that metal culture is fundamentally sexist. Women face three 'dualities' when participating in metal: 'whore/goddess', in which they must prove their knowledge of metal in order to be seen as a 'worthy' fan; 'acting male' / 'looking female', where they need to get the balance of performance right; a 'twilight zone' in which they are not masculine enough to be accepted in metal nor feminine enough to be accepted in the mainstream. They argue that 'men set the agenda for the culture, deciding through initiation rites and questioning which women are "worthy" heavy metal fans' (Nordström and Herz 2013, 464). The contributions of Vasan and Nordström and Herz to understandings of women's experiences are important. But they are partial: both only consider the negative aspects of engaging in metal. These studies, along with those of Kahn-Harris and earlier writers who neglect to consider women's experiences, therefore leave a gap where pleasure ought to be. In this Jamie Patterson's[1] (2011, 2016) work is much more successful.

Patterson reasons that it is important to consider women's gender constructions in metal rather than focus on the male dominance of the genre. Her close readings of the gender constructions in three case studies of women fans prioritise women's passion for the music and examine the benefits of metal for women. Crucially she draws women's metal fandom and metal gender construction into dialogue with their lives outside the metal community (their work and domestic lives). She argues that extreme metal gives women a space to be themselves so that they do not have to worry about mainstream beauty norms or romance narratives, or it gives them a space to experiment with their appearance in ways that transgress normative beauty ideals. This is quite a different portrayal of metal and metal fandom from those offered by other writers. Rather than being sexist, the genre is experienced as a space that frees women from sexism. For instance, pleasure found in clothing is not for its own sake, but for its freeing ability to resist the constraints of stereotypical femininity. Patterson describes how she took to wearing metal shirts around her waist to avoid objectifying looks at her bottom. Within the death metal community wearing shirts around her waist would be seen as 'normal' and a badge of identity, but it also enabled her to refuse objectifying and unachievable mainstream constructions of femininity. Patterson's case studies are carefully analysed with attention both to the differences between the women and the dominant representation of women in the extreme metal community, and to their non-metal lives. It is this attention to the private and personal lives of fans that allows the women to step forward in their own right. No longer anomalies, they are women who love metal music, negotiating their gender identity (and sexism) whilst at metal events and in their everyday lives.

Gabrielle Riches (2011) examines the public space of the concert but uses neither subcultural theory nor scene. She argues that in extreme metal the moshpit is a liminal space with specific rules that allow changes in status for participants and mark a difference from the mainstream. For women the pit can be a subversive place where notions of femininity can be challenged through dress, listening habits, accessories and dance practices. It is not straightforward, however, as when women enter the pit, men are less likely to continue in their moshing practice in the same way because they believe women should not receive the same rough treatment. Gruzelier (2007) may see this as a difficulty for male participants, but Riches argues that it is a problem for women as well. Women enter the pit in order to share the experience: the dancing, the release of anger, the energy, the liberation. If pleasure in subverting gendered notions is also an important part of pleasure in the pit then men's tendency to treat women in the pit differently from male moshers reinforces their feminine gender. Riches' focus on dance also brings attention to the body and the ways the body *feels* in the pit. This means that women and men are theorised as embodied subjects. In this way it marks a change from thinking of hard rock and metal as a genre in which the 'normal' fan is male and women are added in.

Stanley and Wise (1993) argue that just introducing women into existing frameworks is not enough. Studies by Patterson and Riches 'take women seriously' (Stanley and Wise 1993, 18) and consider their experiences important. They are examples of what can be achieved once the straitjacket of subcultural theory and scene are removed. Aiming to 'add women in' has been precisely the problem with the use of subcultural theory and scene because important elements are left out: media representation of women fans and its impact on women fans, and the more intimate ways in which fandom is experienced and enjoyed.

IMAGINARY COMMUNITY

I propose a framework that acknowledges the position of women fans amongst a larger group of fans but that also enables a sense of fandom that takes place in more private spaces, such as the home. 'Imaginary community' moves away from thinking of fandom only in terms of public activities, consumption and ideal of the masculine fan. It acknowledges the private side of fandom and the way the personal fits with the wider group of fans through the imagined existence of a community.

Where 'subculture' is limited to visible fans, usually men in their teens and 20s, 'community' *can* include those whose fandom is usually hidden: women, adults (rather than youths) and children. Where 'subculture' focuses upon specific public practices and on the bodies of participants, 'community' can encompass other expressions of fandom such as listening to music at home, blogging about favourite bands, engaging in creative activities (such as bandom: writing slash fiction about musicians) or reading music magazines, behaviours which are more open to, but not limited to, women fans. For these reasons, 'community' is a more suitable term than 'subculture' for theorising the experiences of women metal fans. But the term 'community' is not as straightforward as it might at first seem. In Tönnies and Harris (2001 [1887]) theorisation, community— the *gemeinschaft*—is modelled against the association—*gesellschaft*—and in this oppositional relationship the idea of a caring, rural, pre-industrial life is set against self-seeking urban industrial lifestyles. This dualism places a higher value on the idealised pre-industrial community. However, as Graham Day (2006) argues, this kind of idyllic pastoral existence was already passing when Tönnies was writing, and his theory was grounded in research that celebrated folk cultures: therefore Tönnies' empirical work is already biased as it affirms a particular lifestyle to the detriment of another. Nostalgia for a 'golden age' is fundamental to theorisations of community: 'the expression bad *gemeinschaft* violates the meaning of the word' (Tönnies quoted in Day 2006, 14). An idealistic vision is therefore embedded within the very concept of community.

In twenty-first century Britain plaintive media cries about the erosion of community tend to nostalgically recall Tönnies' kind of local community, made up of close neighbourly relations, local shops and being on first-name terms with the postman (Friedman 1989). Yet, as Howard Rheingold (2000) notes, we should be wary of wearing rose-tinted spectacles when discussing communities because nostalgia and idealisation obfuscate problems (see Day 2006). Penny Weiss, Marilyn Friedman and Iris Marion Young (1995) argue that nostalgic understandings of community deny difference and ignore structural disadvantages and inequalities within the communities. Any consideration of communities must therefore include an understanding of the ways in which some groups are disadvantaged whilst others are privileged (Weiss 1995). Friedman argues that traditional communities 'have harbored social roles and structures which have been highly oppressive for women' (1989, 277). The nostalgic vision of community ignores the exclusionary practices and the normalising traditions that make power relations appear natural, thereby normalising the exploitation of some community members, for instance, the unpaid labour of women. 'Tradition' is thus used to justify the structural disadvantage women face. To theorise communities without considering the hierarchies within them is therefore problematic. In 'found' communities difference is often not tolerated because, for the community to work, a sense of togetherness is vital; the community is ill equipped to deal with dissimilarity. Furthermore, communities themselves may not exist at all: the kinds of communities that Tönnies portrays are, Day argues, elusive and implausible. In Pahl's words, '[why] does a dead idea refuse to lie down?' (Pahl quote in Day Day 2006, 22). Yet even if a 'real' community does not exist, there is evidence in both *Kerrang!*'s letters pages and in the words of my interviewees that a *sense* of a community exists amongst hard rock and metal fans. Between fans, even those who have never met and will never meet or even know of the other's *individual* existence, some sense of common feeling seems to exist.

Moving away from 'community' a number of researchers working in the field of online fan communities have appropriated Benedict Anderson's concept of the imagined community to fill the gap. Anderson describes the 'community' as follows:

> It is *imagined* because the members of even the smallest nation will never know most of their fellow-members, meet them or even hear of them, yet in the minds of each lives the image of their communion. (1991, 6)

The concept of the imagined community shifts the emphasis away from the question of whether communities actually exist or not, or what the qualities of communities might be, and places importance in the *feeling* of living alongside others. As Hills puts it, 'communities need to be approached not as real or imagined, but in terms of how they are imagined' (2001, 151). Thus the key significance lies in the power that the idea of living in a community holds for those who feel themselves to be members. In distinction to traditional conceptions of community, which are criticised for hiding inequalities, the imagined community of nation 'is imagined as a *community*, because, regardless of the actual inequality and exploitation that may prevail in each, the nation is always conceived as a deep, horizontal comradeship' (Anderson 1991, 7). Moreover, inequalities are not hidden by the concept of imagined community; rather, the way in which they are hidden by the power of the ideal of community is exposed. This *feeling* of being part of a community comes through imagining people simultaneously accessing and digesting information. Key for Anderson are novels and newspapers. The novel because it is structured around the idea of 'meanwhile' so that actions of different characters can be written as if they happen simultaneously, and the newspaper because it recounts events that occur independently and in which the actors are unaware of whatever else is going on. Nevertheless, the events are linked by date and by the reader imagining others reading about the same events on the same day as if in a ceremony.

This concept is appropriate for studying metal fans, between whom there is an imagined relationship across a broad spectrum of media platforms. Furthermore, many of the ways in which metal fans 'consume information' do occur simultaneously: metal clubs, gigs and concerts bring people together at the same time in the same room to experience their fandom together; magazines, especially weekly magazines, are read, if not together, then with a sense that others are reading the same music news at roughly the same time, fulfilling a similar role to that of newspapers in Anderson's theory; television channels such as Scuzz and Kerrang, and metal programmes such as the cartoon *Metalocalypse*[2] (Schnepp et al. 2006–2013) broadcast on cable and satellite television, bringing together people to watch the same music videos simultaneously.

In his discussion of the 'community of imagination', Hills asserts the need for the affective relationship to be considered as central whilst retaining the idea of simultaneity that is key to Anderson's imagined community. Building on this, I propose the term 'imaginary community'.[3] The imaginary community is idealistic and a powerful idea for its members. In drawing attention to the way it is *imagined* as idealistic, the concept opens up the community to scrutiny of its power structures and relations and something of its ideology, all of which have significant impact on women fans' lives. I use the active form of the verb to take in the way in which the idea and ideology of the community are continually repro-duced. In my formulation, the term 'imaginary community' accepts the sense of community that people have, but does not question whether such a community 'really' exists. It acknowledges that this idea of a community is idealistic and nostalgic and exists in contradiction with the experiences of community members so that it portrays an ideal rather than a lived reality. Nevertheless, this sense of community is extremely powerful and carries an ideology with it that affects community members' experiences of participation in the imaginary community and also of their own fandom.

The concept is increasingly being applied to fan groups (see for exam-ple Sandvoss 2005; Bennett 2014) and gaining currency within research on metal (e.g., Lucas et al. 2011; Dawes 2015), replacing problematic frameworks such as subcultural theory and scene. Born (1993) uses a simi-lar notion in her discussion of music and the social. In their work on black metal in Northern England, Lucas et al. (2011), draw on Jean-Luc Nancy (1991) and Anthony P. Cohen (1985) and highlight 'symbolic boundar-ies, tacit knowledge and shared meanings' (Lucas et al. 2011, 281). In my theorisation, the application of the term 'imaginary' to the community allows the tacit hierarchies and power relations to be laid bare for critique. In the following chapter I discuss how the imaginary community works to protect the status quo.

Conclusions

Subcultural theory and the concept of scene both emphasise fan behav-iours in public spaces (the gig, the concert, the club, the festival, the street, and so on). The result is the tacit assumption of particular kinds of fans and particular kinds of fannish activities. Weinstein, Walser and Kahn-Harris all therefore found their research upon a model of male fans. This paradigm ignores the fact that the majority of the most crucial of music fans' behaviours—listening to music—occurs in private (at home, on headphones, in the car) and, as McRobbie and Garber argue, it disre-gards other kinds of fannish activities that also centre around the home.

The ways in which experiences of hard rock and metal fans are gendered are neglected. This means that media representations of women fans are ignored or, worse, reproduced, and women's pleasure in the music is overlooked. To understand how music moves people, and how women hard rock and metal fans negotiate the male-dominated terrain of metal, it is vital to focus on women fans' gendered experiences. In order to do this both private and collective experiences need to be explored. In the following chapter I focus on the metal media to grasp how a sense of collective identity is forged. I particularly grapple with how the media produces and reproduces the ideology of hard rock and metal culture. Paying close attention to gendered assumptions and parameters, I use the concept of the imaginary community to understand women's symbolic 'place' within hard rock and metal. Highlighting the imaginary nature of community brings attention back to the individuals' relationships with their peers and with the music they enjoy, enabling a consideration of fan pleasure.

NOTES

1. Although Patterson utlises the term 'scene', in my estimation this is a misuse: she addresses private aspects of women's fandom in particular rather than attending to gig going or involvement in music making.

2. *Metalocalypse* is a 10 minute cartoon about fictional death metal band Dethklok whose universal popularity makes them the most powerful entity in the world. Their fans are represented as being fanatical to the point of suicide, and the band members themselves have little respect for their fans; their shows frequently result in the deaths of audience members. It is full of in-jokes, such as the fast food restaurant called Burzum and the name appearing on the sign between two burger buns. Burzum are a Norwegian black metal band.

3. My use of 'ideology' and 'imaginary' here are not quite the same as those of Althusser and Lacan. Althusser defines ideology as representing 'the imaginary relationship of individuals to their real conditions of existence' (Althusser 2001, 109). Seductive though this conception is, it leaves little room for us to understand how resistance to capitalist structures can occur because everything we think and do is determined by ideology: there is no way out of it. I use 'imaginary' to denote the creative act of thinking about the abstract world of other metal fans, literally how fans imagine themselves to be part of a community, and not imaginary in the Lacanian sense of the individual's narcissistic self-imaging.

REFERENCES

Althusser, Louis. 2001. *Lenin and Philosophy, and Other Essays*. New York: Monthly Review Press.

Anderson, Benedict. 1991. *Imagined Communities: Reflections on the Origin and Spread of Nationalism*. Rev. and extended ed. London: Verso.

Arnett, Jeffrey Jensen. 1991. Heavy Metal Music and Reckless Behavior Among Adolescents. *Journal of Youth and Adolescence* 20(6): 573–592.

Bayton, Mavis. 1998. *Frock Rock: Women Performing Popular Music*. Oxford: Oxford University Press.

Bennett, Lucy. 2014. Fan/celebrity Interactions and Social Media: Connectivity and Engagement in Lady Gaga Fandom. In *The Ashgate Research Companion to Fan Cultures,*, eds. Linda Duits, Koos Zwaan, and Stijn Reijinders, 109–120. Farnham: Ashgate.

Berkers, Pauwke, and Julian Schaap. 2015. YouTube as a Virtual Springboard: Circumventing Gender Dynamics in Offline and Online Metal Music Careers. *Metal Music Studies* 1(3): 303–318.

Born, Georgina. 1993. Afterword: Music Policy, Aesthetic and Social Difference. In *Rock and Popular Music: Politics, Policies, Institutions*, eds. Tony Bennett, Simon Frith, Lawrence Grossberg, John Shepherd, and Graeme Turner, 265–290. London: Routledge.

Clarke, John. 1976. The Skinheads and the Magical Recovery of Community. In *Resistance Through Rituals: Youth Subcultures in Post-war Britain*, eds. Stuart Hall, and Tony Jefferson, 99–102. London: Routledge.

Clawson, Mary Ann. 1999. Masculinity and Skill Acquisition in the Adolescent Rock Band. *Popular Music* 18(1): 99–114.

Clifford-Napoleone, Amber. 2015b. *Queerness in Heavy Metal Music: Metal Bent*. Abingdon: Routledge.

Cohen, Anthony P. 1985. *The Symbolic Construction of Community*. London: Routledge.

Cohen, Sara. 1997. Men Making a Scene: Rock Music and the Production of Gender. In *Sexing the Groove: Popular Music and Gender*, ed. Sheila Whiteley, 17–36. Abingdon: Routledge.

Cohen, Stanley. 1972. *Folk Devils and Moral Panics: The Creation of the Mods and Rockers*. London: MacGibbon and Kee.

Dawes, Laina. 2012. *What Are You Doing Here? A Black Woman's Life and Liberation in Heavy Metal*. Brooklyn: Bazillion Points.

———. 2015. Challenging an 'Imagined Community': Discussions (or Lack Thereof) of Black and Queer Experiences Within Heavy Metal Culture. *Metal Music Studies* 1(3): 385–394.

Day, Graham. 2006. *Community and Everyday Life*. London: Routledge.

Duffett, Mark. 2014. *Popular Music Fandom: Identities, Roles and Practices*. London: Routledge.

Friedman, Marilyn. 1989. Feminism and Modern Friendship: Dislocating the Community. *Ethics* 99(2): 275–290.

Fyvel, Tosco R. 1963. *The Insecure Offenders: Rebellious Youth in the Welfare State*, vol Rev. Harmondsworth: Penguin.

Griffin, Naomi. 2012. Gendered Performance Performing Gender in the DIY Punk and Hardcore Music Scene. *Journal of International Women's Studies* 13(2): 66–81.

Gross, Robert L. 1990. Heavy Metal Music: A New Subculture in American Society. *Journal of Popular Culture* 24(1): 119–130.

Gruzelier, Jonathan. 2007. Moshpit Menace and Masculine Mayhem. In *Oh Boy! Masculinities and Popular Music*, ed. Freya Jarman-Ivens, 59–75. New York: Routledge.

Hansen, Christine Hall, and Ranald D. Hansen. 1991. Constructing Personality and Social Reality Through Music: Individual Differences Among Fans of Punk and Heavy Metal Music. *Journal of Broadcasting and Electronic Media* 35(3): 335–350.

Hebdige, Dick. 1979. *Subculture: The Meaning of Style*. London: Routledge.

Herek, Stephen. 1989. *Bill & Ted's Excellent Adventure*. De Laurentiis Entertainment Group.

Hesmondhalgh, David. 2005. Subcultures, Scenes or Tribes? None of the Above. *Journal of Youth Studies* 8(1): 21–40.

Hewitt, Pete. 1991. *Bill & Ted's Bogus Journey*. Orion Pictures.

Hickam, Brian, and Jeremy Wallach. 2011. Female Authority and Dominion: Discourse and Distinctions of Heavy Metal Scholarship. *Journal for Cultural Research* 15(3): 255–277.

Hills, Matt. 2001. Virtually Out There: Strategies, Tactics and Affective Spaces in On-line Fandom. In *Technospaces: Inside the New Media*, ed. Sally Munt, 147–160. London: Continuum International Publishing Group Ltd.

Hodkinson, Paul. 2002. *Goth: Identity, Style, and Subculture*. Oxford: Berg.

Judge, Mike, and Yvette Kaplan. 1993–1997, 2011. *Beavis and Butt-Head*. MTV Networks.

Kahn-Harris, Keith. 2007. *Extreme Metal: Music and Culture on the Edge*. Oxford: Berg.

Kitteringham, Sarah. 2014. Extreme Conditions Demand Extreme Responses: The Treatment of Women in Black Metal, Death Metal, Doom Metal, and Grindcore. MA, Faculty of Communication and Culture, University of Calgary.

Lawrence, Janet S. St, and Doris J. Joyner. 1991. The Effects of Sexually Violent Rock Music on Males' Acceptance of Violence Against Women. *Psychology of Women Quarterly* 15(1): 49–63.

Leblanc, Lauraine. 1999. *Pretty in Punk: Girls' Gender Resistance in a Boys' Subculture*. New Brunswick, NJ: Rutgers University Press.

Lucas, Caroline, Mark Deeks, and Karl Spracklen. 2011. Grim Up North: Northern England, Northern Europe and Black Metal. *Journal for Cultural Research* 15(3): 279–295.

McRobbie, Angela and Garber, Jenny. 1991. Girls and subcultures. In Feminism and youth culture: from Jackie to Just Seventeen, ed. Angela McRobbie, 1-15. Basingstoke: Macmillan Press Ltd.

McRobbie, Angela. 1991. *Feminism and Youth Culture: From 'Jackie' to 'Just Seventeen'*. London: Macmillan.

Mitchell, Wendy S., Alan M. Rubin, and Daniel V. West. 2001. Differences in Aggression, Attitudes Toward Women, and Distrust as Reflected in Popular Music Preferences. *Media Psychology* 3(1): 25–42.

Nancy, Jean-Luc. 1991. *The Inoperative Community*. Minneapolis: The University of Minnesota Press.

Nordström, Susanna, and Marcus Herz.2013. 'It's a Matter of Eating or Being Eaten.' Gender Positioning and Difference Making in the Heavy Metal Subculture. *European Journal of Cultural Studies* 16(4): 453–467.

Overell, Rosemary. 2014. *Affective Intensities in Extreme Music Scenes: Cases from Australia and Japan*. Basingstoke: Palgrave Macmillan.

Patterson, Jamie. 2011. When Jane Likes Cannibal Corpse: Empowerment, Resistance, and Identity Construction Among Women in Death Metal. *Home of Metal Conference: Heavy Metal and Place*, Wolverhampton, UK, 1–4 September.

———. 2016. 'Getting My Soul Back': Empowerment Narratives and Identities Among Women in Extreme Metal in North Carolina. In *Global Metal Music and Culture: Current Directions in Metal Studies*, eds. Andy R. Brown, Karl Spracklen, Keith Kahn-Harris, and Niall W.R. Scott, 245–260. London: Routledge .

Phillipov, Michelle. 2012. *Death Metal and Music Criticism: Analysis at the Limits*. Plymouth: Lexington Books.

Purcell, Natalie J. 2003. *Death Metal Music: The Passion and Politics of a Subculture*. London: McFarland.

Reddington, Helen. 2011. The Sound of Women Musicians in the Punk Era. *Music, Politics and Agency Conference*, University of East London, 27 May.

Rheingold, Howard. 2000. *The Virtual Community: Homesteading on the Electronic Frontier*. London: MIT Press.

Riches, Gabrielle. 2011. Embracing the Chaos: Mosh Pits, Extreme Metal Music and Liminality. *Journal for Cultural Research* 15(3): 315–332.

———. 2014. "Throwing the Divide to the Wind": Rethinking Extreme Metal's Masculinity Through Female Metal Fans' Embodied Experiences in Moshpit Practices. *IASPM UK & Ireland Conference*, Cork, Ireland, 12–14 September.

————. 2015. Re-conceptualizing Women's Marginalization in Heavy Metal: A Feminist Post-structuralist Perspective. *Metal Music Studies* 1(2): 263–270.

Rosenbaum, Jill Leslie, and Lorraine Prinsky. 1991. The Presumption of Influence: Recent Responses to Popular Music Subcultures. *Crime and Delinquency* 37(4): 528–535.

Sandvoss, Cornel. 2005. *Fans: The Mirror of Consumption*. Cambridge: Polity.

Schnepp, Jon, Chris Prynoski, and Mark Brooks. 2006–2013. Metalocalypse. Adult Swim.

Sinclair, Gary. 2014. Retreating Behind the Scenes: The 'Less'-civilizing Impact of Virtual Spaces on the Irish Heavy Metal Scene. In *The Ashgate Research Companion to Fan Cultures*, eds. Linda Duits, Koos Zwaan, and Stijn Reijinders, 209–222. Farnham: Ashgate.

Smith, Peter, and Ian Inglis. 2013. A Long Strange Trip: The Continuing World of European Deadheads. *Popular Music and Society* 36(3): 305–326.

Spheeris, Penelope. 1992. *Wayne's World*. Paramount Pictures.

Spracklen, Karl. 2010. Gorgoroth's Gaahl's Gay! Power, Gender and the Communicative Discourse of the Black Metal Scene. In *Heavy Fundametalisms: Music, Metal and Politics*, eds. Rosemary Lucy Hill, and Karl Spracklen, 89–102. Oxford: ID Press.

Stanley, Liz, and Sue Wise. 1993. *Breaking Out Again: Feminist Ontology and Epistemology*. 2nd ed. London: Routledge.

Tönnies, Ferdinand, and José Harris. (1887) 2001. *Community and Civil Society*. Cambridge: Cambridge University Press.

Vasan, Sonia. 2011. The Price of Rebellion: Gender Boundaries in the Death Metal Scene. *Journal for Cultural Research* 15(3): 333–349.

Walser, Robert. 1993. *Running with the Devil: Power, Gender, and Madness in Heavy Metal Music*. Hannover, NH: University Press of New England.

Weinstein, Deena. (1991) 2000. *Heavy Metal: The Music and Its Culture*. Rev. ed. Boulder, CO: Da Capo Press.

Weiss, Penny A. 1995. Feminism and Communitarianism: Comparing Critiques of Liberalism. In *Feminism and Community*, eds. Penny A. Weiss, and Marilyn Friedman, 161–186. Philedelphia: Temple University Press.

Whyton, Tony. 2013. *Beyond a Love Supreme: John Coltrane and the Legacy of an Album*. Oxford: Oxford University Press.

Willis, Paul. 1978. *Profane Culture*. London: Routledge & Kegan Paul.

Young, Iris Marion. 1995. The Ideal of Community and the Politics of Difference. In *Feminism and Community*, eds. Penny A. Weiss, and Marilyn Friedman, 233–258. Philedelphia: Temple University Press.

CHAPTER 3

The Media and the Imaginary Community

INTRODUCTION

Rock fits into a tradition of freeing *men* from societal constraints of caring and responsibility—as exemplified in *On The Road* (Kerouac 2011 [1957]) and songs such as Steppenwolfe's 'Born to be Wild'. Rock offers the potential to be independent of mothers, girlfriends, wives and children (Marcus 1976). But it does not straightforwardly offer women the same liberatory potential of independence (Kruse 2002). Rock music exists in sexist societies, and it reproduces sexist ideas about women and men and sexuality (Schippers 2002). In other words, in spite of its rebellious image and libertarian ideals, rock does not challenge all dominant repressive ideas: of the social constraints that rock rebels against, gender is not one. Music magazines play an important part in communicating these contradictory messages of both rebellious freedom and of a repressive gender order. Kembrew McLeod's (2002) analysis of rock criticism, one of few studies on gender and music journalism, argues that 'writing rock criticism is an ideological act' (McLeod 2002, 94) which is determined by the writers' values—and rock critics are mostly men. Rock criticism sustains 'gender inequality in the music industry' (McLeod 2002, 94) due to the language rock journalists use, which plays a significant role in valorising gendered ideology. In her analysis of music reviews in rock journalism, positive terms (for example violence, masculinity, authenticity) are set against negative terms (for example wimpy, commercial, sentimental). McLeod argues that these terms are sexed, although the music itself does not have essential qualities of, for example, aggression. Evident in McLeod's analysis is that the ideology is not only transmitted by who is talked about and how (it is not the case that all women musicians are derided), but how *all* musicians are described. In McLeod's analysis, music journalists' reporting on music and musicians plays an important role in disseminating particular values that are aligned with the gendered rock/pop divide. Of course, journalists do not work in a vacuum and editors, publishers and magazine owners also exert considerable influence over the values that are communicated through the medium.

McLeod's work tallies with that of Helen Davies (2001). Davies examines articles and photographs of women musicians and fans in UK indie magazines *NME* and *Melody Maker* at the turn of the century. She argues that they were produced within a sexist environment and with a sexist agenda. This has implications for representations of specific women performers (who, she argues, are sexualised and trivialised), especially feminists and those in the riot grrrl movement. Her discussion of the representations of fans explores four categories: women or girl fans of 'teenybop' music; 'serious music' fans; subcultures; and groupies, which she describes in some depth. She argues that according to the music press women fans of 'serious music' are a 'perpetual novelty' (Davies 2001, 313) but not intelligent enough to be serious fans. Instead 'their fandom [is] explained by sexual attraction to a male musician' (Davies 2001), whilst the term 'groupie' is 'often used by the music press to refer to all female fans' (Davies 2001, 315). Metal fans may distance themselves from the indie rock that is the purview of *NME*, but both genres work within the same rock 'n' roll framework and history, although they may claim slightly different lineages. Hard rock and metal media representations produce similar ideas about gender and about women fans, as my case study of *Kerrang!* magazine's letters pages in the 2000s shows.

KERRANG!

As the oldest UK metal magazine, *Kerrang!* has a vital role in giving a unified sense of history of the genre and to giving focus and identity to the heavy metal community (Brown 2007). It was first published in 1981 as a platform for the new heavy metal bands and remains a key part of the metal media. *Kerrang!* is currently owned by Bauer Media Group and before that by EMAP, both global companies. The magazine covers a wide spectrum of subgenres (for example black metal, death metal, emo, pop punk, and so on) although its cover stars tend to reflect the more melodic youth trends. Of the monthly magazines that cover a similar genre, *Terrorizer* has a stronger emphasis on extreme metal, *Metal Hammer* is stricter about its definition of 'metal', and *Rock Sound* tends to cover the hard rock angle rather than metal. *Kerrang!*'s coverage is not always distinct from the UK's other weekly rock magazine, *NME* (for example both magazines have featured My Chemical Romance, the Manic Street Preachers and Metallica on the cover), but *NME*'s focus is more particularly indie.

I examined June issues of *Kerrang!* (the month of major hard rock and metal festivals Ozzfest and Download, which provide a consistent theme) from 2000 to 2008. Around 2000 there was a resurgence in the popularity of hard rock and metal, and sales of *Kerrang!* and other metal magazines rose quickly. After 2008 sales fell to almost half their 2006 high of 85,377 per week, which is commensurate with the general decline of print media in the Internet age. Using this peak time in *Kerrang!*'s readership offers a valuable snapshot of the most popular time in the magazine's existence. It is also a time when a large proportion of women were reading the magazine. Andy R. Brown reports that in 2009 *Kerrang!* had a greater proportion of female readers than the two metal monthlies: 40 per cent as opposed to 36 per cent for *Metal Hammer* and 15 per cent for *Terrorizer* (Brown 2009), whilst in 2006 *Campaign* reported a higher figure of 53 per cent (Campaign 2006). By contrast, only a quarter of estimated readers of *NME* were women (Brown 2007).

Kerrang!'s letters page is cleverly called 'Feedback', punning on the term's double meaning: (one), it refers to the way that the letters are a method by which readers can give their opinions, responses to articles, reviews and other letters published in the magazine; and (two), it refers to the squalling noise made by a sound loop through a speaker and so echoes the onomatopoeic title of the magazine, establishing it within the world of rock 'n' roll. *Kerrang!* readers will almost certainly get the joke. The page plays a crucial role in depicting the imaginary community back to itself. Over the years the page has moved from the rear to the front of the magazine, and changed in size and shape. The design has changed too, but some striking features are consistent: the use of bold colours, particularly black and red. Alongside readers' letters, readers' artwork, photographs of bands (some of which are sent in by readers, some which are promotional shots used to illustrate the letter themes) and other illustrations are also included. Letters reflect on live performances, festivals and albums, and sometimes there are on-going debates about issues important to fans (relationships with other hard rock and metal fans or non-rock fans, for example). The messages are not restricted to letters: 'Feedback' directs readers to communicate with the magazine using email, the *Kerrang!* website and other social media. Some letters are obviously aimed at the magazine's editors, but others are written to other readers or specific letter writers. More letters written by women were published towards the end of the 2000s, but the number of letters written by non-gendered signatures dropped. During the 2000s the magazine was increasingly perceived as a magazine for girls and as 'the new *Smash Hits*'.[1] This suggests that an increase in female readership combined with the magazine's increasing tendency to put youth trend stars on its cover (e.g. My Chemical Romance and Fall Out Boy) were perceived as having a feminising effect on the magazine. Nevertheless, *Kerrang!*'s persistence whilst other magazines stumbled (rock weekly *Melody Maker* closed in 2000) and the controversy roused by coverage of emo and pop punk bands highlight its valued place for metal fans.

Before 2005 debates between letter writers crystallised around themes of relationships between fans and non-fans or around long-running discussions of, for example, the organisation of festivals. After 2004 these kinds of letters became rarer (an exception to this is fans' responses to the disparagement of emo in British newspapers such as *The Daily Mail*: this topic ran and ran). Instead, letters tended to focus on the micro-level of fandom, to praise or denounce particular bands and musicians, describe going to concerts and festivals, or tell stories of meeting a musician. Letters tend to be more self-contained rather than making links across magazine issues. This change in the thematic scope of the letters means that fans are represented as thinking more about the relative merits of various bands. Often this was done in unsophisticated ways, as the brevity of the letters only allows room for one or two adjectives that describe the author's attitude to the band under focus—e.g., 'Papa Roach were amazing at Download!' (Karen 2007, 4)—leaving little room for discussion of community cohesion.

The majority of the photographs in the early 2000s were of musicians. From 2005, a greater proportion of the photographs depicted fans meeting a musician. In part, this change reflects the greater ease with which people can take and send photographs whilst at concerts due to rise of digital cameras and mobile phones. Figure 3.1 shows the consistently low number of women appearing as musicians against the high number of

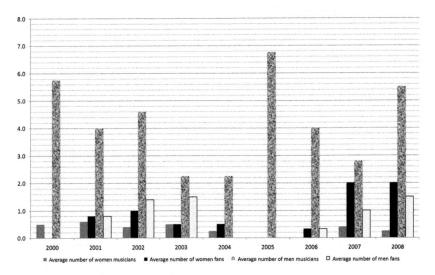

Fig. 3.1   Average number of musicians and fans in photographs, by gender

men. It also shows the low numbers of both women and men appearing as fans. What this says is that when women do appear it is more likely to be as fans than musicians.

Brown argues that, 'the style of the UK's metal magazines owes something to an attempt to translate the defining aesthetics of the genre into a sympathetic textual strategy' (Brown 2007, 645). I would go further and argue that it is not only the aesthetics, but also the ideology of the genre which is being translated. It shows the imaginary community as holding particular ideals and values as essential and unquestioned by parts of the community, ideas and values that on close inspection do not stand up to scrutiny. In this sense, these ideals and values can be read as myths: messages communicated by the magazine which promote a particular ideology and that therefore play a constitutive part in how the community is imagined.

Whilst photographs and letters *are* those of actual fans, the letters pages provide a mediated representation of fans, selected and edited for publication (c.f. Hynds 1992). In general, four criteria guide the publication of letters in newspapers: relevance, that letters should be concerned with timely issues important to readers; entertainment, that letters must 'capture the imaginations of audiences' (Wahl-Jorgensen 2002, 75); brevity, that letters should be fewer than 300 words; and authority, that letters should be from those who are informed and can write well. Although editors seek to appear unbiased in their choice of topic, the rule of authority enables the unconscious proclivities of the editor to play a part in letter selection (Wahl-Jorgensen 2002). These four criteria determine how the letters construct readers as a group by privileging some letter writers over others, resulting in the construction of particular debates (Wahl-Jorgensen 2002), and particular ideas about who readers are and what the imaginary community is like. Other studies treat letters to the editor as windows onto real women's lives and concerns where the letters can be read as texts that reveal beliefs and opinions (e.g. Martínez 2008; Williams 2009). Whilst the letters can be read in this way, the media in which the letters appear needs to be regarded in order to understand the power that the magazine's staff have in choosing how fans appear to one another. Moreover, to ignore the cumulative effect of the repetition of particular representations is to be blind to the way in which representations are engaged in a continual process of constructing the community and in structuring gender (Gill 2007). Therefore, the letters are the words of real women, but because they are selected by the magazine in such a way as to portray a version of the community, they stack up to create a particular representation.

The examples I use in this chapter are representative of the significations in which the myth is grounded, carefully selected after coding. While these representations are the most pertinent to understanding *Kerrang!*'s dominant myths, they are not the only representations; there are letters and photographs that do not fit with the dominant themes (but see Hill 2011). This indicates that some readers attend to the magazine from different standpoints and make meanings of *Kerrang!* that suggest negotiated or oppositional readings (Hall 1980) or resistant readings (Fetterley 1978). Such contradictory signs are infrequent and buck the dominant trend and so have less of a part to play in the accumulation of signs towards the establishment of ideas or values imagined as 'true'. I will return to this point toward the end of the chapter.

Kerrang! tells four myths about the imaginary community of hard rock and metal: that members are equal; that the genre, its people and culture are authentic; its musicians are men and warriors; its fans are women and groupies. Notions of equality and authenticity are fundamental to the representation of the community's core values. The community is portrayed as a 'level playing field' in which all members hold the same status in spite of differences of sex, race and sexuality, and despite disparities between roles (musician/industry, worker/fan). It is represented as an authentic culture based on real talent, hard work and genuine appreciation. These ideas of equality and authenticity are frequently discussed by letter writers, and they are held as self-evident and taken for granted. Authenticity is a quality whose value is held high as an obvious 'good' and has a number of meanings around maintaining personal and artistic integrity ('being true to oneself', not 'selling out' and 'paying your dues'). These markers of 'authenticity' are part of the origin stories of a number of bands and the personal histories of fans. Both equality and authenticity are emotive, politically and culturally charged terms, and they are mobilised to establish the goals of the users as morally right or good. In *Kerrang!*, however, the concepts are used as if they are simple and straightforward, ignoring the fact that they are contestable notions; this is why they are myths.

EQUALITY AND AUTHENTICITY

The importance of equality as a value of the community can be read in a number of aspects of *Kerrang!*: the position of the letters pages within the magazine, the photographs, and, perhaps most forcefully, in readers' letters. The title itself, 'Feedback', makes a contribution towards developing a sense of the community of equals. It acts like an imaginary closed circuit between editors and fans, inviting them into the community circle to discuss *Kerrang!*, implying readers' views are as important as those of the magazine staff. The repositioning of the pages straight after the editorial in June 2004 also gives the impression that readers' views carry similar weight to the editors'. That readers can recognise magazine staff as fans is part of the publishing strategy:

> *Kerrang!* is written by fans, for fans [...] As long as *Kerrang!*'s view is from down the front of the gig, we'll stay fresh without trying too hard. (Stuart Williams, *Kerrang!* Publishing Director quoted in Campaign 2008)

The 'by fans, for fans' approach is not presented as a marketing strategy, rather it is proffered as if it comes naturally because staff are writing what they themselves want to read because they are *just the same as* the readers. Williams presents *Kerrang!* as being a magazine of the fans—a grassroots publication—but actually it is a product of an international media company.

Equality between Fans and Musicians

Where the letters pages produce an imagined intimacy between fans and magazine staff that generates a sense of sameness, the photographs do similar work between fans and musicians. Photographs sent in by fans showing meetings between fans and musicians, especially from 2005 onwards, form a major part of the page. Photographs tend to look spontaneous, like 'snapshots', and are often taken backstage at a concert, but sometimes outside next to a tour bus, or inside a concert auditorium. Fans in the photographs are women and men, usually young (late teens/early 20s) and white. Musicians are nearly always men, white and, often, older than the fans. These images record a meeting that is likely to be exceptional in a fan's life. The photograph records a unique occasion, and yet a number of elements signify a close relationship based on similarity and implied parity between the fan and the musician.

Chloe's photograph (Fig. 3.2) records her meeting with Ginger, the lead singer of The Wildhearts (issue 1162, 2007). The pair are inside a dark public room, probably at a concert. Their clothes match: both wear black hoodies with logos and black tops. Their postures and gestures, her arm extending behind Ginger as if patting his waist, his hand reaching towards her elbow and the other giving a thumbs up, their smiles give a sense of a happy meeting, of long-parted friends reunited. In these smiles, close proximity and touching, as well as the mirroring of outfits, Chloe and Ginger give an impression of friendly camaraderie, of sameness and of equal status.

Fig. 3.2   Chloe (right) meets Ginger of The Wildhearts (*Source: Kerrang!*)

This image contains many of the same elements as other fan-musician photographs, and it is sometimes hard to tell which is the fan and which the musician. The shared style signifies that the musicians remain part of the community and that their musical success has not changed them (that is, they do not now wear Armani suits). It is common for musicians and fans to stand with their arms about each other's shoulders or to be touching in some way: there *appears* to be no hierarchy or star system here.

The suggestion is that most metal musicians are just like any other community member: their musical success is down to their hard work, and any fan could achieve the same success. Nor, as the naturalness and the ordinary clothes imply, has success changed them: they remain grounded and ordinary. Similarly, letters often record a meeting between a fan and musician. Such letters tend to declare that the band members are nice, ordinary people. In this example, Small Hyper Blonde records a happy encounter with musicians:

> After the show, even though the band were obviously tired they came outside and talked to the fans. They signed stuff and were actually listening to what the fans had to say. (Small Hyper Blonde 2001, 58–59)

The musicians, as presented by Small Hyper Blonde, respect their fans to the extent that they put their own needs to one side: they delay resting to talk to fans. As with the photographs, the musicians are presented as unpretentious and down to earth. On the rare occasions when stars did not take time to meet fans or were rude, letters tend to be derisive of the musicians.

Egalitarian Utopia?

The letters frequently assert that the community is equal and not subject to the major societal faultlines that affect mainstream society (sex/race/disability/age and so on). Claims about the equality of the genre appear in the references to 'looks', where 'looks' relates to race and dis/ability. Lisa of Nottingham, describing abilist abuse she suffered at a concert, writes of other rock fans: 'I thought you were supposed to see people for what they are—not what they look like' (Lisa 2001, 59). nads6666 claims that discrimination is not an intrinsic part of the community, writing, 'other rock fans have never commented on the colour of my skin, although I am the only Asian rock fan round my way' (nads6666 2002, 67). Lisa's surprise signifies that she believes the hard rock and metal community's values prevent it from making judgments based upon people's looks, whilst nads6666's letter disavows racism. These letters show how the community is imagined to prioritise love for the music as the central so that 'rock fan' is the central category of similarity, unifying participants across differences.

Westen argues that the modern Western concept of equality refers to like treatment of like people, but that within that definition there is a tautology:

> Equality is entirely "[c]ircular." It tells us to treat like people alike; but when we ask who "like people" are, we are told they are "people who should be treated alike." Equality is an empty vessel with no substantive moral content of its own. (1982, 547)

Equality therefore rests on sameness and does not accommodate difference, and the idea shapes Western thinking and discourse on human rights. It is this concept of equality that is mobilised in *Kerrang!*'s letters pages, articulated as something which *ought* to be accorded to all hard rock and metal fans—at least in terms of respect—but rarely do the letters specify how it is to be enacted.

In the imagined community, the nation is thought of as a community of equals, and real discrepancies or inequalities are not accounted for (Anderson 1991). Yet communities naturalise inequalities under the guise of traditions so that such discrimination is overlooked or not seen. Tradition is vital in maintaining a sense of cohesion, and this requires a feeling of sameness amongst community members (Weiss and Friedman 1995). Sameness is prioritised and differences hidden. In *Kerrang!* the sameness that binds is taste in music. This aesthetic equality reaches across a number of divisions within the community and is a crucial part of *Kerrang!*'s successful creation of a sense of community amongst hard rock and metal fans. Equality refers to two slightly different but linked things: the way in which musicians, fans and journalists are imagined to be of equal status and accorded the same respect; and the way in which the community is thought of as different from wider society and therefore does not feature the same areas of discrimination. In this way the hard rock and metal community is imagined to be a society of equals with no one, whether musician, journalist or fan, man, woman, gay, straight, black, white, and so on, occupying a higher position than another.

As the letters make evident, similarity of musical taste is the primary unifying factor of the community. Aesthetic appreciation trumps other lines of similarity, such as gender, race or age, along which solidarity may be constructed. This is the way in which the community is *imagined*, but equality is a myth. The photographs and letters depicting meetings between fans and musicians belie the sameness of musicians and fans. Almost unwittingly, even as the letter writers write of the ordinariness of the musicians they encounter, the fact of the letter reveals that there is something special about the men: they *are* stars. Furthermore, letters that highlight musicians' respect for fans do not take into account the way in which cultivating a fanbase is 'work'. Fiscal success and credibility as a band relies upon dedicated fans; a reputation for arrogance or neglect of fans can impact on sales. The relationship between fans and musicians is therefore not straightforward. Whilst some musicians do have genuine and caring attitudes towards fans, there is also a good deal of necessity in creating this image. It is not so important whether musicians are actually caring, or not, but that they are seen to be.

Furthermore, for *Kerrang!* to maintain its position in the community it is vital that its editorial staff and writers are *perceived* as fans. It is a marketing strategy and vital to selling magazines. This does not mean that the staff are *not* fans but that creating a feel of fandom is the crucial feature in establishing the sense of community. This is further elaborated in their published marketing strategy:

> Our research painted a clear picture of a world where it doesn't matter what colour you are, what your background is, what you wear, what your sexuality is. A world defined by its attitude to life. In Generation K!, credibility was found to be the key. (Marketing Society Awards quoted in Brown 2007, 648)

Kerrang! aims to appeal to potential readers by representing the community as already invested in an 'attitude to life' (non-discriminatory, rock and metal-loving). But the letters, like Lisa's, that claim that the hard rock and metal community is non-discriminatory are written when something has occurred that challenges the writers' perceptions of the community as equal. Indeed these events signal that the equality on offer is not only based on the similarity of musical taste, but also on the body of the fan or musician. Semblance to a white, able male body is required for 'equality'. Parity in the imaginary community is therefore a myth: a naturalised idea that serves the needs of the corporation publishing the magazine and the bands appearing in the magazine's pages, and an idea that reproduces the white male dominance of the genre.

The idea of the imaginary community as a level playing field is, however, linked to other ideas which are distinctly gendered. Equality is discussed in terms of loving similar music, but on further investigation this 'similar music' requires an additional element beyond musical semblance: it has to be 'authentic'. The myth of authenticity works in collaboration with the myth of equality and reinforces the myth of the warrior. Whilst at first glance this myth looks fairly innocuous, it relies upon gendered notions of rock and pop, and so validates the dominance of men as musicians and the exclusion of 'feminine' qualities. It colludes with the myth of equality because it is through its story of musicians being fans who progress through hard work and remaining 'true' to their musical values that authenticity is established. It is linked to the myth of the warrior because it determines who is 'authentic' enough to become a musician. Considering which individuals are represented as musicians is important because it is a key indicator of the differing levels of access to musical participation different groups have, and therefore the kinds of freedom they enjoy. On the letters pages realistic design elements, promotional photographs that give the appearance of capturing real moments, and letters about pop music, or other feminised subgenres, that contrast the genre with hard rock and metal all establish the community as 'authentic'.

Realism and the Authentic Magazine

Kerrang! uses skeuomorphism, the inclusion of design features that no longer have practical use, to give a feeling of realism in its design schemes. For example, in the early 2000s the letter of the week was set on a pale blue box positioned slightly out of the vertical line. The box was crosscut with faint grey lines and across the top were regular white circles, some of which break the top line. This blue box looks a lot like writing notepaper, but the text is typeset and the blue box is graphically created: it looks like a piece of notepaper stuck to the page, like a scrapbook. A number of other graphic techniques are similarly skeuomorphic: the re-creation of the website's message boards as if displayed in a web browser, beige rhombuses that evoke parcel tape, and drop shadows which give the effect of the photographs taped to the page rather than being printed. These techniques give a fanzine or scrapbook feel, as if the page has been created using paper, scissors and glue rather than on a computer. They are not used exclusively by *Kerrang!* and can be found in many magazines, but in *Kerrang!* they evoke a sense of the do-it-yourself (DIY) history of the genre (see Kahn-Harris 2007; Delfino 2007) and emphasise the notion of the magazine as a fan creation. *Kerrang!* thus builds upon its myth of equality by ensuring its appearance resonates with fanzine aesthetics, and it summons this shared history through such 'realist' techniques, thereby invoking tradition.

Musicians are portrayed as sincere members of the hard rock and metal community through the printing of promotional photographs that show them in their rock/metal garb in everyday settings, creating a sense that band members live a real hard rock and metal lifestyle. For instance, the band Finch (issue 1061, 2005) (Fig. 3.3), wearing jeans and T-shirts, loiter next to a wall at the side of the road, appearing as though they are waiting for a bus. The musicians do not look at the camera, implying that

Finch, au naturel and laughing in the 'painted face' of MCR'S Gerard Way, yesterday

Fig. 3.3   Finch (*Source: Kerrang!*)

the photograph has caught them unawares—it is not obviously posed. These realistic postures and casual clothes contribute towards an idea of the musicians living the hard rock and metal lifestyle: that this is their normal life. There is no sense that the musicians have dressed up especially for the photo shoot and that when the cameras have gone they will change their attire. In this way the musicians are represented as sincere and genuine members of the hard rock and metal community.

Rock versus Pop

Whilst musicians present themselves as authentic members of the community, they are also drawing upon the way in which the music is positioned in opposition to pop music. This antagonistic relationship is sited within a binary in which pop is seen to be 'manufactured' whilst hard rock and metal is 'authentic'. Here's The Voice of the Next Generation arguing that British people have bad taste in music:

> The British public's taste in music sucks; what with all this boy band, teen-pop shit it's like we're being force fed crap until we grow to like it while the real musicians out there go without any recognition. (The Voice of the Next Generation 2000, 50)

The Voice mobilises the idea of mass culture as the creation of an elite that is used to dupe the working class and stifle authentic folk cultures. This Marxist position is famously associated with Adorno and Horkheimer (1997 [1944]), who theorise mass culture as produced with the purpose of subduing the working classes and helping them to adapt to their exploited position in capitalist society, thus reducing the threat of socialist revolution. Those who fall prey to the capitalist message are the 'deceived masses' (Adorno and Horkheimer 1997 [1944], 133) who love the culture which is sedating them. The Voice sets her/himself outside of 'The British Public' (even whilst using 'we') by claiming that they (The British Public) do not understand the way in which they have been duped. The Voice is virulently dismissive of all pop music: it is a genre-based critique, with *all* pop music bad and *all* music discussed in *Kerrang!* 'real', which, in the context of authenticity, means 'good'.

It is not only pop music that comes under fire, however. Emo and My Chemical Romance are criticised for their lack of authenticity, and such letters often rely on distinctions between which music is suitably 'metal' and which is not. The latter comes to be positioned as 'other' regardless of the sound of the music. The following two letters, published side by side, work together to try to push My Chemical Romance out of the pages of the magazine:

> This whole dark scene of rock is so overrated. Not only is the word "black" overused way too much in rock, but there's so much rock nowadays that's all about self-harm, suicide, or death, so it wouldn't hurt to have a few cheery articles would it? (Elliott 2007, 4)

Elliott's letter implicates My Chemical Romance by reference to *The Black Parade*, the band's 2006 album which is about death and hints at suicide, plus British tabloids have described the band as leaders of a suicide cult (Sands 2006). This implication is picked up in the headline to the next letter: 'Stop crying your hearts out'. In the letter, Little Harry Hardcore writes, 'one message to all My Chemical Romance fans: STOP IT AND GET SOME SLAYER' (Little Harry Hardcore 2007, 4, capitals in original). Slayer are a longstanding band with an established place in the canon of hard rock and metal. *Kerrang!*'s letter headline links the two letters and thereby establishes the magazine as supportive of the view of My Chemical Romance as excessively involved in misery. It stresses a need for coverage of more canonical bands, calling My Chemical Romance's fans' place into question and affirming Slayer's.

In part, inclusion and authentic status is dependent upon the gender make-up of a band's audience. Emo and My Chemical Romance have been popularly feminised, partly via the bands' lyrical emphases on 'heartache, weakness, longing and loss' (Williams 2007, 146), but My Chemical Romance has also been feminised because of the band's use of make-up, its feminism and its large female fan base (Hill 2011). Paul Brannigan, editor of *Kerrang!* between 2000 and 2009, reads the contested place of emo as a result of prejudices around gender and age, and a protectionism by older, male fans of more established metal bands:

> Emo fans are the whipping boys of the moment. [...] There's a misogynistic air to it. A lot of the credible metal bands have got an older, very male following and they see teenage girls getting into bands like MCR and think they've not earned the respect to be called a rock fan. (Brannigan quoted in Boden 2006, 53)

'Respect' from male fans of 'credible metal bands' is something teenage girls must *earn*, not something that is accorded automatically as a right, an argument that certainly belies the myth of equality. Brannigan puts the lack of respect down to both age and sex of My Chemical Romance fans, but he also implies that bands 'like MCR' are not 'credible'. So whilst Brannigan seems to condemn older fans' misogyny, he betrays his own disbelief in My Chemical Romance's authenticity. The derogatory comments are the result of sexist attitudes which perceive women as inauthentic or not serious rock fans, echoing Davies' (2001) assertion that serious fans are treated as anomalous. But, moreover, because anything associated with women or with femininity—for instance a large female fan base—is positioned as suspect, pop and emo, with their large female followings, present a significant danger to the ideology of hard rock and metal as authentic.

The association of cultural authenticity with masculinity has been well established by Andreas Huyssen (1986), who clearly explained how mass culture and art have been positioned as antithetical and how this relationship relies upon a gendered binary. This association is obvious too in Adorno's work: he describes pop fans quite specifically 'as girls' (Adorno quoted in Frith 1983, 44). Whilst I am reticent to use subculture's theoretical framework, Sarah Thornton's (1995) extension of Huyssen's argument to subcultures and mainstreams is valuable for understanding how 'authenticity' works amongst music fans. She notes how members of subcultures create a communal identity defined against a demonised 'other' and, in the case of 1990's dance culture, the outsiders belong to the 'mainstream'. 'Mainstream' is a label given to the culture that is currently most popular, to the extent of being considered 'the norm'. It is not only feminised but fundamentally devalued. It is 'derivative, superficial and *femme*' (Thornton 1995, 5), and it is associated with pop music, fashion, herd mentality, passive consumption and lack of discernment or real taste.

'Subcultures', on the other hand, are authentic, intelligent, original and independent. Coates (1997) makes a similar argument about the rock/pop divide. The trouble is that femininity proves a threat to authenticity so that anything which is associated with women needs to be restrained from rock to preserve its authenticity. Frith (2007) hints at this in his discussion of rock critics' disdain for James Blunt. He concludes that the contempt shown for the musician is intertwined with the status of the fans:

that James Blunt CDs are displayed in music shops as 'Perfect for Mothers Day' is enough to deter people from buying them. Blunt lacks respect, Frith argues, because his target audience is (older) women. Pop music fits into this schema, and the genre is freely vilified by *Kerrang!*'s letter writers. My Chemical Romance, with its young audience and sympathy for feminine topics, also falls within the 'pop' or 'mainstream' side of the dichotomy, as implied by Brannigan. Authenticity is therefore dependent upon a sharply marked difference between 'feminine' and 'masculine' and requires the feminine to be expunged. This fits in with Connell's (1995) theorisation of hegemonic masculinity, which relies upon the expulsion of the feminine in order to maintain a powerful position of dominance. Masculinity is therefore not an essential quality which some men have more of than others; it is continually being negotiated within gender relations. Similarly authenticity is not an essential characteristic of some music and musicians. It is chimeric, mythical. If it were a real or natural quality of hard rock and metal then contact with any amount of femininity would not damage it. As a result, women's place in hard rock and metal is precarious: any claims they may make to authenticity will always be challenged (Nordström and Herz 2013).

In the letters, *Kerrang!* readers discuss equality and authenticity as values that are embodied by the community and that are axiomatic. This is in spite of their sometimes contradictory experiences at hard rock and metal events and in reading the magazine. However, even if 'real life' does not always live up to the idealistic community brought into being in the letters pages of *Kerrang!*, that does not (necessarily) make the community and its values less real for letter writers. The myths are so powerful that they work to make incongruous experiences seem like exceptions. That is not quite the case with the messages that *Kerrang!* delivers about gender. The myths of equality and authenticity are held to be self-evident by letter writers in *Kerrang!*, but the messages delivered by the myths of the warrior and the groupie are not transmitted through open discussion of the roles of men and women. They are communicated through the visual elements of the letters pages—the design and the photographs—and through the topics and tones of, in particular, women's letters. This means that they are 'obvious' in a different way to the values of authenticity and equality that appear in the letters themselves, because it is about how women and men *appear* rather than what they *say* the community ought to be.

WARRIORS

Working in tangent with notions of authenticity as essentially masculine, designs and photographs in the magazine signify war in order to naturalise the expulsion of the feminine. In common sense understandings of battle, femininity is a liability. In the design and images of the letters pages, red and black are prominent in transmitting this message. Their heavy use, especially after 2004, makes a significant impact upon the eye, as they are combined with striking effect. This combination can be seen frequently on hard rock and metal album artwork, T-shirts and in music videos, but the two colours also resonate with the signifiers of westernised warrior masculinity: red signifies blood, sex, debt, Satan, communism, danger, fire, aggression and confidence, while black signifies death, funerals, apocalypse, war, evil, nights, and fear (Dabner 2004). When used together (for example, in the Nazi flag, on poisonous or dangerous animals, a roulette wheel, a pack of cards) new meanings are created: risk, danger and amorality, but also forbidden pleasures and freedom from societal constraints. They also signify 'rage and intensity' (King 2001, 16) and so reflect the anger and intensity of the music. The sans serif font[2] of the letters implies modernity and signifies youth and newness, whilst serif fonts can appear more traditional (Frost 2003) and 'authoritative' (Dabner 2004, 83); the difference is like that between 'shouting and talking' (Frost 2003, 94). As with the use of red to imply aggression and speed, and thus reflecting the music, so the 'shouting' sans serif fonts mimic the loud, aggressive vocal delivery of many hard rock and metal bands. *Kerrang!*'s letters pages' colours therefore prominently signify danger, death, war, gore, youth, power and high volume. This gives a general sense of danger, and also connotes masculinity whilst *not* implying femininity: on the letters pages there are no soft pinks (except for the HMV logo) and no curly fonts. There is no graded shading: colours are bold with hard edges and no soft lines. There is little white space as the pages are full, creating a visual onslaught. The designs thus create an immediate visual impression and form a dramatic backdrop against which images are placed. It is a battlefield to be populated by warriors.

Photographs of musicians are generally photographs of men, and they tend to signify strength, masculinity and aggression. Musicians wear black, their hair is often long, and many have beards and tattoos. The look is strikingly different from the neater, short-haired and clean-shaven ideal of contemporary hegemonic masculinity.[3] These photographs use

Fig. 3.4 Robb Flynn
of Machine
Head (*Source: Kerrang!*)

postures, costumes and facial expressions that signify anger, aggression or intimidation in some form. Different kinds of aggressive and intimidating miens and gestures appear across the period. Machine Head's Robb Flynn (issue 1214, 2008) (Fig. 3.4) is a particularly good example. His imposing muscular massiveness fills the page. He is pictured against a background so dark that his black hair fades into it. His T-shirt is black, his beard is black and his eyes are black. His beard grows only on the underside of his chin, like a shadow. His arms are tattooed and he looks unsmilingly into the camera. His nose is pierced through the septum and a ring hangs in it, reminiscent of a bull. This implies that he is dangerous, virile and in need of careful handling. When militaristic postures, gazes and attire are not present, other indications of physical prowess, bravery and power are visible: tattoos; muscular frames emphasised by bare chests or upper arms; long hair, signalling defiance of convention. Long hair is also reminiscent of Anglo-Saxon and Viking warrior culture, both of which are crystallised in the British imagination as invading forces wielding bloody axes. Gestures and expressions evoke horror films and villains and seem designed to shock and to strike fear into the viewer (although of course seasoned metal fans will *not* be afraid). The people these images are intended to shock are some unnamed group outside of the hard rock and metal community that might comprise authority figures such as parents, teachers, employers, police, the Church or the government ('The Man'). For example, Slipknot wear grotesque masks that reference horror films such as *The Texas Chainsaw Massacre* (Hooper 1974), *Motel Hell* (Connor 1980), *It* (Wallace 1990) and *Hellraiser* (Barker 1987), films whose characters are murderers, torturers and predators.

The predominance of male musicians indicates that in the imaginary hard rock and metal community, musicians are male. Moreover, they embody bravery, strength, power and aggression in a context of war, on a bloody and gore-strewn battlefield. It is an image that affirms the masculinity of the genre of hard rock and metal and its musicians. Trafford and Pluskowski (2007) argue that the popular cultural representation of the Viking has been prevalent in heavy metal since its inception and forms an important motif in both lyrics and artwork, so it is not surprising to see it in *Kerrang!*. The use of Vikings (rather than other images of warriors such as chivalric knights) is important because it means that particular attributes can be attached to the hard rock or metal musician, and these qualities bolster the masculine status of the musician. The list of salient characteristics of Vikings is violent and masculine: 'bloodthirsty and rapacious attackers'; 'barbarian disrupters of civilized life'; 'hyper-masculine'; energy and dynamism; physical (and military) strength; and they are unlikely to 'submit […] easily to any acknowledged authority' (Trafford and Pluskowski 2007, 58). So whilst the Vikings are dangerous, they are also regarded as strong and independent: traits that are still valued within the context of contemporary Anglophone masculinity. Warrior masculinity is therefore something to which men have greater access and which also works to exclude the feminine. The myth thereby functions as a barrier to women's participation in the genre as musicians, resulting in fewer opportunities for women fans. I am not arguing that women cannot utilise warrior masculinity in order to be successful musicians (Angela Gossow might be regarded as one example) but rather that women's feminine socialisation and the ways in which women's femininity is regulated on a day-to-day basis places them at a disadvantage when seeking to become successful musicians. Of course not all women desire to take to the stage and wield an axe on the battlefield of rock, but they should feel able and have the opportunity to express themselves musically if they wish.

Clifford-Napoleone (2015b) uses a Butlerian performance framework and argues that masculinity in metal is nothing more than a performance: metal is queer in its performance of masculinity. In fact, she argues, what is actually going on is a 'drag show' (Clifford-Napoleone 2015b, 11) in which misogyny and homophobia are used to mask the desires of performers. Although Clifford-Napoleone and I may be coming at the topic from different theoretical perspectives, we are in agreement about metal masculinity: the warrior myth is a clear example of the way in which masculinity is 'done' for effect. In fact, I think it is overdone. Where Clifford-Napoleone and I differ is in the impact of masculinity on gender hierarchy. For Clifford-Napoleone, masculinity can be used by women who seek to participate in metal (her examples are Joan Jett and Otep). For me, the opportunities of performing masculinity are so evidently more open to men—trained to it throughout their lives—that women are distinctly disadvantaged. Nor are material barriers to be ignored. Clifford-Napoleone also neglects the representation of women who do not perform masculinity in metal. Looking at this is crucial for understanding how masculinity works with the gender division.

GROUPIES

The three myths of equality, authenticity and warriors set a scene in which masculinity is reified and femininity is excoriated: hard rock and metal appear as men's playground/battlefield. Yet women read *Kerrang!* in large numbers and are known to be fans. How are they represented in the magazine's version of the imaginary community? On average less than ten per cent of musician photographs appearing on the letters pages show women, but slightly more photographs of fans show women than men. When women do appear in *Kerrang!*'s letters pages, therefore, it is more likely to be as fans than musicians, and because photos of men are usually photos of musicians, female fan pictures eclipse those of males; therefore, hard rock and metal music fandom has a feminine face. To some extent, the greater proportion of photographs showing men as musicians corresponds with the smaller number of women making hard rock and metal music as signed artists. However, the overwhelming maleness of musicians in the representation is an important factor in band formation: musicians have to 'look' right. *Kerrang!*'s lack of women musicians does nothing to change the maleness of musicians, and it does not provide aspirant women musicians with role models. Moreover, the fan portrayed is a particular type of fan, more interested in musicians than in music: the groupie.

The comic strip *Pandora* is a prominent representation of women fans. The strip follows the exploits of a female fan called Pandora (Fig. 3.5), who makes excellent cheese and pickle sandwiches, often for musicians. The strip uses humour and irony to characterise Pandora and her aunt, Auntie P, as independent women who are primarily music fans. However, the visual portrayal uses exaggerated sexual features combined with states of undress to present a highly sexualised image of a female fan. Pandora

Fig. 3.5   *Pandora* comic strip (*Source: Kerrang!*)

and Aunty P both wear a lot of makeup, have large, perky breasts, and their extreme cleavages are usually offset by the word 'bitch' on their tops. Pandora is sometimes drawn naked or with breasts or pubic region exposed (on the toilet, masturbating, in bed where she sleeps without nightclothes): her large, high breasts, her rosebud mouth and big eyes fit into modern ideals of feminine sexual attractiveness. Aunty P (the initial suggesting that she too is called Pandora and that there is a continuum of women fans), is older, has wrinkles and chain-smokes. Aunty P is a veteran of the glam metal era, indicated by skin-tight clothes, back-combed hair and make-up, and the suggestion of sexual hedonism. Neither Pandora nor Auntie P are ever depicted playing instruments or as involved in other creative pursuits: they 'hobnob' with musicians, engaging in banter or make them cheese and pickle sandwiches. This portrayal of female fans as sexualised and in the service of male musicians continues in the photographs of women fans.

Photographs of women fans appear frequently, often depicting meetings between women fans and men musicians. Two example snapshots depict happy, smiling women alongside taller, older men who frequently touch the younger women. Fan Sarah of Wakefield (issue 855, 2001) is photographed in a busy Leeds record shop, posing next to Roger Manganelli of Less Than Jake (Fig. 3.6). Manganelli towers above her, leaning in. He gives a Johnny Rotten-esque stare. Sarah wears a white and red Less Than Jake T-shirt and she looks directly towards the camera. She is aged around 15 years old and appears happy to have met Roger. In a later issue

Fig. 3.6 Sarah (left) meets Roger Manganelli of Less Than Jake (*Source: Kerrang!*)

Fig. 3.7 Fans meet Jordan Pundik of New Found Glory (*Source: Kerrang!*)

(907, 2002), a photograph of women fans meeting Jordan Pundik of New Found Glory shows the musician is a head taller than his four female fans (Fig. 3.7). His arm is draped around one of their shoulders. He smiles slightly, but his body is turned away from the camera and he is leaning back a little, suggesting that he wants to be elsewhere. The four fans, aged around 15–17 years old, stand grinning in front of him. Two wear New Found Glory T-shirts; one stretches upwards as if standing on tiptoes. Two girls hold their hands up: one to her throat as if trying to contain her excitement, the other to her chest. The four girls stand close together and all look elated. The photographs of women fans meeting male musicians show that this is an unequal relationship. The men musicians touch the fans around the shoulders, they lean in to close proximity: the musicians encroach upon the young women's bodies and space. They are physically more imposing—taller, wider, older—and with facial expressions that are staring, tight-lipped and 'playing-up' to the camera. They are obliged to have their photographs taken whilst the young women desire to have the meeting recorded. Meanwhile the women are smaller in size, often stretch up, lean into or look up at the musicians. They smile or grin. The musicians' reticence and discomfort is in discordance with the women's pleasure: the women are more interested than the musicians in the meeting and the photography.

The sense of women's passion for their favoured bands is also evident in their letters defending the bands from detractors, and My Chemical Romance are a good example of a well-defended band. Becca positions the band as misunderstood, and her defence rests partly on the experiences of the musicians. Crucial is the rejection of the potentially very damaging accusation that the band has caused young people's deaths:

> One of those bands who helped me through this [bullying and depression] are MCR. They had been through so much as a band, and they pulled through it all. Their lyrics have such hope, they hold one important message, to keep going, whatever it takes. So people who brand their music as "depressing" and the band as possible leaders of a "suicide cult" can shove it up their ... well ... you get the point! (Becca In Norwich 2007)

My Chemical Romance were also the focus of an organised defence by fans when UK tabloid newspaper *The Daily Mail* linked the band to the suicide of emo fan Hannah Bond in 2008 (Hill 2011). Issues from May of that year include many letters that are supportive of the band, and a photograph of fans protesting outside *The Mail*'s offices (issue 1214) shows that the majority were young women.

Meanwhile, other letters from women express sexual desire for male musicians, such as Millie writing about Simon Neil:

> The pictures of Biffy Clyro in last week's issue (K! 1159) are absolutely gorgeous. Did it take long to wash all those inky equations off of Simon Neil's delicious body? (Millie 2007, 4)

Millie's 'delicious' suggests food and so signifies mouths, tongues, lips, taste buds and oral sensuality. Letters such as Millie's intimate that women fans gain a good deal of pleasure from their attractions to male musicians; the inclusion of such letters also positions women as willing participants in sex with musicians. The defensive letters champion the music of all-men bands, and women are signified as protectors of their musical and personal reputations, loving them seemingly unconditionally and without requitement. The letter writers are emotionally invested in their favoured bands' value, and their own identity is tied in with it. There is an unbalanced relationship between women fans and male bands which is also evident in the desiring letters. Women seek relationships with their favourite bands, stating that they *love* them and that they will act on their behalf. This relationship does not work both ways; individual fans are not of interest to bands: it is *the number of fans*, and so numbers of record, ticket and merchandise sales, that matter. The musician is always special to the fan; the individual fan is rarely special to the musician. Thus the relationship between musicians and women fans is an unequal one.

Whilst female fans are represented as desiring, loving and protecting male musicians, and whilst men musicians are photographed in ways that signify the fearsome warrior, photographs of women musicians tend to emphasise heterosexual attractiveness. Typical of this representation is the image of Paz Lenchantin, bassist of A Perfect Circle (issue 805, 2000) (Fig. 3.8).

In the photograph Lenchantin looks up, away from the camera, her dark hair falling wispily over her face. Her lips are full and slightly apart signifying sexual readiness. Her eyes, 'coy', look up and towards the top of the frame rather than directly out at the viewer. Her make-up, smooth skin and sculpted eyebrows are part of a beauty regime that is not part of

Fig. 3.8 Paz Lenchantin of A Perfect Circle (*Source: Kerrang!*)

the preparation that most male musicians undergo before a photo shoot. The letter alongside the image further sexualises Lenchantin:

> GOD DAMN, that baby from A Perfect Circle is one hot mama. I would appreciate it if you would forward her phone number and address to me... or maybe just a 10ft poster of her grabbing her breasts. What a babe! (Someone else 2000, 50)

The author, who *Kerrang!* addresses as 'sir' in their reply, uses three common monikers for attractive women—'baby', 'babe' and 'hot mama'—all of which refer to bodily attractiveness. He (assuming *Kerrang!* is correct) then exercises his male privilege and makes an unsolicited advance towards the object of his lust by asking for her contact details. Failing that, he requests a larger-than-life poster of Lenchantin in a sexual pose. Someone else's request positions *Kerrang!* as a sexual mediator—a pimp—which further objectifies Lenchantin. This portrayal shows men as sexually autonomous and works with the predominant representation of men as musicians, whilst women are reduced to their sexual use value. Letters from women fans that express desire for male musicians, on the other hand, show the female fan as sexually invested in musicians rather than objectifying men because the dominant vision is of women as fans, watching, listening, rather than music making.

These images and letters naturalise a certain kind of relationship between the depicted women and men: because representations of women in *Kerrang!*'s letters pages are primarily of women as fans, this marks a gender divide in the roles members of the imaginary community can play. Women are placed in the role of camp followers or cheerleaders. This gives musicians a symbolic *carte blanche* whilst the women are symbolically willing in whatever their favourite musicians wish of them. Those women who are fortunate enough to become successful as musicians, are not represented in the same ways male musicians are (as warriors). Women musicians are heterosexualised for a male audience and, although men musicians are also sometimes positioned as objects of desire, they primarily appear for a male viewer: as a warrior to be admired and emulated. When women fans defend musicians from what are framed as personal attacks, and when they express desire for male musicians, they reinforce the message that women are primarily interested in the persons of musicians over the music. What this amounts to is a myth of women as always sexually willing. This chimes with the cultural understanding of women who participate in rock music as the reward for male rock stars' travails on the road. It echoes what Cheryl Cline (1992) and Lori Twersky (1981) describe as the ways in which any woman involved in rock music, whether as fan, musician, journalist or wife, is referred to as a groupie. Schippers defines a groupie as 'one who is sexually accessible to rock musicians, or someone with whom rock musicians have sex' (2002, 26). It is obvious from this definition, however, that this representation doesn't apply to the vast majority of women involved in rock music. Furthermore, the representation aligns 'groupie' with 'slut' (Cline 1992, 83) and is used to scorn women. Plus not all women musicians or fans are groupies, nor wish to be, but all hard rock and metal-loving women are defined in this stereotype by their availability for male pleasure rather than their interest in the music. This message, along with the myth of the warrior, establishes distinct and hierarchical roles for women and men that are rooted in understandings of women as subordinate to men.

The dominant representation of women in hard rock and metal as groupies is dangerous. Pamela Des Barres (2007) repositions the groupie as muse, and this rethinking of what 'groupie' means is important work that needs to be done within feminist understandings of rock music (but see Coates 2003). Des Barres (2007) is right that it is a problem when women who want sex with musicians are condemned; women should be able to pursue their desires without facing sexist disapprobation. However, when *all* women are represented as groupies this is dangerous for three reasons.

First, because it assigns only the role of fan to women who love hard rock and metal. Brill (2008) identifies a similar problem in the highly sexualised images of women in goth, arguing that it reproduces the inequality it represents. Male musicians benefit from their status via access to creative and sexual expression, group bonding, the power to affect people's lives through their artistic endeavours, increased self-worth and, possibly, financial rewards. In the words of Brill, 'the greatest honour a woman may hope for in this order of things is to be chosen as a muse or a cover model by the male artist' (Brill 2008, 164). Not all fans wish to be musicians or to express themselves musically, but, should they wish it, they ought to have access to musicianship and to the rewards of being in a band. As things stand, the lack of role models in *Kerrang!* for women who wish to become musicians is just one of many barriers to overcome.

Secondly, it enforces a heterosexuality, which is built upon the common sense idea of women fans as interested in the person of the male musician rather than the music. Cultural meanings are 'not only "in the head". They organise and regulate social practices, influence our conduct and consequently have real, practical effects' (Hall 1997, 3). Representation produces meanings that affect social practices because 'they define what is "normal", who belongs—and therefore, who is excluded' (Hall 1997, 10). The media encode messages, creating discursive knowledge that makes our real lives intelligible (Hall 1980, 131). The myths in *Kerrang!*, then, play a crucial role in determining how the community is imagined; they have consequences for women fans (and for men musicians) outside of the magazine's pages. Women fans' passion for the music may incorporate aspects of sexual desire for musicians, but it is not limited to it, and nor should it be assumed to exist. Furthermore, this representation relies upon the idea that particular sexualities flow from particular bodies, a notion that enforces heterosexuality. In doing so it asserts that women are ruled by their (heterosexual) bodies and their 'base' desires and cannot appreciate music in a cerebral manner, as it should be in Kantian aesthetics. That kind of understanding depends upon the man/woman and mind/body binary so that women's pleasure is first and foremost a bodily delight—and this kind of fleshy gratification is devalued. Proper appreciation of music is supposedly intellectually 'pure' and occurs in the mind, untainted by corporality. This means that women fans are not—cannot—be taken seriously as music fans because their appreciation of the band is first determined by their feminine crushes on the musicians: it is seen as fortuitous if they like the music as well, but even then the enjoyment is 'suspect' (Davies 2001, 313).

Thirdly, the myth of the groupie has implications for women who wish to meet musicians and may be attracted to them. In her discussion of the reporting of the crimes of Jimmy Savile (the British television presenter of Top of the Pops during the 1960s and 1970s, posthumously found guilty of raping and sexually assaulting hundreds of people, many young women), Karen Boyle (2015) describes a context of male sexual entitlement within popular music culture. The photographs in which women fans are being touched by musicians are vivid examples of this entitlement. Boyle links such unsolicited touching to a 'continuum of sexual violence' (Kelly 1987) that constitutes a range of controlling behaviours of men over women, from verbal harassment and unwanted touching to rape and incest. Women fans, as represented in *Kerrang!*, are put in a position in which embarking on a sexual encounter with the musician is considered 'natural', expected. They are assumed to be sexually willing and consenting. Women fans are put in vulnerable positions in which there is an unequal power relationship that is ripe for exploitation. Recent UK investigations into sexual crimes committed by rock musicians and other media figures, some historical, some more recent, are awful examples of how female fans are targeted. For men musicians, exploiting sexual opportunities is required for their status as musicians, and therefore *expected*, whether their partner is willing or not (Forrest 2010). The roles of groupie and musician are not just complementary; they are a necessary part of the culture (Schippers 2002). Rock is founded on the basis of this contempt for women. When *Kerrang!* represents women fans' pleasure in hard rock and metal as determined by attraction to musicians, or by representing women musicians as only valuable for their heterosexual attractiveness, the message that hard rock and metal is a masculine genre in which men make music for men dominates. Its homosociality is affirmed whilst threats of homosexuality are headed off with excessive heterosexual activity.

CONCLUSION

The dominant message of *Kerrang!*'s letters pages is of an imaginary community in which women are designated as heterosexual bedmates rather than taken seriously as fans. So whilst the community is imagined as equal and authentic, it actually represents women as groupies and men as warrior-musicians. The reifying of authenticity and of male musicians is predicated on the diminishing of the feminine so that woman cannot be full community members, either as fans or as musicians. They have a role, and that role is to provide an adoring mirror for male musicians. *Kerrang!*'s myths ultimately bolster male dominance and reinforce the subordinate position of women in the imaginary community. And yet these myths are communicated within an imaginary community that values equality, rendering this particular inequality difficult to see and hard to challenge because it means challenging the whole culture of the hard rock and metal genre. Gill defines such representations and practices of power in which inflexible ideologies find subtle ways to maintain their authority as 'flexible sexism' (2011, 62). Women are no longer exscripted (written out of) from hard rock and metal, but they are not accepted on the same terms as men either.

There are other messages in the letters pages of *Kerrang!*, and there are letters and images which do not fit into the myths. These myths are the dominant messages, not the only messages; I have discussed elsewhere some of the ways in which women letter writers employ devices that can be associated with the warrior myth, such as flyting and sounding (engaging in verbal insult battles with fellow readers) (Hill 2011). The use of these techniques suggests that women letter writers are able to access masculine forms of address, although these kinds of letters are overwhelmed by the defensive and celebratory letters that are more typical of women letter writers. Furthermore, it is unlikely that *Kerrang!*'s letters pages are encountered by all readers or all the time and in the same way; other kinds of readings are possible (Hall 1980), and the sex of the imagined and real reader makes a difference (Fetterley 1978). The power of the myths is in the immediacy of their messages, making the relationship between women, fandom and sexual availability seem natural. Barthes describes such naturalisation of ideas as 'ideological abuse' (2009 [1957], xix), implying that when we encounter myths we are damaged by them. But as Hall (1973) argues, although producers of media texts may encode a preferred message, readers of the text may not 'get' it. Each reader's cultural milieu will affect how they engage with the text, impacting on whether they accept the preferred or dominant reading, whether they challenge it outright or whether they accept aspects of the preferred reading, but not all. Melanie Lowe's (2003) study of tweens' engagements with Britney Spears adds to this understanding of the processes of meaning making. She argues that media readings are a complex process in which we knit together a number of differing discourses, some of which may be contradictory. In her example, feminism is part of young women's debates about Britney—they condemn the sexualised images of the singer—but so too are empathetic feelings towards her, as they consider the work and pressures upon her. Lowe's valuable work highlights the complex ways in which we make meaning when we engage with media texts. Women fans' readings of *Kerrang!* may therefore identify and challenge the naturalisation of gendered roles in metal, questioning not only the roles, but also the relationship between metal, masculinity, authenticity, equality and gendered roles. There may be queer readings that celebrate the queer potential of metal for female masculinities (Clifford-Napoleone 2015b) or that read the groupie as evidence of liberated feminine sexuality (Shirazi 2010).

Clearly, the theory of many possible readings raises a challenge for Barthes' theory, in which myth seems to have a life of its own, able to get inside our heads like a parasite and make a home there. The agency of the media text producers—and their willingness to change the story or rewrite the myth—has no place in the theory. The questions of how much editors 'know', how consciously representations are made or how much media workers rely on conventions remain, and more research would be valuable. It could be argued that the presence of women on *Kerrang!*'s letters pages echoes the increased female readership and is a sign of women's involvement in metal. That would challenge Walser's description of metal as 'worlds without women' (1993, 110), and the presence and topics of the letters could be read as changing the agenda for hard rock and metal to include more feminine aspects. Yet, the photographs and the single-gendered portrayal of musicians undermine this reading as women's role is so limited—there is no change in the agenda. Women are always outside and need to fight for their place, whilst men are making hard rock and metal music for one another as if it is the natural order of things. In this way, the male experience of hard rock and metal is assumed by *Kerrang!* to be the normal experience; women are there to enhance the male experience, not to share in it. If this is the preferred reading, then because it asks the reader to identify with a male position (Fetterley 1978), it may be taken on board by men more often than by women. Women's readings would require more negotiation as they are asked to identify against themselves, and so they may be more likely to have oppositional or negotiated readings. Engaging with the media is a gendered experience expressly because of the gendered ideology of the imaginary community that it represents: women and men are highly likely to 'read' the myths differently.

NOTES

1. *Smash Hits* was a pop music magazine. It ran from 1978 to 2006. Its readers were supposed to be teenage girls: 'teenyboppers'. A number of forum comments reveal this attitude and a small sample can be read at: http://www.kerrang.com/blog/2009/12/kerrang_magazine_02122009.html
2. A serif font (e.g., Times New Roman) includes ornamentation on the characters, while a sans serif font (e.g., Arial) does not.
3. Not all photographs show hard rock and metal musicians looking like warriors: metal has its fashions. In the early years of the century, many images show very short cropped hair on nu-metal artists. The concept of aggression

remains in the challenging and threatening looks cast at the camera, and black clothes are prominent. Fashions associated with emo reject aggressive expressions; hair falls in straightened 'floppy' fringes, often black with streaks of blond, and they wear eyeliner. This more polished appearance, which requires daily maintenance of hair and make-up, is associated with women's beauty regimes and signifies femininity. Emo fashion receives gendered criticism, reinforcing the angry, long-haired fashion as hegemonic.

REFERENCES

Adorno, Theodor W., and Max Horkheimer. 1997 [1944]. *Dialectic of Enlightenment*. London: Verso.

Anderson, Benedict. 1991. *Imagined Communities: Reflections on the Origin and Spread of Nationalism*. Rev. and extended ed. London: Verso.

Barker, Clive. 1987. *Hellraiser*. Entertainment.

Barthes, Roland. 2009 [1957]. *Mythologies*. Translated by Annette Lavers. London: Vintage.

Becca In Norwich. 2007. Letter to the Editor. *Kerrang!*, 23 June.

Boden, Sarah. 2006. Nobody Likes Us. We Care. *Observer Music Monthly*, December.

Boyle, Karen. 2015. Hiding in Plain Sight: Sexism as Disguise in the Jimmy Savile Case. *FWSA Biennial Conference*, Leeds, 9–11 September.

Brill, Dunja. 2008. *Goth Culture: Gender, Sexuality and Style*. Oxford: Berg.

Brown, Andy R. 2007. Everything Louder Than Everything Else. *Journalism Studies* 8(4): 642–655.

Brown, Andy R. 2009. 'Girls Like Metal, Too!': Female Reader's Engagement with the Masculinist Ethos of the Tabloid Metal Magazine. *Heavy Metal and Gender International Congress*, Cologne University of Music and Dance, 10 October.

Campaign. 2006. Magazine ABCs Jan–Jun 2006: Film and Music. Last modified 25 August. http://www.brandrepublic.com/Campaign/News/589406/Magazine

———. 2008. Media: Double Standards—There's Much More to Music Television than MTV. Accessed 27 October 2008. http://www.brandrepublic.com/Campaign/Features/Analysis/779641/Media-Double-Standards---Theres-music-television-MTV/

Clifford-Napoleone, Amber. 2015b. *Queerness in Heavy Metal Music: Metal Bent*. Abingdon: Routledge.

Cline, Cheryl. 1992. Essays from Bitch: The Women's Rock Newsletter with Bite. In *Adoring Audience: Fan Culture and Popular Media*, ed. Lisa A. Lewis, 69–83. London: Routledge.

Coates, Norma. 1997. (R)evolution Now? Rock and the Political Potential of Gender. In *Sexing the Groove: Popular Music and Gender*, ed. Sheila Whiteley, 50–64. Abingdon: Routledge.

———. 2003. Teenyboppers, Groupies, and Other Grotesques: Girls and Women and Rock Culture in the 1960s and Early 1970s. *Journal of Popular Music Studies* 15(1): 65–94.

Connell, Raewyn. 1995. *Masculinities*. Cambridge: Polity.

Connor, Kevin. 1980. *Motel Hell*. United Artists.

Dabner, David. 2004. *Graphic Design School: The Principles and Practices of Graphic Design*. London: Thames & Hudson.

Davies, Helen. 2001. All Rock and Roll is Homosocial: The Representation of Women in the British Rock Music Press. *Popular Music* 20(3): 301–319.

Delfino, Robert A. 2007. Justice for All? Metallica's Argument Against Napster and Internet File Sharing. In *Metallica and Philosophy: A Crash Course in Brain Surgery*, ed. William Irwin, 232–244. Oxford: Blackwell.

Des Barres, Pamela, ed. 2007. *Let's Spend the Night Together: Backstage Secrets of Rock Muses and Supergroupies*. London: Helter Skelter Publishing.

Elliott. 2007. Letter to the Editor. *Kerrang!*, 2 June.

Fetterley, Judith. 1978. *The Resisting Reader: A Feminist Approach to American Fiction*. London: Indiana University Press.

Forrest, Rebecca. 2010. Mud Shark: Groupies and the Construction of the Heavy Metal Rock God. In *The Metal Void: First Gatherings*, eds. Niall W.R. Scott, and Imke Von Helden, 135–148. Oxford: Inter-Disciplinary Press.

Frith, Simon. 1983. *Sound Effects: Youth, Leisure, and the Politics of Rock*. London: Constable.

———. 2007. The Unpopular and the Unpleasant: Thoughts Inspired by the Work of James Blunt. *New Directions in Popular Culture Conference*, Leeds, 21 March.

Frost, Chris. 2003. *Designing for Newspapers and Magazines*. London: Routledge.

Gill, Rosalind. 2007. *Gender and the Media*. Cambridge: Polity.

———. 2011. Sexism Reloaded, or, It's Time to Get Angry Again! *Feminist Media Studies* 11(1): 61–71.

Hall, Stuart. 1973. *Encoding and Decoding in the Television Discourse Birmingham Centre for Contemporary Cultural Studies*. Birmingham: The University of Birmingham.

———. 1980. Encoding/Decoding. In *Culture, Media, Language*, eds. Stuart Hall, Dorothy Hobson, Andrew Love, and Paul Willis, 128–138. London: Hutchinson.

———, ed. 1997. *Representation: Cultural Representations and Signifying Practices*. Milton Keynes: The Open University.

Hill, Rosemary Lucy. 2011. Is Emo Metal? Gendered Boundaries and New Horizons in the Metal Community. *Journal for Cultural Research* 15(3): 297–313.

Hooper, Tobe. 1974. *The Texas Chainsaw Massacre*. Bryanston Pictures.

Huyssen, Andreas. 1986. *After the Great Divide: Modernism, Mass Culture, Postmodernism*. Basingstoke: Macmillan Press.

Hynds, Ernest C. 1992. Editorial Page Editors Discuss Use of Letters. *Newspaper Research Journal* 13: 124–136.

Kahn-Harris, Keith. 2007. *Extreme Metal: Music and Culture on the Edge*. Oxford: Berg.

Karen. 2007. Letter to the Editor. *Kerrang!*, 30 June.

Kelly, Liz. 1987. The Continuum of Sexual Violence. In *Women, Violence and Social Control*, eds. Jalna Hanmer, and Mary Maynard, 46–60. Basingstoke: Macmillan.

Kerouac, Jack. 2001 [1957]. *On the Road*. London: Penguin Books.

King, Stacey. 2001. *Magazine Design that Works: Secrets for Successful Magazine Design*. Gloucester: Massachusetts Rockport Publishers Inc.

Kruse, Holly. 2002. Abandoning the Absolute: Transcendence and Gender in Popular Music Discourse. In *Pop Music and the Press*, ed. Steve Jones, 134–155. Philedelphia: Temple University Press.

Lisa. 2001. Letter to the Editor. *Kerrang!*, 23 June.

Little Harry Hardcore. 2007. Letter to the Editor. *Kerrang!*, 2 June.

Lowe, Melanie. 2003. Colliding Feminisms: Britney Spears, 'Tweens,' and the Politics of Reception. *Popular Music and Society* 26(2): 123–140.

Marcus, Greil. 1976. *Mystery Train*. New York: Dutton.

Martínez, Katynka Z. 2008. Real Women and their Curves: Letters to the Editor and a Magazine's Celebration of the "Latina Body". In *Latina/o Communication Studies Today*, ed. Angharad N. Valdivia, 137–159. New York: Peter Lang Publishing, Inc..

McLeod, Kembrew. 2002. Between Rock and a Hard Place: Gender and Rock Criticism. In *Pop Music and the Press*, ed. Steve Jones, 93–113. Philedelphia: Temple University Press.

Millie. 2007. Letter to the Editor. *Kerrang!*, 2 June.

nads6666. 2002. Letter to the Editor. *Kerrang!*, 29 June.

Nordström, Susanna, and Marcus Herz. 2013. 'It's a Matter of Eating or Being Eaten.' Gender Positioning and Difference Making in the Heavy Metal Subculture. *European Journal of Cultural Studies* 16(4): 453–467.

Sands, Sarah. 2006. Emo Cult Warning for Parents. *The Daily Mail*, 16 August.

Schippers, Mimi. 2002. *Rockin' Out of the Box: Gender Maneuvering in Alternative Hard Rock*. London: Rutgers University Press.

Shirazi, Roxana. 2010. *The Last Living Slut: Born in Iran, Bred Backstage*. New York: itbooks.

Small Hyper Blonde. 2001. Letter to the Editor. *Kerrang!*, 2 June.

Someone else. 2000. Letter to the Editor. *Kerrang!*, 10 June.

The Voice of the Next Generation. 2000. Letter to the Editor. *Kerrang!*, 17 June.

Thornton, Sarah. 1995. *Club Cultures: Music, Media and Subcultural Capital.* Cambridge: Polity.

Trafford, Simon, and Aleks Pluskowski. 2007. Antichrist Superstars: The Vikings in Hard Rock and Heavy Metal. In *Mass Market Medieval: Essays on the Middle Ages in Popular Culture,* ed. David W. Marshall, 57–73. Jefferson: McFarland & Co.

Twersky, Lori. 1981. Devils or Angels? The Female Teenage Audience Examined. In *Rock She Wrote: Women Write About Rock, Pop, and Rap,* eds. Evelyn McDonnell, and Ann Powers, 177–183. New York: Delta.

Wahl-Jorgensen, Karin. 2002. Understanding the Conditions for Public Discourse: Four Rules for Selecting Letters to the Editor. *Journalism Studies* 3(1): 69–81.

Wallace, Tommy Lee. 1990. *Stephen King's It.* Warner Bros. Television.

Walser, Robert. 1993. *Running with the Devil: Power, Gender, and Madness in Heavy Metal Music.* Hannover, NH: University Press of New England.

Weiss, Penny A., and M. Friedman. 1995. *Feminism and Community.* Philedelphia: Temple University Press.

Westen, Peter. 1982. The Empty Idea of Equality. *Harvard Law Review* 95(3): 537–596.

Williams, Megan E. 2009. "Meet the Real Lena Horne": Representations of Lena Horne in Ebony Magazine, 1945–1949. *Journal of American Studies* 43(1): 117–130.

Williams, Sarah F. 2007. A Walking Open Wound: Emo Rock and the "Crisis" of Masculinity in America. In *Oh Boy! Masculinities and Popular Music,* ed. Freya Jarman-Ivens, 145–160. New York: Routledge.

CHAPTER 4

Women Fans and the Myth of the Groupie

INTRODUCTION

Many of my interviewees shared *Kerrang!*'s view of the community as equal and recounted that at hard rock and metal events they were less likely to encounter gender-based prejudice or outright sexism than at mainstream events. In my estimation, a powerful form of sexism exists in the myth of the groupie, although it is not widely discussed as such in the letters pages. It is a gendered division that serves to ensure that the high-status role of musician is reserved for men and provides those men with women to bolster their egos and cater for their heterosexual desires. Indeed, the concept of the rock musician is predicated upon the heterosexual division of labour, and the woman fan is thereby naturalised as heterosexual. To be a lesbian fan of a male musician does not make sense in the imaginary community because women's fandom is inextricably tied to an assumption of heterosexual interest in the male musician. Only one of my interviewees made reference to being anything other than heterosexual. Because I did not ask my interviewees to define their sexuality, I do not want to assume that this means the majority *were* heterosexual, however, most of the discussion around love lives and sexual attraction did place men in the role of sexual partners. The one exception was Hazel, who said she had had a 'bisexual phase'. The heterosexist ideology of hard rock and metal *may* have resulted in some women being reticent about discussing other kinds of sexual feelings.

© The Editor(s) (if applicable) and The Author(s) 2016   83
R.L. Hill, *Gender, Metal and the Media*, Pop Music, Culture
and Identity, DOI 10.1057/978-1-137-55441-3_4

To be a woman fan, then, is to be assumed to be sexually attracted to musicians and if not actively seeking sexual contact with a musician, at least desiring it. Thus, whilst not all women *are* groupies, all women are seen as potential or actual groupies. Cheryl Cline asked in *Bitch* magazine 'are female fans the same as groupies?' (1992, 76) and concluded that rock journalism shows no difference—all women involved in rock are groupies, whether a fan, journalist or even a musician. Nor is the term without its problems: 'it's used as an all purpose insult' (Cline 1992, 77).

What is wrong with being represented as a groupie? Rock's most famous groupie, Pamela Des Barres, has, in her autobiography and edited collection of 'backstage secrets' (Des Barres 2005, 2007), made an effort to reclaim 'groupie' as a feminist concept, arguing that 'I still considered myself a true feminist in the early days of women's rights because I was doing exactly what I wanted to do. I loved music and the men who made it' (2005, 12). More recently Roxana Shirazi's (2010) autobiography presents her groupie experiences as a sequence of adventures in which she explores her own sexuality, reclaiming it from the double standard that condemns women who pursue 'sexual pleasure and sexual adventure' (Shirazi 2010, 2). Shirazi and Des Barres position themselves as sexually liberated feminists, and although I find elements of their stories problematic, it is clear from their narratives that groupie experiences can be joyful and exciting—choices freely made rather than exploitative relationships. The tales are not about the exploitation of women's bodies (unlike Jenny Fabian and Johnny Byrne's *Groupie* [1969]), but about free sexual expression and passionate engagement with music and musicians. Nevertheless, for most women music fans who do not wish for sex with musicians, groupie is used as a stick to beat them with, synonymous with 'slut'. Additionally, as Shirazi notes, slut is still used to moralise and police women's sexual behaviour. 'Slut' may be the focus of some reclamation (for example, via the slutwalk movement), but it remains a derogatory term in its common sense usage.

Cline is critical of the stereotype but acknowledges some truth in the tales of sexual exploitation by bands; however, she argues that women who do become groupies are *not* uninformed about what awaits them. In the lower ranks of the groupie hierarchy are

> The "totally disposable" girls who provide "room service or 'in-flight entertainment'—ready and willing to be used or abused as the fancy dictates." This is the more realistic description of the groupie's lot, and girls know it. (Cline 1992, 82, citing Herman)

Also problematic is that the term 'groupie' prioritises women's sexuality (or rather assumptions about it) over their musical interests because women fans are believed to be more interested in the person of the musician than in the music. This disparagement of the seriousness of women's interests should not, perhaps, come as a surprise: after all, mass culture theory denigrates both the cultural products and the audience of those products when the audience is feminine. The devaluing of women hard rock and metal fans is part of the same misogynistic thinking. The result is not only that they are not accorded respect for their musical tastes, but they are also denied other roles and face derogatory comments from other community members. In short, they suffer a lower status. The kinds of sexism that arise from this are detailed by Nordström and Herz (2013) and include persistent 'testing' of women fans' knowledge and taste. What's more, any sexual pleasure that they may gain in addition to musical joy from their fandom is treated as a lesser form of fandom and not taken seriously.

What impact does all this have on women fans? To challenge negative portrayals of women fans, the visual and sexual pleasures that women gain from fandom need to be considered, as well as the aural pleasures. As Liz Stanley argues, myths and ideology are powerful forces, not just in everyday practices, but in thought processes too:

> Cultural politics sees the material and ideological as symbiotically related, recognising that ideas have a material origin and that the ideological has importance through the expression of ideas in concrete material practices. (1992, 3)

The ideology of hard rock and metal has a part to play in women's lives as it creates expectations and colours their understanding of what happens to them—their experiences are created by this collision of events and ideology. In analysing the words of my interviewees I treat their responses as stories of experiences formed through their rememberings and retellings of what has happened to them, and made sense of within the ideology of the imaginary community (and other competing 'world views' such as feminism and socialism). This meaning is to be treated as important and as 'real' because the structure that serves the purposes of the genre's male dominance has real effects upon their lives. The myth of the groupie thereby has import in creating different musical experiences for women and men; it creates a climate in which women's fandom is always played out against the backdrop of their imagined sexuality—that is, others' sexist stereotypes and prejudices. The myth of the groupie is communicated through *Kerrang!*'s letters pages; but it is also evident in the rock media more broadly as it forms a crucial part of the genre's culture.

Films such as *Almost Famous*, rock memoirs of canonic bands (for example, Mötley Crüe's *The Dirt* [Lee et al. 2014] and *Hammer of the Gods* [Davis 2005] about Led Zeppelin) and banal descriptions of women fans in gig reviews and interviews with musicians (for example the depiction of Lindsay Lohan as a sexual prize [Johnson 2007]) all contribute to the idea of women as primarily interested in sex with musicians. The ideology of hard rock and metal is therefore evident in a range of cultural texts; one single text is not responsible for communicating the imaginary community's shared values and myths. When I asked my interviewees about the myth of the groupie, therefore, they did not only reflect on *Kerrang!* but upon the general media figure of the groupie.

I asked my participants three questions about the groupie myth:

1. Have you ever met your favourite band?
2. Do you know what a groupie is?
3. Would you call yourself a groupie?

My interviewees expressed discomfort with the representation of women fans, and none took on the moniker 'groupie'. For example, Patti gave me a detailed description of the musical elements that she loved when she listened to Coheed and Cambria, and then said,

[Patti] I do quite fancy Claudio Sanchez. That's not true, but I like him very much indeed.

[Rosemary] Do you fancy him or not? I'm a bit confused...

[Patti] Yes I fancy him a lot, Rosey, yeah. (Patti)

Patti's self-contradiction exposed the discomfort and complicated thinking behind whether or not to disclose her attraction, and she initially implied that her attraction was not strong. 'Like' removed the sexual connotations of 'fancy' and changed her attitude to one of non-sexual admiration, perhaps more for his musical and lyrical abilities. Her clarification, in response to my probing question, was given in a very direct manner, with two affirmatives, and a quantity ('I fancy him a lot'). Patti's discomfort with a discussion of attraction to the musician is evident in the way in which she changed her mind about telling me of her desire. In her initial response to my question her reasons were musical reasons. The retraction of her statement of the sexual pleasure she gained suggested that she viewed the musical pleasure as the more important, that physical appeal was not suitable for discussion. Patti's unease is typical of the responses of my interviewees when discussing the concept of groupies and their own attraction to musicians.

THE CONCEPT OF THE GROUPIE

Cline (1992) argues that women rarely claim the groupie title, and, given the media representation of the groupie as someone with little agency or self-respect, it is perhaps unsurprising that it was the same with my interviewees. In general there was an age split in how groupies were discussed, but all my interviewees positioned them as women distinct from themselves. Some women were critical of what they understood to be groupie behaviour. Not because they perceived the groupie to be a 'slut': *that* kind of criticism was not prominent. Dolly's description of a groupie sets the tone for most of my interviewees' ideas about groupies:

> [Dolly] I'd say that a groupie's usually female, who kind of hangs 'round dressing rooms and, er, goes on, follows them 'round on tours and tries to get behind the scenes; maybe I'm wrong, I don't know, but I wouldn't class myself as one. [...]
> [Dolly] I don't think it's a fan as such I just think it's somebody, yeah a fan of course, they have to have an interest in the band, but just somebody who wants to hang on every word they say and sleep with the band and I would class that as a groupie.
> [Rosemary] You're saying groupie quite, it sounds like you don't approve...
> [Dolly] [pause] No maybe not, maybe I don't. I don't know why I don't. I just think, could you be bothered? To spend your life just following somebody around, it's a bit stalkerish to be honest. Yeah I'm not into that. (Dolly)

Dolly's description, and particular phrases like 'hangs 'round' and 'hang on every word', all evoke a sense of desperation and self-abasement. 'Stalker' is especially degrading: when used to describe women it is reminiscent of the Alex Forrest character in the misogynistic *Fatal Attraction* (1987), whose sexual desire turns to murderous mania. Dolly's depiction of a groupie is of a woman who finds meaning in her life via her interaction with musicians, but it is not a complimentary portrayal. Her phrase 'I don't think it's a fan as such', although she corrects herself, fits in with the myth that groupies are interested in musicians, not music. Although Dolly does not consider herself a groupie—clearly challenging the idea that all women fans are groupies—she accepts that groupies exist and are to be disdained. This negotiated reading of the myth enables Dolly to choose her own identity without challenging the ideology of the imaginary community.

Music First

Bert shared Dolly's idea about groupies as pathetic, but she did acknowledge their interest in music. It was for this reason that sleeping with musicians could be a damaging experience:

> [...] they're [...] gonna sleep with you and [...] not call you, you know "your cheque's in the mail", kind of, 'bye!', and you're gonna feel really bad and then probably lose that music cos it's not gonna have the same effect on you anymore; you've ruined it by sleeping with this person. (Bert)

For Bert, the groupie risks her relationship with the *music* (because in her view groupies' relationships with musicians are hopeless). In desiring a musician there are no positive outcomes. Bert positioned the groupie as someone with false expectations of a romantic relationship with the musician and who was exploited by the band; 'your cheque's in the mail' suggests prostitution rather than a mutually satisfying experience. For Bert, the groupie is deluded, the 'dupe' caricature of rock journalism. Sally and Hazel made similar comments.

Bert, Sally and Hazel's depictions of a groupie imply that love of the music is the most valuable kind of fandom. This works to create the groupie as inauthentic because she is aligned with maligned feminine pleasure. All three women therefore position their own fandom as authentic because they place value on musical pleasure, untainted by sexual attraction. This careful negotiation around fandom is symptomatic of the vilification of groupies and of the way in which all women fans' motives are questioned in the light of the groupie myth. Distancing themselves from a mode of fandom they regard as inauthentic is a mechanism to ensure that their own fandom can be regarded as authentic. Negotiating the myth by putting music first enables Bert, Sally and Hazel to avoid the demeaned groupie identity; but it relies on the myth of authenticity, which is a crucial part of maintaining the gender segregation within the genre. This serves to create a division between different kinds of women and different kinds of fandom. It reinforces the cleavage between musical pleasure and other kinds of pleasure that fans may experience.

Critiquing the Representation

A small number of women made the *concept* of the groupie the focus of their ire, interpreting it as a sexist representation that was damaging to women; they did not challenge the way the concept split their fandom. Laura and Gwen's censure was based on the way in which the stereotype was used to demean *all* women fans. And since they were fans, they were angry about how the concept reflected badly upon them. Gwen maintained that the stereotype of the woman fan as groupie was one propagated by the music industry and that this resulted in the institutionalised sexist treatment of women fans as consumers:

> It ties into this idea that, I suppose, like society and especially record labels have of women as fans [...]. It's the reason why boy bands get created and everything because it's the idea that girls don't [know] what the music's about, they don't care what they're listening to, they only care that they're looking at somebody pretty. Whereas guys, you know, well they're actual fans, they care about the music and what it's like and everything and it frustrates me more than anything cos it's like it's tying into this stereotype of women as not being important as consumers because all women want to do is buy shoes and look at pretty guys. And it doesn't matter what they're singing as long as they look pretty while they're doing it. (Gwen)

Gwen's sarcastic and angry tone delivered a scathing critique of music industry and societal sexism. She was frustrated by the common sense idea—the myth—that the women are not interested in music and linked the sexism she saw in the music industry to a more general sexism; the music industry was therefore no better than other industries. Laura, too, described herself as 'frustrated' by assumptions that if you like a band as a woman you must want to marry the lead singer. She found it 'offensive'. Both Gwen and Laura were critical of the sexist ideas held about women's fandom, and they contrasted it with their own experiences of being women fans. They did not match up. The result was that both women felt anger about the way they were positioned as women fans. This oppositional reading 'calls out' the myth as a sexist misreading of women's fandom.

Attacking the Underlying Sexism

Although Gwen in particular dissected the way in which the groupie concept demeaned all women fans, neither she nor Laura made any defence of the figure of the groupie. Criticising a stereotype is one thing, but perhaps it is not the groupie herself who should be the focus of these evaluations. Susan, my eldest interviewee, and three of the younger women, Alexa, Jessica and Éowyn, all sought to rethink what it means to be a groupie.

Susan had been a reader of *Spare Rib*, a UK feminist magazine in the 1970s, and holds an MA in Women's Studies. She said she would never use the term 'groupie' to describe a woman because it had 'very sexist overtones' and was 'tantamount to calling them a slag' (Susan). However, it was the term itself she objected to, not the actions:

> I think probably I wouldn't, I'd never use, I never use the phrase. I don't think I've ever used it, and I think that's probably because it's got very sexist overtones to it, which, so it's probably a term I'm really uncomfortable with. [...] When you read things in the press about groupies that would sleep with any member of the band deda deedar deedar but I, it's not something I really wanted to get into because I would think more of, they could sleep with whoever they wanted to, it was their choice anyway. [...] It always seems to me a right-wing press term, a *Daily Mail* term. (Susan)

To Susan the term 'groupie' was underpinned by misogynistic ideas about women's sexuality, and she argues for women's choice of sexual partner, rather than the kinds of exploitation detailed by Bert and Hazel in their more scathing depictions. She was aware that her views ran counter to dominant representations of groupies, introducing a UK right-wing tabloid newspaper, *The Daily Mail*, to serve as a shorthand for explaining how 'groupie' is used to propagate and naturalise misogynistic ideas about women.

These diverse criticisms vary in strength, but all rely upon feminist understandings of women's experiences as running counter to hegemonic representations. Whilst Gwen and Laura defended women as able to be fans without reducing that passion to wanting to sleep with musicians, Susan defended women by arguing that they could 'sleep with whoever they wanted to', critiquing the double standard that valorises men's sexual promiscuity and denigrates the same behaviour in women. All three argued that women should be able to act without being subject to sexist interpretations of their behaviour. Because myth works to naturalise an idea, as if it is universally correct and accepted, little room remains for thinking about other perspectives or that things could be another way. Dissent is difficult to put into words and thoughts (Fetterley 1978). Feminism was crucial in helping my interviewees to make sense of the myth of the groupie and their relationship to it. It gave them the conceptual tools and language with which to express their opposition to a sexist representation.

Reinterpreting 'Groupie'

Not all of the women I spoke to believed that being a groupie was fundamentally associated with sex, however. All of the women over 25 defined a groupie as a woman who was seeking sex with a band, but the younger women defined it neither as gender specific or necessarily about sex. In fact Éowyn, Jessica and Alexa all interpreted the term in a positive way, seeing 'groupie' as something that women or men could be and that heightened the pleasure in their fandom. For these three women (and for Aime), being a groupie involved travelling to gigs in other cities (not just local gigs), wearing all the 'merch' (i.e., merchandise: T-shirts, belts, and so on with the band's logo or artwork), attempting to meet the band, and maybe, but not necessarily, sexual activity with the band. In this sense 'groupie' was about pleasure in the music, travel, friendship, and the experience of the gig, as Alexa made clear: 'I think it's just enjoying a band and following 'em cos you like 'em, enjoy going to the gigs' (Alexa). Alexa implied that these were activities that anyone might do, rather than being extraordinary or remarkable.

Both Éowyn and Jessica said that 'groupie' only had sexual connotations in other people's interpretations, laying the blame for the groupie's poor reputation on the media, just as Susan did. Jessica had an idea of what a 'true groupie' is:

> [Rosemary] Do you think there's a sexual element to it, the term groupie? [Jessica] I would say "no", but I know that a lot of people do perceive it as that, but I, I don't think a true groupie, as it were, would. It would then be anything to do with sex. I think that's just, I think that's something the media's influenced rather than people themselves actually being like that. Erm, and like, in books and stuff in fiction books, you might, there's a lot of times they'll sort of make a perception of them that is a sexual nature, but I don't think it is to be honest, in my opinion.

And like Susan, she recognised that her attitude and her views were different to other people's, using tentative language ('I don't think', 'as it were', 'I think', 'sort of', 'to be honest', 'in my opinion') to signify the difference between her opinion and what she understood to be more commonly held beliefs.

Both Éowyn and Jessica were critical of the way in which groupies are *perceived* as wanting sex, but they did not believe there was any truth in this. Furthermore, they did not understand 'groupie' to refer exclusively to women. Rather 'anyone could be a groupie' (Éowyn). It seems incredible that the term that has been used to powerfully denigrate women fans could lose both its sexual *and* its gender meanings. Perhaps it is not the common sense interpretation of the word that is changing, but rather it is these young women's *informed decision* to reinterpret the meaning of the term and that thereby reveals feminist sensibilities. Both women were politically active in left-wing campus politics, and Éowyn described herself as socialist and was a National Union of Students (NUS) women's officer. Both expressed other feminist ideas through the course of the interviews and were clearly aware of the disparities between representations of women and women's experiences. Susan's understanding of a groupie's behaviour may not have been similar to the younger women's, but they shared the interpretation of the media usage of the term to sexualise and undermine women. It is significant that all three retained the belief that women fans should not be defined in a sexual way when they expressed their passionate engagement with the music, whether that be via sex with band members or travelling to watch gigs.

These young women's reinterpretations of 'groupie' were also quite different to the way in which Des Barres reclaims 'groupie' as 'muse'. The young women sought to reappraise 'groupie' to take in ordinary fan activities. I recognise the activities in the redefinition from my own experience: I have travelled around the UK and once went to Germany to see The Darkness as a birthday treat. Yet I would not call myself a groupie, even in the non-sexual sense that the young women outlined. The activities of the 'groupie' defined by Alexa, Jessica and Éowyn look to me more like the behaviour of very keen fans, and perhaps there is an age gap between our understandings. For Des Barres, the rethinking is around what musicians gain in the musician/groupie encounter. But it is also about removing underlying sexist notions that denounce women who have many sexual partners (Des Barres 2007). Susan's argument has more in common with Des Barres' attitude, and perhaps these ideas are more commonly found amongst feminist women who grew to adulthood during the late 1960s and early 1970s, that is, when the women's liberation movement was growing in influence. Such a range of resistant reading strategies is evidence of the variety of different positions that can be adopted. But it also makes apparent how the universal 'reader', or hard rock and metal participant, is positioned as male with women as objects rather than as subjects of the culture.

THE IMPACT OF THE GROUPIE MYTH

The groupie myth was not just an abstract concept for my interviewees, however. A number of the women, some of whom critiqued the concept, evidenced differing ways in which the myth of the groupie impacted upon them as music fans.

Asexual Activities

Carol, in her 50s, made oblique, careful responses to my questions about groupies. She said she 'made it her business' to speak to members of bands she loved but was horrified when I asked if she was a groupie:

[Carol] [slightly offended] Absolutely not! I'm not interested in having sex with these people because they're too young for a start, ha ha!

[Rosemary] So being a groupie means having sex with the band?

[Carol] Yes, to me that is exactly what it means and it always has done.

[Rosemary] And that's not something that's appealing to you?

[Carol] No. I don't want to have sex with rock musicians.

[Rosemary] So, erm, are you attracted to them physically?

[Carol] Sometimes, yes.

[Rosemary] And that's as far as it goes?

[Carol] Sometimes, yes! (Carol)

Carol laughed to offset the directness of her responses, but there was no room for discussion. She was teasingly, playfully vague, and her guarded comments about sexual relationships with musicians revealed just how much she believed to be at stake when negotiating her status as a female fan. 'Groupie' was something she was *not*, and in order to maintain that position it was necessary to deny the possibility of sexual activity.

Not only did the women distance themselves from expressing sexual desire for musicians, but they also distanced themselves from *being seen* to be sexual by male audience members at gigs. Aria, the one woman I spoke to who had achieved success as a musician, felt it was important to avoid sexual encounters even when she was attending gigs as a fan:

> The reason I was there wasn't to meet people; I was there because of the music. And because the UK death metal scene was relatively small, it's the same people at all the gigs. So you go there and you're "alright, how's it going?!" So it was never really, never really about that. And if anybody did try and sort of crack onto me they got a very terse comment back, and then they'd leave me alone. (Aria)

For Aria meeting people was *not* the reason for her attendance at gigs and concerts. I inferred from the context that the size of the scene meant that protecting her sexual reputation was important, because in a small scene gossip was likely to be rife. In her hypothetical scenario 'if anybody did crack on to me', 'crack on' has negative connotations: the metaphorical undertone of 'cracking a nut' places women as in need of being 'cracked' and makes sex into a challenge for men. This negative attitude towards male sexual attention at concerts was reiterated when Aria stated, 'they'd leave me alone'. In this those men who had approached her resembled irritating flies, and their attention was clearly unwanted. Like the men that Jeanette encountered, who she said were at gigs only for the music, Aria went to gigs for the music. Thus she aligned herself as a 'real fan' rather than a groupie, ensuring her authentic and disinterested aesthetic appreciation was paramount.

Protecting Reputations

Laura and Gwen were aware of the negative portrayal of women in the concept of the groupie, but it still affected them when it came to wanting to meet their favourite bands. Laura would like to meet My Chemical Romance, but said,

> I would have to think very carefully about what I would want to say cos at the end of the day I'm not going to say, "I really like your music, thank you for making good music; please continue to do so…" I don't really want to have the thought of […] "oh, I love you" erm […] yeah. (Laura)

She drew up a hypothetical situation in which the opportunity to meet My Chemical Romance had arisen, and said she would have to think rationally about whether to go. The band's hypothetical misinterpretation of her motives, that all that would be heard would be 'oh I love you', chimes with the myth of the groupie and plays a role in her decision. Whilst there was exasperation in Laura's response to my question, there was also comedy in her ideas of what she would not say to the band, building up a sense of the meaninglessness of the meeting in which she had no effect upon the band: 'I really like your music, thank you for making good music; please continue to do so'. The comic effect comes from the repetition of 'music', which is then unmatched in the final clause, creating a disjuncture between what is expected and what occurred. Meanwhile, the inconsequentiality of the terms verged upon the asinine. If the meeting would seem to be meaningless there must be other advantages in a meeting that Laura had to 'think carefully about', but that she did not specify.

The impact on Gwen was more definite:

It's one of the things I sort of think about female fans is that female fans are very often seen as only there because they fancy the band, and that really frustrates me cos if I went to meet Panic! At The Disco, even if I was there saying I love the music, I love the fact that [it's] different, and all the things I've said to you about why I love their music, "this drumming in this one song just makes me kind of go wow!", you know all that would be heard would be "hi, I really fancy you". And I really hate that and so I would not go and meet them for that reason. (Gwen)

As in her critique of the groupie stereotype, Gwen's response was characterised by a lack of pauses and stops as her fury overtook the sentence. Just like Laura, Gwen drew up a hypothetical situation within which to explain her feelings about meeting Panic! At The Disco and her anger about the myth, but she also returned to things she had said previously. By reminding me of what she liked about the band, she drew a sharp contrast between her feelings about the music and the way she was perceived, which was *because* of her female status.

In the previous chapter I asserted that one of the ways in the myth of the groupie works is to construct male musicians as heterosexual and exploitative, and they are expected to have sex with female fans. This perception of male musicians plays its part in Gwen and Laura's ideas about what musicians are like and how musicians perceive their female fans. Therefore, being seen *not to be a groupie* in the eyes of their favourite musicians was important to both women as they aimed to position their fandom as authentic. They thought the concept of the groupie was damaging to women fans, and they understood that moniker to be so powerful in the minds of their preferred musicians that it would discredit their fandom. They were careful to sidestep the appearance of adhering to the groupie stereotype, and in doing so they hoped to avoid its implications and to maintain a sense of themselves as 'real' fans. This is reminiscent of how Bert and Sally portrayed groupies as missing out on the pleasure of the music.

Preferring Bands that Eschew Misogynistic Representations

Laura identified hard rock and metal as a genre in which women are mistreated. However, these were not her own analyses (although her comments about groupie culture show that she was well aware of problems of sexism in the genre). Rather, they were criticisms voiced by My Chemical Romance singer Gerard Way. She noted Way's tirade on the subject of musicians who use their power to sexually exploit young women:

> There's a [...] DVD that they have, like, life on the road concert DVD and a two hour tour diary, and one of the stories that they tell in that is about them touring with some other band [...] pushing them [roadies] to go into the crowd before the show and tell girls to show their tits for backstage passes, and Gerard Way got really angry about that because he went on a whole rant during the concert about stupid rock kids [...] who think they're great [...] and there's [...] a number of examples of him getting really annoyed about the way women are treated in rock music. (Laura)

Laura's use of 'some other band' is telling. It indicated that the name of the band was unimportant; indeed it could be any other band because sexist attitudes are so standard in rock. The unnamed band members were positioned as villains, driving a culture which sexualises young women fans, turning roadies into accomplices in this objectification. There is also the intimation of an exchange—'tits for backstage passes'—in which young women are vulnerable objects of unfair exchange. Furthermore, 'stupid rock kids', who base their identity on their musical allegiance, accept the bad treatment of women without challenging it. Way therefore goes against the grain of rock culture and his emotions convey his authenticity as a feminist rather than as a metal musician.

What is fascinating about this is that Laura (also a fan of Queen and U2) used the words of a rock band to make clear her own concerns about rock and metal's gender politics. The ideology of the genre might be sexist, but *she* had found a band who were openly critical of it. Indeed, Laura's preference for My Chemical Romance was due specifically to the singer's declared feminism:

> I admire Gerard Way very much. And he's a feminist. I enjoy the music, but, a large part of my enjoyment is [because of his feminism]. (Laura)

Laura's measured tones ('I admire', 'a large part') and the passive voice of the final clause make her preference for My Chemical Romance a rational choice, rather than a passionate love. Her reasons are clearly intellectual. She did not find him physically attractive or particularly like his voice or his lyrics, but she liked his politics. Along with her careful thoughts about meeting the band, Laura's rationalisation of her fondness for My Chemical Romance reveals her perception of the importance of not being seen to be a 'typical girl fan', someone whose emotional attraction is the primary cause of fandom, someone whose sexuality is suspect (Busse 2013).

Also very evident is how the myth of the groupie rests on a binary distinction that attributes major differences to women and men. The binary associates women with emotions whilst men are viewed as superior rational thinkers. The binary is the subject of feminist critique as it encodes value, raising up those qualities that fall on the left side of the binary (male, mind, good, reason) to the denigration of those that fall on the right (female, body, bad, emotion) (Lloyd 1993). In spite of these criticisms, it is clear that the idea that women are more emotional and more closely tied to their bodies than men remains a powerful force in the popular imagination and in popular culture. The binary relegates women's mythical fandom (that is groupiedom) to an inferior place in the rock hierarchy. The women I spoke to were aware of that position and read it oppositionally or in negotiated ways. In terms of their own identities, they worked to sidestep it. However, the binary *itself* is the problem, not that women fall on the wrong side of it.

The question *must* be asked: what is so wrong with being attracted to musicians? Why can this not be viewed as a valid form of fandom and of musical engagement? It is widely acknowledged that the performer contributes to the value of the music: the musician's role is uncontested.

If the musician is acknowledged as important then a range of responses to the music *and* the musician should be possible, including those that are around sexual attraction.

DESIRE

Although there was discomfort in discussing the figure of the groupie, as well as criticism and negotiation, a number of women did express attractions to musicians. For Hazel and Gwen this was quite a straightforward physical attraction, but for Aime in particular desire was described in ways that rendered it complex.

Attraction to Musicians

Hazel described her feelings for Tura Satana singer Tairrie B, and also made an aside about Manic Street Preachers bassist Nicky Wire. The two desires were not quite the same, and Hazel's attraction to Tairrie B was specifically linked to the way the singer broke out of traditionally subordinate femininity to take on a 'dominant role':

[Rosemary] When you say that you were attracted by [Tairrie B], what, in what way were you attracted?

[Hazel] I liked her look, I liked the way that she was there to lead the band rather than just be eye candy.

[Rosemary] So it wasn't, or was it like a sexual attraction? Or was it a mixture of things?

[Hazel] Well at that time I was going through my "I might be bisexual" phase [...], and it was almost like a sexual attraction because I just thought "wow this woman's stunning and she's taking such a dominant role".

Hazel used 'look' in the singular rather than the plural 'looks', implying clothing style and accessories rather than particular facial or bodily characteristics. This sense of Hazel as attracted by personality was compounded by 'she was there to lead the band' and later 'she's taking such a dominant role'. For Hazel, Tairrie B was different from other women singing in bands, who she determined were 'eye candy', implying something sweet but without substance, easily devoured and quickly forgotten. Tairrie B was *not* like this. Hazel contextualised her attraction with reference to everyday understandings of sexuality ('bisexuality"), normalising her own attraction within the musical context. This also gave a sense of Hazel as 'normally' heterosexual and her desire for Tairrie B as out of kilter with her usual sexual self, but then it was only 'almost like sexual attraction'. This added to Hazel's assertion that her attraction was part of a 'phase' and reaffirmed the heteronormativity of the hard rock and metal genre, rather than raising a significant challenge to it. However, the ambiguity of whether Hazel's attraction to Tairrie B was sexual underlines the complexity of how fandoms are constructed in ways that do not only rely upon musical appeal.

Despite being critical of the groupie concept, Gwen also said that there was at least one musician with whom she did wish a sexual encounter, but she was quick to manage this desire with the assertion that it was the music that was important and physical attraction a bonus:

> The drummer of Panic! At The Disco I would happily take home 12 times a day. [...] I listen to this music and the fact that the people in the band are attractive or not attractive doesn't change for me the enjoyment I get from it. Like, I actually prefer My Chem's music [over] Panic's music, even though there's nobody in My Chem that I find attractive and there is in Panic. So yeah, for me it's not about what they look like, that just happens to be something that is there. (Gwen)

Gwen placed the emphasis of her attraction on *this particular* drummer so that what was important was her attraction to *this* musician and not to any other. Her 'take home 12 times a day' romanticised the encounter because 'take home' suggests a close bond and is reminiscent of 'take home to meet the parents'. But her attraction to some musicians did not govern her passion for the bands: her attraction was 'just something that happens to be there', which minimised the importance of the physical admiration by implying that her attraction to the musicians was a fact that had no bearing on her enjoyment of the music.

Gwen may have been quick to negotiate the groupie stereotype and what it meant when a woman declared a sexual attraction to a band member, but actually she and Hazel, who expressed desire for Nicky Wire of Manic Street Preachers, were the only women who explicitly declared that they would sleep with musicians, although others expressed attraction. Aria had described her dismissive attitude to male sexual attention at concerts, but later in the interview I introduced the topic of physical attraction by reference to the visual pleasure I gain from *Metalocalypse* character Skwisgar Skwigelf. Aria shared this attraction and began to discuss the appeal of the warrior image more generally. There was clearly a difference between the face she presented in her local scene, and the one she felt able to present to me, a fellow fan, feminist, musician and an early career academic:

> For my personal taste in men I find the warrior type very, very attractive. [...] Tall, broad shoulders, long hair, or just some kind of hair, beard. Nice chunky forearms. Very sexy. Absolutely. And I kind of put it akin to, I don't know whether it's something in me, I just find the warrior type very, very attractive and I think there's a lot of, irrespective of metal, I think there's a lot of women find that attractive. (Aria)

Aria mobilised mainstream romance discourse in her opening sentence: 'for my personal taste in men' and 'warrior type', which worked within the common sense understanding of people having a particular 'taste' and 'type'. This language is familiar, and it established Aria as a woman who knew what she wanted from life, and her taste and type are presented as a matter of fact. Aria's sexual identity was therefore bound up with her musical identity so that the 'warrior type', constructed as hegemonic and allied to the representation of musicians in *Kerrang!*, was for her very attractive. Jackson and Scott (2010) theorise the sociality of sexuality and Aria's sexual and musical tastes have a relationship in which neither one can be reduced to the other.

Although the complementary position to the warrior musician is 'groupie', Aria was also a musician and for her 'warrior type' may not only have been attached to the male bodies of musicians, but also to male fans. Schippers (2002) argues that when women are the musicians this has the potential to destabilise the musician/groupie dichotomy. Although I think her evaluation can be useful, I do think that she misses an important point. Disparaging forms of musical pleasure which involve sexuality leaves those women who describe their attractions to musicians as voiceless and 'in the wrong'. I argue that it is vital to think about the ways in which women's musical pleasure is formed not through their ears alone, but also through their visual and erotic pleasure.

Mixing Music and Desire

Aime's attraction was mixed up with her appreciation of her favoured musician's, Avenged Sevenfold's drummer, musical ability:

> I fancy the balls off them! [...] Er... yeah [both laugh]. They're not necessarily good looking guys in a way. I mean the main singer, yeah, he's obviously

sort of good looking and so is maybe Zacky, but the drummer, he's not good looking, not that good looking. He's actually quite weird looking! But it's almost the way he plays his instrument, the way he talks, the way he sings that attracts me to him, and it's just the different things, it's not necessarily how they look, which is what most people usually go for. (Aime)

Aime vividly described her attraction as a voracious desire and appetite, but in describing the members of the band she appealed to an objective measure of handsomeness. She compared her attraction to other people's reasons for feeling desire—visual appeal—thus rendering her own attraction more genuine than that of 'most people'. Crucially, her attraction is bound up with his musicianship and his personality, expressed through his talk. Thus she constructed her sexuality as one that was sophisticated rather than shallowly based on appearance.

This echoes Schippers' (2002) findings in the Chicago hard rock scene in the 1990s, where a fan may state an attraction to a musician, but would then claim that attraction as due to musical ability so that both the musician and their musicianship were sexualised. However, Schippers accounts for this by positioning this move as a strategy that fans would engage in so that they were not perceived as a groupie in a scene that was radically anti-sexist (for a rock scene) and defiantly against the 'girls, girls, girls' culture of the preceding popular hard rock and metal subgenre, glam metal. This strategic redesignation of desire seems to me to force sexual significance on to music and musicianship, and it does not resemble Aime's depiction of her attraction, which is more spontaneous and does not apologise for the physical desire. For Aime desire was mixed up with musical pleasure in complex ways. Her attraction was to the musical performance of a particular musician, and this enabled her to overcome his 'weird looks'. On another level, it also suggests that we need to try to understand musical joys in ways that acknowledge pleasures other than aural or intellectual enjoyment. This argument is also made by Fast (1999): she describes a similarly complicated relationship between women's love of Led Zeppelin and desire for the musicians. She positions women as the (hetero)sexual subject looking at, listening to, and gaining erotic pleasure from Led Zeppelin, as well as musical pleasure. They are neither solely concerned with the musicians, nor are they only interested in the music. Erotic pleasure is given an equal position alongside musical pleasure. Importantly, this reinstates women as subjects so that they cannot be thought of in terms of being passive sexual objects ready and willing to be exploited by careless musicians.

CONCLUSION

The women's discussions of sex, sexism, music and musicians are complex and show clearly that women fans' experiences of being hard rock and metal fans cannot be reduced to simple interpretations. Women hard rock and metal fans' decoding of the myth of the groupie is more likely to be oppositional or negotiated than to accept the dominant or preferred reading. Nevertheless, they are powerfully affected by it, and there is a necessity of finding ways to distance themselves from it. For some women this meant positioning the groupie as extraordinary, for others it meant contesting the validity of the concept, and for still others it resulted in rethinking the meaning of 'groupie'. The myth impacted directly upon the women in differing ways: it caused some to seek out bands that did not rely on ideological notions of femininity; it meant distancing themselves from their favoured bands; it caused them to carefully position their pleasure in the music as asexual. Finally, in spite of the discomfort that many of the women showed in discussing the concept of the groupie, a number did express desire for musicians. This desire was complex and bound up with the music. Because women fans are sometimes attracted to some musicians (although they may not all want sex with them), the myth alienates women from free expression of their music fandom. This alienation is entrenched because women are already marginalised in hard rock and metal in a number of ways and so avoiding the denigration of groupies is vital to preserve their reputations and self-esteem.

Returning to Stanley's assertion that rather than identifying how ideology produces 'false consciousness', we need rather to consider how ideology operates in people's lives. This examination of women's negotiations of the myth of the groupie provides a clear example. The women fans I spoke to do not accept the dominant representation of themselves as groupies, and many are very aware of the unfairness of the representation and the damage it does. The myth of the groupie has an impact upon the ways in which women fans understand their own fandom. It has to be negotiated so that the implications of excessive sexual desire and frivolous fandom do not 'stick' to them. For some women this meant downplaying their passionate desires and attempting to construct their sexuality as one was neither promiscuous nor drew attention away from their serious engagement with the music. Part of the power of the myth of the groupie is that it distorts the ways in which women hard rock and metal fans feel able to express their fandom and their sexuality. Damage is done to women fans' sexual reputations (when 'groupie' means 'slut') and to their status as music fans (when 'groupie' means 'not serious'). Cline (1992) has unpicked the misogyny that has led to the term's usage as a way to demean all women fans, thus potentially liberating women fans from its yoke, and my younger interviewees had redefined the term. However, I am not totally won over by their renewed version of 'groupie', as the impact of the denunciation that women fans face is evident in the ways in which it affected my other interviewees. The power of the myth of the groupie means that women fans still feel they must negotiate the negativity of the stereotype and position themselves as serious or authentic fans. In claiming, or aiming to claim, the position of the 'real fan' they step outside of the fan role that the ideology of the genre prescribes for them (or at least imagine that they are able to do so). They do not see themselves as groupies and they reject the positioning of their sexuality as easily readable (that as a woman fan they are *naturally* attracted to the musicians in their favourite bands and that this sexual attraction *exceeds* their intellectual engagement with the music) within the heterosexual world. They are determined not to be sexually or musically positioned 'simply' because of their gender. This negotiation and repositioning of their identities as women and fans, however, is not a simple or safe manoeuvre. For some it requires the suppression of any desires they may have for musicians and other community members, meaning that they are unable to express themselves freely.

Ignoring our embodied and sexual experiences of music seriously limits understanding of fandom. Believing that there is a right way to be a fan, which assumes a rational and intellectual musical appreciation, represses or denies a large part of our pleasure. As Rosemary Overell's (2014) work on grindcore shows, that goes for men fans as well as women fans. Sex must form part of the questions asked of hard rock and metal fandoms if a better understanding of the complex ways in which we make connections to particular musics is to be had. They must be probing and inspiring questions—and scholars must be ready to hear the answers, no matter how ambiguous.

REFERENCES

Busse, Kristina. 2013. Geek Hierarchies, Boundary Policing, and the Gendering of the Good Fan. *Participations* 10(1): 73–91.
Cline, Cheryl. 1992. Essays from Bitch: The Women's Rock Newsletter with Bite. In *Adoring Audience: Fan Culture and Popular Media*, ed. Lisa A. Lewis, 69–83. London: Routledge.

Davis, Stephen. 2005. *Hammer of the Gods*. London: Pan Macmillan.

Des Barres, Pamela. 2005. *I'm with the Band: Confessions of a Groupie*. London: Helter Skelter.

————, ed. 2007. *Let's Spend the Night Together: Backstage Secrets of Rock Muses and Supergroupies*. London: Helter Skelter Publishing.

Fabian, Jenny, and Johnny Byrne. 1969. *Groupie*. London: Mayflower.

Fast, Susan. 1999. Rethinking Issues of Gender and Sexuality in Led Zeppelin: A Woman's View of Pleasure and Power in Hard Rock. *American Music* 17(3): 245–299.

Fetterley, Judith. 1978. *The Resisting Reader: A Feminist Approach to American Fiction*. London: Indiana University Press.

Jackson, Stevi, and Sue Scott. 2010. *Theorizing Sexuality*. Maidenhead: McGraw-Hill International.

Johnson, Lisa. 2007. Anarchy in the USA. *Kerrang!*, 13 January, 27–29.

Lee, Tommy, Vince Neil, Nikki Sixx, Mick Mars, and Neil Strauss. 2014. *The Dirt: Confessions of the World's Most Notorious Rock Band*. New York: HarperCollins.

Lloyd, Genevieve. 1993. *The Man of Reason: 'Male' and 'Female' in Western Philosophy*, vol 2. London: Routledge.

Nordström, Susanna, and Marcus Herz. 2013. 'It's a Matter of Eating or Being Eaten.' Gender Positioning and Difference Making in the Heavy Metal Subculture. *European Journal of Cultural Studies* 16(4): 453–467.

Overell, Rosemary. 2014. *Affective Intensities in Extreme Music Scenes: Cases from Australia and Japan*. Basingstoke: Palgrave Macmillan.

Schippers, Mimi. 2002. *Rockin' Out of the Box: Gender Maneuvering in Alternative Hard Rock*. London: Rutgers University Press.

Shirazi, Roxana. 2010. *The Last Living Slut: Born in Iran, Bred Backstage*. New York: itbooks.

Stanley, Liz. 1992. *The Auto/Biographical I: The Theory and Practice of Feminist Auto/Biography*. Manchester: Manchester University Press.

CHAPTER 5

Listening to Hard Rock and Metal Music

INTRODUCTION

Question: if hard rock and metal is so problematically sexist, as Vasan (2011), Nordström and Herz (2013) and my study of *Kerrang!* posit, and 'masculinist' as Weinstein (2000 [1991], 130) asserts, why do women like it? Answer: social interactions and sexist encounters are not the only experiences of the genre. For many of my interviewees, music listening took place in private: on headphones, at home, in the car, whilst commuting, cleaning and gardening. Hard rock and metal-specific social interactions in these circumstances were therefore limited: the focus was on the music itself.

Pleasure in music has only recently become the primary interest of those studying hard rock and metal. This is an odd omission, but its roots can be traced back to the subcultural framework used by many scholars. Hesmondhalgh (2005) notes that subcultural theory was never about music anyway; but without considering the music, knowledge about people's participation in such groups (united by music) is lopsided. As Riches argues,

> Failing to incorporate pleasure into music and leisure discourses obfuscates the ways in which we can explain why women, appearing to consent to dominant and patriarchal practices and expectations, engage in contradictory activities within forms of popular culture. (2011, 327)

© The Editor(s) (if applicable) and The Author(s) 2016   105
R.L. Hill, *Gender, Metal and the Media*, Pop Music, Culture and Identity, DOI 10.1057/978-1-137-55441-3_5

If pleasure is overlooked then the ways in which gender works in musical engagement cannot be fully examined, nor can we gain a rich understanding of women's participation in the male-dominated metal sphere.

Exemplary of this omission are Leblanc's (1999) discussion of how punk girls construct femininity, deal with sexual harassment from within and outside of the punk subculture, and negotiate their public performance of punk, and Vasan's (2011) argument that women engage in 'cost reduction' mechanisms in order to reduce the personal impact of the misogyny at gigs. These are both vitally important studies that contribute enormously towards understanding the gendered nature of subcultural experience. But they tell only a part of the story. Kahn-Harris (2007) briefly discusses pleasure in music, focussing on fans' difficulty in articulating what they like about extreme metal. In the main, his discussion of women death and black metal fans focuses on their marginal status. He describes the way in which black metal's ideological prioritising of the music eschews discussions of politics, and so prohibits challenges to sexism in the scene. However, I argue that focussing solely on the problems of access that women fans face does an injustice to those fans. Because they always position female fans by their gender, Vasan and Kahn-Harris sell women fans short by not considering how they too love the music 'for its own sake'. Thus loving the music whilst taking their sex for granted becomes a position that is only open to male fans. The male model of fandom is thereby presented as 'normal'. An assumption of the male hard rock and metal fan as the norm produces women as extraordinary so that the ways in which they are *different* becomes the focus of study, rather than any similarities. Women's engagement with the music is therefore forgotten or treated as of lesser importance. This is surprising given long-held common sense understandings of hard rock and metal as 'masculine' (Bayton 1998, 40; Weinstein 2000 [1991], 106).

Recent work by Riches (2011, 2014, 2015) and Overell (2014) provides a more nuanced portrayal of gendered experiences at hard rock and metal events, with pleasure the centre point around which participants revolve. Overell investigates masculinity in Melbourne's grindcore scene through the lens of 'brutal' musical experience. 'Brutal' is coded as masculine, but Overell argues grindcore music cannot simply be read as masculine: in some ways it is disembodied, particularly in the vocal delivery of lyrics. The vocal delivery is characterised as 'all noise' (2010, 206), and its 'excessive' screamed vocal style can be coded as feminine. This places pleasure in grindcore at centre stage and thereby brings gender into focus.

Riches' work on women and the mosh pit responds to previous work that has emphasised masculinity, violence and aggression in relation to the mosh pit. Because of her specific focus on the pleasurable aspect of participation in the mosh pit, her study positions women as normal subjects within the mosh pit at the extreme metal gig, rather than as exceptions, problems or victims. These studies do not shy away from discussing the problems of sexism at events, but it is clear that sexism is only one part of the participants' musical experience.

The work of Riches and Overell demonstrates that thinking about pleasure can offer fresh perspectives on women fans' experiences and on constructions of women and men within the social spaces of metal. If this were a study of male fans, it would not be extraordinary to discuss men's interest in music. But to think of women fans as interested in *music*, rather than musicians, runs counter to how women fans are commonly understood. To discuss women's interest in music is not to attempt to elevate my interviewees' reputations to 'authentic fans': rather taking their engagement with the music seriously shows that notions of the 'authentic fan' are inadequate for understanding women's—and men's—fandom.

Previous studies that have examined women's engagement with popular culture have typically considered those cultural forms that have been thought to be damaging, in many cases reinforcing a destructive ideal of femininity (see for example Radway 1984; Ang 1985; Geraghty 1991; Stacey 1994; Skeggs 1997). These authors show that the pleasures women experience are complicated for a variety of reasons and that textual readings produce a multiplicity of meanings. These include resistant readings that allow texts to be reconceived so that messages with which women find it difficult to identify become more palatable and even enjoyable (Fetterley 1978). Furthermore, as Radway (1984) shows with regards romance readers, examining pleasure is a successful means to challenge demeaning stereotypes of women's cultural engagement. In this chapter, then, I prioritise women's experiences of the music and examine how they discuss the pleasure they derive from their favourite bands. Using discourse analysis to consider the language that women use to describe hard rock and metal music, a complex picture of women's musical experience emerges: language that echoes the ideas underlying the myths of the warrior and authenticity is heard, but so is unexpected and creative language that challenges understandings of the genre as only enjoyed as a masculine pleasure.

HARD ROCK AND METAL AS A 'MASCULINE' GENRE

Walser's (1993) work on heavy metal and gender centres around the way that the genre 'excripts' women, writing them out and creating a fantasy world for men in which women do not exist. Musically, he characterises heavy metal as masculine music due to its 'virtuosity and control', articulation of 'a dialectic of controlling power and transcendent freedom', 'vocal extremes, guitar power chords, distortion; and sheer volume of bass and drums' (Walser 1993, 109). This conception of the music as masculine is evident too in Kahn-Harris's analysis of fans' descriptions of what they like about the music. He concludes that fans are 'inarticulate' (2007, 54) and that they have limited language available to them. The lexicon they do use is bounded by the extreme metal scene which values 'aggression, brutality, energy, etc.' (Kahn-Harris 2007, 53). 'I just liked it' (quoted in Kahn-Harris 2007, 54) asserts one of Kahn-Harris's interviewees, and he leaves it at that. He then moves on to consider other (non-musical) aspects of extreme metal fandom. But understandings of musical pleasure are poor if they can only rest with phrases such as 'I just liked it'. The opacity of this speech proves an obstacle to greater understanding and 'just' works to foreclose any follow-up questions. Allowing such a wall to remain in place means relying on received, inaccurate ideas about the music and about women fans' involvement in hard rock and metal.

In my interviews with women fans I began by asking them to describe heavy metal, then enquired about their favourite band that featured in *Kerrang!*, and followed this with, "what do you like about them?" Far from being inarticulate, the women eloquently described both heavy metal and their reasons for favouring a particular band. Their descriptions shed light on the intersection of the ideology of hard rock and metal with gender. Like Kahn-Harris, I found that women's descriptions of their pleasure did sometimes echo the ideology of the genre via notions of warrior masculinity and ideas of authenticity. However, I also ascertained that where Kahn-Harris found that the discursive limits curtailed fans' descriptions when it came to describing their favourite bands; by contrast, my interviewees were not so restricted.

Defining Heavy Metal: Using the Language of the Warrior Myth

Responses to the question, 'what do you think heavy metal is?', were very varied. Some women gave a list of instruments and band names, but others depicted sounds or atmospheres. Still others talked of how the music made them feel. Karen's response was particularly excited, and in her enthusiasm she encapsulated one or two of the main ideas that most of my interviewees described:

> Oh! That's really difficult isn't it! Erm, it's loud—life is loud, *Kerrang!*—no it's, it's loud. I wouldn't say it's aggressive. How would you describe it? It's just great! Lively! It's not boring! RnB is so dull! God, heavy metal's got, it's got oomph about it! And to be fair there's the odd band that doesn't and the odd song that doesn't, but generally it's got oomph. There. That's how I'd describe it: it's got oomph. (Karen)

Karen's exclamations ('oh!', 'it's just great!', 'lively!', and so on) demonstrated her passion for the genre in general. As she thought over what it was that defined heavy metal, in order to come up with an answer she first used 'loud' and realised in doing so that she was echoing the tagline on the cover of *Kerrang!*: 'Life is Loud'. Hunting for a more original response, she countered depictions of metal as 'aggressive'. She then made a value judgement ('It's just great! Lively! It's not boring!') and compared the genre to one she considered more mainstream one (RnB). In her struggle for words she turned to the onomatopoeic 'oomph', which described the feel of the music and the impact it had on her. For her, 'oomph' was the determining factor in heavy metal.

Karen was the only woman to use the word 'oomph' (although Susan's description of the vivacity of Led Zeppelin gave a similar impression), and most women were more measured in their tones. However, in comparing the genre to a more mainstream one (RnB), in emphasising the volume of the genre ('loud') and determining that it was 'not boring', Karen drew on the same sort of language as a large proportion of my other interviewees. Most women used some of the words, or similar terms, in the following list: 'loud', 'heavy', 'hard' 'severe', 'raw', 'power', 'grunty', 'strong', 'faster', and expressions related to anger or aggression such as 'fiercer' and 'angry' were also employed. These were by far the most frequent adjectives in descriptions of metal. Kahn-Harris (2007) found that his interviewees used the language that was available within the scene to describe the music, and the terms I heard do indeed fall within the discursive framework of hard rock and metal. These are all qualities that can be associated with the myth of the warrior in *Kerrang!*. They connote masculinity in its furthest position from femininity: high volume and fast speed were evident in the designs of the letters pages; 'severe' and 'hard' have a part to play in developing fearsomeness, and they were indicated in the

photographs of musicians; 'strong' and 'power' describe physical prowess and endurance and are reminiscent of the stances of musicians that
emphasised their physical strength. 'Heavy' refers to the low sound of the
music and is complicit in the strength and power as something difficult to
move. 'Raw' signifies an open wound and suggests cries of pain and anger,
such as might be heard on a battlefield. 'Grunty' has an animalistic quality,
and its use here is a reference to the death growl vocals, which are a low
roaring sound and perhaps not dissimilar to a battle cry. These descriptors
are consonant with *Kerrang!*'s warrior imagery, in which glaring faces and
intimidating poses are *de rigueur* for metal musicians, usually coded as
masculine. This language therefore echoed the visual and audible qualities
of the music and emphasised the symbolic masculinity of heavy metal.

Eleven women referred particularly to guitars in their descriptions of
heavy metal and what they liked. For some women it was the guitar solos,
for others the riffs, and for some their simple presence. For example,
Hazel said, 'I like anything that has an electric guitar in it, I like the sound,
I like the noise. The noise is pleasing to my ears' (Hazel). For Hazel the
importance of the music lay in its 'sound' and 'noise', implying that there
was not a particular style of playing that she liked, nor that the sound was
either beautiful or especially melodic. It did not particularly *exclude* those
qualities, but it also included the kinds of sounds that some people may
call, in a derogatory sense, 'noise' rather than 'music'. It later became
apparent that Hazel did not like just *anything* with an electric guitar in it,
but the presence of the guitar caught her attention and allowed her to dis-
criminate between bands who used the instrument and those who did not.

That the women described electric guitars and not acoustic guitars is
significant. The electric guitar is iconic and popularly romanticised and
personified—both as a woman's body to be made love to and as a man's
penis to be masturbated through the guitar solo to orgasm. Queer readings are possible, but dominant readings of the symbolism of the guitar
announce the guitarist as male. Drawing on Ruth Oldenziel's historical
work on technology, race and gender, Monique Bourdage (2010) considers the way in which technology, and in particular the electric guitar,
has been masculinised. She argues that through the electrification of the
guitar as a 'technophallus' (Waksman 1999, 188) women musicians have
become alienated from the instrument. Acoustic guitars, on the other
hand, are 'feminine-coded' (Bourdage 2010, 7), and they are associated
with singer-songwriters such as Joan Baez and Joni Mitchell (Bayton
1997). Women guitarists are expected to play acoustic rather than electric
guitars (Bayton 1997). The use of acoustic guitars in rock usually occurs

in ballads or slower sections: songs about love and romance that are introduced in the concert setting as 'this one's for the ladies'. On the other
hand, in its masculinity the symbolic use of the electric guitar works alongside the myth of the warrior to reinforce the masculinity of the hard rock
and metal musician. Moreover, the guitar is also linked intimately with
the myth through its nickname. The colloquial term for a guitar within
hard rock and metal is 'axe'; throughout Seb Hunter's humorous metal
memoir (2004) the author uses 'guitar' and 'axe' interchangeably. 'Axe'
in this case signifies the weapon rather than the household tool as, within
the context of the warrior imagery and language, an axe resonates with
understandings of Viking invaders fighting with axes (rather than swords).
It connotes powerful, dangerous and frightening masculinity.

My interviewees' frequent references to guitars therefore indicate the
sound of the genre and the symbolic construction of its musicians as masculine, echoing how musicians are depicted in *Kerrang!* as warriors. The
invocation of the guitar as a characteristic of heavy metal therefore works
within the recognisable ideology of the genre.

Defining Heavy Metal and the Myth of Authenticity

A number of the women I spoke to maintained a frosty intolerance
towards music they described as manufactured or 'pop'. For example,
Dolly claimed 'a poppy song is nothing', whilst Kimberley described
attending a Westlife concert to please her sister: 'there are some things we
can do for our sisters, and that was the most severe one I've had to do'
(Kimberley). For a large number of my interviewees pop music was not
only something they disliked. Many women placed hard rock and metal in
an oppositional relationship to pop: the instruments used were more 'real'
than in pop, the quality of musical ability was greater, the lyrical content
was more meaningful. In this sense, the symbolic relationship between
rock and pop played an important role in thinking about and enunciating
musical preference. Nine of the women distinguished between the music
they liked and 'pop' music. For example, Sally described hard rock and
metal musicians as 'poets' and drew a contrast with 'stuff in the charts' (a
very loose definition of pop):

> Whereas stuff in the charts, it's much more manufactured and it's all a set
> formula and it's all very samey, whereas there's a lot more sort of change
> of tempo and you know the music fits the lyrics better and things like that.
> (Sally)

Sally represented pop music as a single unified genre without internal differences. 'Set formula' implied that the music was made without thought or creative passion—it was made to a formula. This developed her use of 'manufactured' to give the sense of the songs being mass produced like a McDonald's meal: that is, no love had gone into the generation of the product. Metal's wider range of tempos and stronger music and lyrical fit, although sounding like concrete musical elements, are actually quite vague. They are also framed by the discourse of pop as manufactured and simplistic, whilst a hard rock or metal band would be expected to write lyrics and music which would therefore provide a better emotional 'fit' (as if it were an automatic relationship). The metaphor 'poets' implied that the lyrics were better, with more beautiful phrasing and word choice, and a more serious perspective on the world. In establishing what pop is (manufactured, prosaic, routine and formulaic) hard rock and metal easily slipped into an antagonistic relationship with it: hard rock and metal becomes everything that pop is not.

The use of particular instruments is a powerful motif in hard rock and metal and part of the mythology that divides the genre from mass-produced music, signalling it as 'authentic'. Referring to the instruments that are used in the music, in particular bass, drums and guitars, as *real*, and contrasting their use with music made on computers or using synthesisers, was a common theme amongst my interviewees. For instance, in describing what she liked about the genre, Jessica emphasised the *realness* of the instruments:

> I consider metal to be, it has to be real metal for me, like they have to play their own instruments and it's not, it can't be all computerised cos that's just not real music for me.
>
> [Rosemary] What sorts of instruments?
>
> [Jessica] Erm, guitars mainly, but that's, I play myself so that's something I have a passion for, and it has to be real drum kit and it has to be a real, their real voice, not autotuned or anything like that.

Jessica's definition of metal explicitly relied on the use of particular instruments and the musicians' ability to play them. All of the values she turned to are about the production of the music and the performance of the musicians, rather than the sound of the music. She repeated 'real' five times in this short response and, although Jessica did not define precisely what she meant by the word, it was placed in contrast with music made using computers ('all computerised', 'autotuned'), suggesting that it was a particular use of technology that was problematic in her estimation. This clearly linked the definition of the genre to the ability of the musicians, but it also reinscribed the binary between what was metal ('real') and what was not ('unreal'). Ironically, in the digital age nearly all music-making utilises computers in some way during the recording process. In his discussion of recording drummers, metal record producer Mark Mynett (2013) has debunked the idea that metal musicians always play their own instruments. He argues that expectations of drum parts have become so high that many musicians cannot actually play the parts that appear on the records: these parts have been created using computer software.

Why is it important that a drum kit be made of metal, wood and skins (or synthetic skins) rather than a machine? Why should a traditional manner of playing (with sticks and brushes) be valued above a skilled musician using a synthesiser kit and programming a drum line into a computer? Why does it matter how a song is made? Although *I* pose these rhetorical questions, for the majority of the women, the way in which the music is created was crucial. 'Realness', an imagined quality that probably bears little relation to the real conditions of music production, was set against pop music and other kinds of music: genres such as electro/electronic, dance or hip hop, in which the music is made using synthesisers, keyboards, samplers and computers. Such modern technological means of making music are associated with the manufacturing of songs because they are understood as more easily mastered than traditional instruments. This underestimates the skills involved in programming and sampling, lending intrinsic value to traditional musicians and devaluing newer forms of musicianship. (There may also be a raced and classed element to this denigration, if metal is viewed as a middle class form.) Making the distinction with pop music was consonant with the ideology's stress upon authenticity and a key element in proving that authenticity.

The quality of the musicianship, particularly of guitarists, was highly valued, as Aime revealed in her description of Synyster Gates' guitar playing:

> When he was little he taught himself to play it, his dad's guitar, upside down but he wasn't left-handed, but he taught himself to play it upside down [...]. Then when his dad bought him a guitar he played that and then flipped that upside down and then learnt his dad's guitar so he can play it both ways and upside down. (Aime)

Aime noted that Gates was a guitarist from a young age, implying that he was naturally drawn towards the instrument, had a 'good ear' and natural aptitude. His ability and desire to learn, and his voracious appetite to play the instrument all complement this depiction of Gates as a natural musician. The verb 'flipped' suggested a quick and easy process of fast, almost immediate learning, emphasising the supposed naturalness of his skill. Aime's use of the repeated 'taught himself', 'he played that', 'then learnt' and 'he can play it' all omitted any teacher in the learning (his dad merely provided the instruments and there was no mother in Aime's tale), further reinforcing the sense of the guitarist as an autodidact with natural ability. Aime drew attention to Gates as an unusually skilful musician by repeating his particular skill, 'upside down', four times and linking it to 'both ways' so that it was clear that Gates could play both left and right handed guitars. This multiple-playing ability connoted a high level of musicianship that is above the usual standard for guitarists. The description stood in for a more technical discussion of his ability which might have drawn on musical terminology, but nevertheless indicated the value she placed upon his skill.

Ruby's discussion of Killswitch Engage's Howard Jones' vocal talent was similarly devoid of technical language, instead emphasising the effect it had upon her:

> It's a little bit like opera, […] but when you do see just the power that comes out of somebody's body, sort of voice, it makes the hairs stand up. And it's kind of a similar thing really. (Ruby)

Ruby's 'opera' drew a comparison between Killswitch Engage and a high art form that is well known for the virtuosic singing of its performers. 'Power' implied strength and force, suggesting that his voice was loud and confident, but the word also connoted that he had control over the audience. Unusually, she referred to both Jones' singing body and her own listening body, so that he is conjured as also having bodily power as well as vocal power. This was echoed in her rough descriptor 'sort of voice' so that it was not only his singing that was causing such an effect, but the body too. The power he had was to cause her body to react, 'the hairs stand up'. Jones' voice gave Ruby a visible physical reaction in her body so that the music moved her in a very deep way. It was not possible for Ruby to explain this reaction further except to liken it again to opera. Thus she connects her somatic reaction to the music to the power of the singer's voice, and uses the incident at the festival as an exemplum of his musical ability.

Many women commented upon the ability of the musicians in their favourite bands. Drummers were 'amazing' (Gwen, Bert, Aime), 'fearsome' (Carol), 'phenomenal' (Aria); singers were 'amazing' (Bert), 'powerful' (Ruby), 'great' (Karen); guitarists were 'amazing' (Bert) 'fantastic' or 'magnificent' (Carol); bassists were 'amazing' (Aime). Although the women only used a limited language to describe the impression that musicians made upon them, that so many *did* refer to musicianship is significant. These descriptions of musical performance highlight the extraordinariness of the musicians: as men who are determined and have the perseverance to practise hard; who are autodidacts; who can play their instrument in a variety of (unconventional) ways; or who can make sounds that produce physical responses in the listener. These musicians are, for their admiring fans, above the ordinary musician in terms of their ability. They are *virtuosos*, and, in knowing the difference between good playing and virtuoso playing, the fans separate themselves from those who cannot tell the difference.

Walser (1993) discusses virtuosity as a key attribute of heavy metal, particularly in the context of the influence of classical music. Virtuosity clearly holds meaning within hard rock and metal fandom, and Walser identifies it as reinscribing 'familiar constructions of masculinity and individuality' (Walser 1993 107). The appreciation of virtuosity fits in with the ideology of hard rock and metal, in which the guitar solo holds a defining place, and in which high-quality musicianship is generally valued (in comparison to, for example, punk, in which it is energy and politics that are valued). Riesman argues that an appreciation of virtuosity is something that is associated with the 'minority' of 'more active listeners' (1991 [1950], 9), a group which is defined in opposition to the 'majority' who are 'undiscriminating' (Riesman 1991 [1950], 8). Identifying the genre as one in which virtuosity is valued therefore reinforces the dichotomy between rock and pop, and rock's concomitant authenticity.

Lyrical content was another area in which hard rock and metal was described as contrasting to and, importantly, *better than* pop music. For Hazel this meant that the lyrics dealt with themes she perceived to be more serious than the romantic lyrics typically found in pop songs. Here she describes Tura Satana:

[Hazel] I always preferred the lyrics to say the lyrics to pop songs because they were less frivolous and they had more to say.

[Rosemary] What do you mean by frivolous?

> [Hazel] Well it wasn't all about, just like "oh I want a boyfriend, I love my boyfriend" and it was… you know, cos I happen to, I'm not a love song person, I'm not a mushy sort of sentimental person at all. (Hazel)

Hazel characterised all pop as 'frivolous' due to its preference for lyrics about romance. She described pop songs as referring to wanting a boyfriend, which, in the terms of heteronormativity, feminises the singer. Her tone as she mimicked the imagined song lyrics was scoffing: 'oh' implied that the singer was daydreaming whilst the repeated 'boyfriend' suggested the reduced scope of the singer's life. Hazel showed further derisiveness towards pop lyrics through her use of the adjectives 'frivolous', 'mushy', and 'sentimental'. The latter two words implied the expression of emotion not felt (false emotion), whilst the former signified that the subject matter was not serious or worthy of concern. This was emphasised in her contrasting description of hard rock and metal songs having 'more to say' (although on what topics she did not define). She put her dislike of pop lyrics down to a personal preference for songs that were not about love, because she identified herself as not a 'mushy' person. In dismissing romance themes she echoed the ideology of hard rock and metal as it seeks to diminish the feminine and to raise the music up as more serious.

For Bert it was the concept album format used by Avenged Sevenfold that was preferable to an album of unconnected songs:

> It had a story throughout the whole of it, and you can listen to [it] from beginning to end and know what that exact story is just from listening to the songs. And I love that; I love that you can go completely out there, yeah? And sometimes it doesn't work, sometimes it does, but it's just always amazing that you can do that, because if somebody did that in pop people would be there just "oh my god" you know, they just wouldn't get it. (Bert)

This suggests the high-quality songwriting ability of the band: that they could write song after song, that they were so skilled that they could create a large number of songs. Bert viewed the band's experimental approach as brave and progressive. Hard rock and metal was then constructed as *the* genre that permitted experimentation, rather than pop, because pop fans would be flummoxed. Bert's 'people' and 'they' referred to an undiscriminating mass of pop fans, and she directly reported what she imagined they were thinking: 'oh my god'. This was an expression of disbelief, disdain and unwillingness to try to understand due to pop fans' repudiation of non-conformity. Her final phrase, 'they just wouldn't get it', signified that Bert believed pop music fans to be not bright enough understand the concept of the album and the point of the experimentation.

For Bert, being able to appreciate a concept album was a sign of a hard rock and metal fan because the concept album would not be understood in pop. Pop fans' appetite for three-minute hit songs means that the story needs to be told within the confines of a single song. A concept album tells a story or explores an idea over an album of perhaps 45 minutes and maybe ten songs. Bert suggested that genre expectations of pop fans prevented them from understanding other ways of storytelling in music, hinting that, because pop fans do not 'get it', they lack sophistication in their music fandom.

Some other lyrical themes in hard rock and metal that the women discussed were death (Bert), bipolar disorder (Jessica), sexism, racism and homophobia (Alexa). These preferences are marked by the way that they are thought of as 'universal' and as being of interest to anyone, regardless of gender, race, sexuality, age and so on. Love and romance, in contrast, are not thought of as universal: they are a woman's interest alone. Drawing attention to the difference in the themes of lyrics compared to the lyrics in pop songs was not a neutral 'different but equal' judgement: it meant placing a higher value on the lyrical themes of rock and metal and judging them as more valuable because they were more serious. These kinds of descriptions of pop music echo the language of the myth of authenticity as, in disparaging pop lyrical themes, the women relied upon the dichotomous construction of rock and pop.

Such terminology is parallel with the mythological framing of hard rock and metal, and, in particular, the myths of the warrior and authenticity. By referring to objects and positions that are commonly represented as masculine (love of the guitar, virtuosity, the disparagement of pop music) there appears to be a rejection of femininity, which is due to its relationship with pop music. This appears to be problematic: by asserting rock's value to the detriment of pop, culture that is associated with women is positioned as being less valuable and women as producers, artists and enjoyers of culture are seen as less important. Thus the idea that only men have something important to say, be it artistically or politically, is maintained, and this then feeds into the perpetuation of women's subordination despite the rhetoric of equality. Furthermore, it positions women fans as involved in the disparagement of their own gender as they align themselves with a masculine culture that writes out the feminine.

FEMINISM AND HARD ROCK AND METAL'S MASCULINITY

Common sense understandings of hard rock and metal as masculine owe much to the way in which certain sounds are *construed* as 'masculine'. However, it is important to remember that 'masculine' sounds are only 'masculine' because they have been understood as such: they have no inherent masculine qualities. In his description of metal as masculine, Walser clarifies his position by asserting that the description is not due to any essential gender qualities of the music:

> Underpinning all semiotic analysis is, recognised or not, a set of assumptions about cultural practice, for ultimately music doesn't have meanings; people do. There is no essential, foundational way to ground musical meaning beyond the flux of social existence. (1993, 32)

In ascribing qualities to masculinity, Walser makes it clear that these meanings are constructed rather than inherent, a perspective shared by Susan McClary. In the foundational feminist musicology text *Feminine Endings* (1991), McClary investigates the way in which music has been divided along gender lines so that, for example, major keys are linked to the masculine and minor to the feminine (McClary 1991, 11). Throughout traditional musicology she finds that gendered binaries abound. Whether or not composers are consciously choosing to musically construct femininity or masculinity, the gendered codes are 'taken to be "natural"' (McClary 1991, 9), even by those composers. Moreover, they are *heard* as natural by the listener, too. Gendered interpretations of music therefore affect our understandings of, and pleasure in, the music, as well as our thoughts and feelings about musicians and about fans. This is clear from my interviewees' descriptions of music that use language that emphasises the *masculinity* of hard rock and metal. Their gendered hearings of the music were part of their experience and part of their pleasure. However, that pleasure has not been treated as neutral and has been politicised by groups of non-fans.

The perceived hypermasculinity of heavy metal and the virulently misogynistic lyrics to be found in some rock and metal songs (Grant 1996) have led to criticism of the music. This has come from conservative quarters, particularly in the USA, including the powerful PMRC campaign that led to the famous 'Parental Advisory' stickers, and also from some feminists in the early days of the Women's Liberation Movement (Wise 1984; Baumgardner 2005; Rat 2013 [1970]). Some feminists in the 1970s assumed that rock music was 'bad for women' and contributed to oppression via negative representations of women and sexual objectification; images of women as deserving victims of male violence or as out to deceive and harm innocent men; or as sexually passive (for an overview of these 'repressive representations' see Whiteley 2000). In her introduction to the compilation of the Chicago and New Haven Women's Liberation Rock Bands' recordings, Jennifer Baumgardner states that there was a general feeling of rock as a problem:

> Rock was part of the revolutionary language, and feminists were squeezing out the sexism there too. They were challenging the Rolling Stones—or at least talking back to their lyrics—She's "under your thumb"? Oh, yeah? Screw you, sexist pig! (2005, n.p.)

This was reflected in a comment made in the 1970s by a male friend of one of my interviewees. He was confused that as a *Spare Rib* reader and feminist Susan could enjoy the music of Led Zeppelin and other heavy metal bands:

> I can remember having a conversation with a friend who said, "you know I find it really uncomfortable that you like this sort of music". A male friend. [...] Yes, he said "because it seemed to me to epitomise everything that you stand against". (Susan)

The conversation, although it had occurred in the 1970s, had clearly stayed in Susan's memory and had made an impact upon her, although it did not stop her listening to Led Zeppelin, Deep Purple and other 1970s heavy metal bands. More recently, Vasan's feminist research is underpinned by incomprehension, causing her to 'ponder why women are drawn to death metal in general: why women choose to associate themselves with a male-dominated and overtly misogynistic subculture' (2010, 70).

These kind of criticisms place women who enjoy hard rock and metal music, despite its sexisms, in a minority amongst feminists and have led to criticism of those women who want to make rock music (Baumgardner 2005) or listen to it (Willis 1977). Sue Wise (1984) felt pressure from feminist friends to drop her fandom of Elvis, as if being an Elvis fan and being a feminist were incompatible. Liking Elvis was a state of false consciousness to be rejected. Norma Coates (1997) draws attention to this problem when considering her own attachment to The Rolling Stones, but for her it is not only the misogynist attitudes or lyrics that are problematic, but the music itself:

> A feminist fan of the Stones and rock like myself is faced with an immediate conundrum: if indeed it is the phallic power of the sound that draws me to it, then I am complicit in my own submission to that power. I accept and at the same time reinforce it. Some might say that when I describe the Stones' sound as sexy, I am operating under 'false consciousness', simply accepting and reinforcing hegemonic tropes of male and female sexuality. This is an unsatisfactory explanation (1997, 50–51).

False consciousness may be an unsatisfactory explanation for her Stones fandom, but she does not offer another.

The argument that rock is bad for women is rooted in the construction of rock and pop as dichotomously oppositional, which results in a cyclical relationship: thinking of metal and rock as 'masculine' means thinking in ways that are inevitably compelled to hang upon the gender binary. Furthermore, interpreting metal as masculine misses out some of the more interesting aspects of the genre, such as the queering discussed by Whiteley (2006) and Clifford-Napoleone (2015b). When hard rock and metal is thought of as 'masculine', its more 'feminine' attributes are hidden: the high voices of bands like Led Zeppelin and Budgie; the make-up of, for example, My Chemical Romance and many glam metal bands; the ubiquitous long hair. When these elements are considered, the heteromasculinity of hard rock and metal looks more complicated, as Sheila Whiteley argues:

> In essence, metal is about men being manly, and while Walser relates this to the codes of misogyny, exscription and the fraternalistic culture of bands and fans, problems arise when connecting the sweaty gods to their often androgynous images—the long hair, mascara, spandex, and leather. (2006, 257)

Whiteley also makes an important point about the dangers of interpreting metal *only* as masculine: that is, the genre is more open to feminine play for its male musicians than Walser admits, and this needs to be taken into account.

Susan Fast (1999), too, finds a good deal to worry about in conceptions of rock music, Led Zeppelin in particular, as masculine. She argues that leaving the masculinity of rock assumed and unquestioned misses an opportunity to engage with the ways that both female and male fans make sense of Led Zeppelin's music. She writes that in the assumption of the masculinity of the music and the fans there is no place for her own fandom of the band. Similarly, the identification of Elvis as 'butch god' (Wise 1984, 395) by feminists did not correlate with the Elvis beloved of Sue Wise. She argues that this macho Elvis rejected by her feminist friends was the Elvis of 'men who depicted this phallic hero as having worldwide cultural significance' (Wise 1984, 397). As Fast argues in her discussion of how the 'masculinity' of Led Zeppelin and their music has been maintained, the key players in the media and academia who have contributed to this reading are male (1999, 247). Representations of hard rock and metal music are written and sanctioned by men (music journalists, the musicians, editors) or by those whose job it is to ensure the ideological perspective of the genre is maintained (albeit with some female industry workers or musicians) (Bayton 1998; McDonnell and Powers 1995). For this reason, Fast argues, it is vital that women's perspectives on rock and metal be considered. Picking up on Coates' notion of the gender binary of rock/pop and the effect of interpreting rock as masculine, she writes, 'in reading these words I felt enormous sorrow that her pleasure had been compromised by an essentialist view of how gender might work in music' (1999, 252). Considering hard rock and metal as exclusively masculine eclipses women fans' own interpretations that challenge the notion that the genre is only an arena for hypermasculine posturing, which excludes or demeans women. For this reason I now consider how my interviewees described their pleasure in hard rock and metal in ways that did *not* fit in with the ideology of this imaginary community.

Articulating Pleasure in Music

When describing their enjoyment of their favourite bands, only five women used the same kinds of language employed in their descriptions of heavy metal. More women invoked 'dissimilarity' between the music of their preferred bands and others. In addition, my interviewees used quite novel and imaginative descriptors, so that they were able to articulate why their favourite bands moved them in language that often contrasted sharply with the sort of terminology that is typically associated with hard rock and metal. They described the music as allowing transcendence, as enabling shared experiences; they also used romantic terms, and two women discussed their simultaneous love of pop musicians alongside their hard rock and metal fandom.

Transcendence and Transportation

Three of the women articulated the ways in which the music allowed them to transcend their immediate surroundings. For instance, Aime described Avenged Sevenfold's unusual musical choices in order to elucidate her listening experience:

> In "Beast and the Harlot" they go verse chorus solo verse chorus chorus so that's weird: I found it weird that they put the solo within the first half of the song and that's how they experiment. And it's like one of the greatest riffs of all time, and they don't just do the riff, they do things in the background, which makes it even more interesting. You're listening to it and the bass is different; it's not just going along with the chords, and it's an adventure to listen to in a way. (Aime)

At first Aime was specific about the construction of the song, determining that the format was 'weird' in order to emphasise the difference between this song and more traditionally constructed songs. What I found most intriguing, however, was her use of 'adventure' to describe her listening experience. Listening to the band was akin to going on a journey. Sections of the song led her through the musical landscape: the positions of the instruments and other effects in the mix meant that there was much of interest to experience each time the voyage was made, and the unusual bass melody meant that the passage was an extraordinary one in comparison to other musical journeys. In my interpretation, 'adventure' does not just mean 'journey'; it also connotes excitement, quests and tasks to be accomplished, with potentially the thrill of meeting wizards and the risk of encountering dragons! 'Adventure' is romantic and, in describing 'Beast and the Harlot' in this way, Aime created a sense of the song as able to transport the listener to another world that was more exciting than everyday life in twenty-first century Britain.

Jeanette described seeing her favourite band, Red Sparowes, and the effect of the political images of China that they used as the backdrop for their music:

> It was visually absolutely stunning, but it was also very disturbing images at the same time. Together, combined with extremely melodic, beautiful

music in front of you, so it transports you as well. I mean I certainly didn't, during that show I didn't think political thoughts, but makes you think very creatively, erm. Yes, it just opens up, erm, it lets your mind flow. (Jeanette)

Jeanette's use of 'visually stunning' and 'together combined' provide a sense of the concert as more than simply an aural event; it was a fuller sensual experience. The strong adverbs, 'absolutely', 'very', 'extremely', 'certainly', all signify how powerful the effect of the concert was for her. The beautiful music had the impact of allowing her mind to 'flow' in ways that she considered creative. Hard rock and metal is not generally thought of as allowing space for *thinking*. As I infer from Overell's work on the way in which grindcore 'blows away' (2012, 202) its listeners, the genre is often thought of as allowing the listener some sense of obliteration. Hard rock, in particular, is not associated with the intellect. Rather it is often associated with the life of the body: sex, drugs and alcohol. This attitude is epitomised in Hebdige's off-the-cuff denunciation of 'heavy metal rockers' as being distinguishable by their 'idiot dancing' (1979, 109, 155), in which the movement of bodies in time to the music is the notable characteristic. In Jeanette's remarks there was an impression of images crossing her consciousness, as if in a meditative state and that this kind of creative thinking was not the kind of thinking she could access easily in her daily life. Red Sparowes' music and imagery enabled this and it was extraordinary and central to her pleasurable experience. Furthermore, Jeanette used 'melodic' and 'beautiful', words that are not usually associated with hard rock and metal. Hard rock and metal is not typically thought of as 'beautiful': common sense understandings of the genre by non-metal fans sometimes interpret the music as harsh and ugly (Weinstein 2000 [1991] compiles a range of sources which characterise the music in this way). The density and pace of the songs can make listening a difficult experience for new listeners and, in these cases, they may not hear a melody at all. Furthermore, these terms do not fit into the ideological language of the genre, as they do not refer to speed, heaviness, hardness or aggressiveness; in fact they are more associated with femininity and with art.

Susan described listening to Led Zeppelin as enabling a feeling of being different from normal when normal is 'mundane': 'it lifts you out of the mundane. I mean cleaning or ironing can't be anything but mundane can it? So a well-chosen piece of music just lifts you above that' (Susan). Susan used the verb 'lifts' to describe the way in which music can affect someone doing housework. In this she implicitly placed cleaning and ironing in the position of bringing one down, that is, that such tasks are depressing. 'Mundane' lent an air of transcendence to the way in which music functions. This presentation of music as enabling transcendence of boring tasks is a view shared by Lawrence Grossberg (1984). He argues that rock enables young people to find some sense of empowerment in their adolescent powerlessness, but Susan's description of the way music 'lifted' her was rooted in her experience of being a single mother with young children. For Susan, it was not powerlessness that needed to be overcome but the boring and endless task of housework. Susan was not alone in finding that hard rock and metal music helped with housework: Ruby found that energetic metal helped her with the gardening, and Jessica said that it aided her in cleaning. However, for Susan the music's power to 'lift her above' the mundane was not just to motivate her to engage in house or garden work, rather it meant that she could feel outside of the tasks. Although men's work in the home has increased over time, women remain responsible for and spend more time on domestic labour (European Social Survey 2013). Hard rock and metal therefore have import for women's ability to accomplish household tasks with some level of pleasure, and this is a crucial way in which musical experience is shaped by the gender system.

However, transcendence itself is associated with gendered qualities. Kruse (2002) argues that music critics—mostly male—have assumed that rock is a male genre and that their readers are male. They have treated women fans as unable to really understand rock as a transcendental art form, in which transcendence is taken to mean universal and timeless, that is, outside of social conditions. Yet, she argues, musical meaning is fundamentally tied to our lived experience and to social conditions. This argument makes a case for the polysemy of music and plurality of musical experiences—and gender must therefore be one important component of shaping those experiences. When gender plays a part in limiting our lives to the 'mundane'—as it certainly does when it comes to unpaid domestic labour—fans' experiences of hard rock and metal's ability to 'lift' us out of mundanity is a clear refutation of the problems with the notional universality of transcendence that Kruse elaborates. Hard rock and metal is experienced in this case *because* of the very particular social conditions of women's lives.

Musical beauty was credited with the power to expand these women's minds, enabling them to think more 'creatively', lifting them above mundane employments, or taking them on a journey into a fantasy land. All of these descriptions give an impression of pleasure in hard rock and metal that is quite different from those descriptions that characterise the genre as masculine or negative. My interviewees described positive elements that enhanced their thinking and meditative lives.

Shared Experiences

Ruby found that sharing the emotions or experiences with the musicians was an important component of her musical experience. She enjoyed the way in which she could relate to what the musicians were singing about.

> It's an affiliation. [...] when I got divorced [...] obviously it was a highly emotional time. I think, you know, that a lot of, a lot of the metal music I listened to at the time was, especially with Killswitch Engage, was about heartbreak and sorrow and it kind of makes you feel like you're not the only person in that situation. It's almost like having a heartbreak buddy there on your iPod. (Ruby)

Ruby used 'affiliation' in the sense of sibling love and friendship. This was signified also through her use of 'not the only person', 'buddy' and 'there on your iPod', all terms which worked to create a sense of how Ruby felt about the music at the time of her divorce: that the music could provide intimacy, friendship and stability in a time of difficulty. Ruby's vocabulary—which is readily found in pop music—brings forth the question to what extent does vocabulary cross genre boundaries? Ruby called Killswitch Engage her 'heartbreak buddy' as she found that the songs resonated with her own feelings at the time of her divorce. She felt that she was not alone, even when she was alone with her iPod headphones.

Jenny gained happiness from what she saw as the enthusiasm and enjoyment of the band; in this case in the gig environment when she went to see/hear Slabdragger:

> Really like enthusiasm and commitment and energy. And particularly if their lead singer's got that, I mean I don't necessarily make out the words they're singing, but I like commitment, and that respect and they played really well as a band. You could really see they were all enjoying themselves, and it's nice when it works both ways. (Jenny)

Jenny ascribed her affection for Slabdragger to the merits of the band in performance. The three qualities that she liked about the performance were not musical merits, rather they were about the attitude of the performers. For Jenny, the enthusiasm was combined with what she interpreted as the commitment of the band and 'that respect'. The phrase, 'it's nice when it works both ways', implied that the audience gained pleasure from hearing and witnessing the band's performance, and the band too gained satisfaction and enjoyment from their own performance. In the words 'both ways' Jenny intimated that the band's joy was also inspired by seeing their audience's enthusiastic response.

Jenny made the suggestion that bands can convey their own feelings of exuberance and enthusiasm to fans: that music has the power to transmit emotions. This idea of joy in the performance implies that there are times when bands are unable to enjoy the music they perform. On these occasions the performance itself may be note-perfect, but there is some *je ne sais quoi* missing. The joyous performance is therefore very important: happy, socially shared and overwhelmingly positive. This brings to the fore ideas about music as a communal experience that allows for personal feelings to be explored in musical companionship. These pleasures do not necessarily fit in with the language that echoes the ideology of hard rock and metal in, particularly, the myth of the warrior. However, the women were not describing a whole-community experience: Ruby and also Susan were feeling a quite personal communion with the band.

Romance Language

Aime told me that her first encounter with Avenged Sevenfold had been via music television. This occurred after having just read a review of the band:

> It was just a review of a gig, and I thought, "oh that gig sounded cool; [I] might go on YouTube and have a find out a bit" and, er, just before then I was watching *Kerrang!* on TV and I flipped over the channel, and just that second a song of theirs came on, and it was this kind of like husky bit where he sings, and I was like ah! It was just I felt [breathy] that moment and I was like, it was really nice, it was kind of like a fairytale. (Aime)

Aime began by saying 'it was just a review', where 'just' ascribes little importance to her encounter with the piece (it came to have more significance later). The synchronicity of reading the review and then seeing the band on television seems to have suggested a magical or romantic relationship between herself and the band, as indicated by her use of the word 'fairytale' (she seems to have forgotten that she was intending to 'go on YouTube' where she may very well have chosen to watch the same video). The romance came from her somewhat erotic response to the 'husky' quality of the singing. 'Husky' is associated with throatiness and can be read as 'sexy', particularly if used about women (Churcher 2007). Aime struggled to put her response into words, using instead 'ah!', sighing breathily and intimating a short time of arousal, 'that moment'. The use of 'fairytale' with Aime's narration of the story, which presents it as an encounter like love at first sight, relying on magical synchronicity, works within a discourse of romance language. There is a distinct sense that Aime's musical experience of Avenged Sevenfold was a romantic one. Although Aime's storytelling might well work to bolster ideas of young women fans as groupies by ascribing a romantic relationship to her attitude towards the band, her response to Avenged Sevenfold is not as straightforward as a passion for particular band members; her previous comments signaled that it was a relationship with the music *and* how she imagined the musicians. It was a complex affection that intertwined her intellectual musical pleasure with her erotic musical response and with her imaginative thoughts about the band.

Upheaval at the Pop/Rock Divide

Many of my interviewees made generalisations about pop music and its fans that contrasted pop unfavourably with hard rock and metal music and its fans. Most did not describe the ways in which pop music and rock music can both defy their ideological construction as separate spheres. Yet although the women tended to be invested in the notion of difference between rock and pop, ambiguity remained in delineating that difference. Thus the rock/pop dichotomy impacted on their thinking in some ways but not in others. For instance, Gwen insisted that she rarely knew the name of songs or the bands that were singing them, thereby showing little interest in the accumulation of band-related knowledge so important for demonstrating 'real' fandom. Nor was she uncomfortable about this lack of cultural knowledge.

Two women, Alexa and Aime, both spoke of their passion for pop singers (Adam Lambert and Britney Spears respectively) and acknowledged how this was unusual. Alexa said she felt slightly guilty about her passion for Adam Lambert, and I asked why. She responded:

> I don't know. I think it's just because, with him being, erm, like an *American Idol* runner-up and loads of people are like, "oh it's all manufactured and it's not real music, it's just processed". I think that's the problem with it that a lot of people have, but I think he is actually one [of] the few that has defended his position, and he is quite unique and original from it, and he does actually sing live and put on a good show [laughs]. (Alexa)

Terms Alexa imagined 'loads of people' have used to describe Adam Lambert very much fit in with ideas of a rock/pop divide ('manufactured', 'not real', 'processed'), and she summed up that it was these imagined ideas that caused her guilt: 'I think that's the problem'. In acknowledging these criticisms of Adam Lambert, Alexa deftly positioned herself outside of such concerns. Her defence of the singer may in some ways have paid homage to ideas about what 'counts' as authentic music ('unique', 'original', 'sing live'), but Lambert remains a pop musician. In openly discussing her love for his music and in challenging stereotypes about pop she shook the divide between pop and rock, perhaps not to its foundations, but certainly with the effect of worrying its 'truth' claims.

For Aime, also, liking hard rock and metal *and* pop was not always easy:

> You don't often find someone like me [...] I like such a massive group of bands and different types of music and stuff like that, and I suppose I'm just a part of a lot of communities in a way, depending on who I'm going to see. Avenged Sevenfold it's all moshers, and then I like, erm, Britney Spears. I love Britney Spears. I got her album on my phone and [My Chemical Romance], and then both get criticism, and I'm like "oh I feel bad now!", but I like the bands or the singers so they can get over it. (Aime)

She posited herself as unusual and explained that a wide range of eclectic tastes marked her out as different within her peer group. Aime's taste was clearly unusual, and she saw herself as shifting between different groups of music fans. She was initially tentative about naming Britney Spears, but then she announced confidently that 'I love Britney Spears', adding as an exemplum of her passion that she had 'got her album on my phone'. She carried her phone with her everywhere, so this indicated that the album was always available to her. However, when Aime found that others could not understand her genre crossing, she employed a rock 'n' roll 'fuck you' non-conforming attitude to fend off criticism and bolster her wavering self-esteem. So whilst she enjoyed music from the 'wrong' genre, the 'right' attitude made sense of her tastes.

These young women transgressed the boundaries of rock and pop so that they were able to enjoy the music they chose. In my semiotic readings of *Kerrang!* magazine's letters pages, I found that in the early 2000s a number of letters contained an ethos of 'just like what you like', meaning that one should not feel bounded by genre classifications, and one should feel free to enjoy any kind of music (Hill 2014b). This worked within a framework of authenticity and equality in which being true to musical taste was valued and equality translated into respecting other fans. In practice, however, the letters pages demonstrated numerous occasions when fans *did* denounce other fans for their genre-crossing musical pleasures. These squabbles over genre and preference work to reinforce the myth of authenticity because, ultimately, enjoying pop music marks out a hard rock and metal fan as not really an authentic fan. That these women broke through the anti-pop prejudice was remarkable, and these examples highlight the way fans are placed in a straitjacket by the ideology of hard rock and metal, particularly women fans who are more in need of proving their fandom, being seen generally as second-class fans or groupies. For a woman hard rock and metal fan to admit to enjoying pop music was to lay herself open to criticism from other fans as not being serious about hard rock and metal, as Aime described. In speaking openly and without (much) shame about their preferences, Aime and Alexa challenged the myth of authenticity.

CONCLUSION

Coates (1997) meditates on whether being a feminist fan of The Rolling Stones is a state of false consciousness, a concept that Fast (1999) finds problematic. However, women's fandom cannot be reduced to understandings of women hard rock and metal fans as cowed by the music or as 'betraying' women or feminism. Deeper consideration of women's pleasure in hard rock and metal music is vital in challenging assumptions about the genre and its fans. Kahn-Harris (2007) notes that extreme metal fans, when describing or explaining their love of the music, use language that is limited by the scene itself. I too found that amongst women fans, the use of language that fits neatly within the ideology of the genre *was* prominent in their descriptions of heavy metal. Terms such as 'fierce' and 'heavy', the emphasis on noisy electric guitar, the love of virtuosity and musical ability, and the comparisons to pop music which stressed hard rock and metal's authenticity against pop's manufactured nature are intrinsic in the way in which hard rock and metal music is understood as symbolically masculine. But when particular qualities are ascribed to a gender, the male dominance of the genre is maintained via the reification of male-associated qualities and the denigration of those linked to femininity. The result is the alienation and exclusion of women from the genre and the presumption of an underlying male norm for musicians and for 'real fans'. When only these 'masculine' qualities are taken into account, metal appears to be 'naturally' associated with men; but as Riches (2014) shows, such qualities are not exclusively available to men: aggression is a human quality not a male one.

However, my interviewees' language was not limited by these conventions. When asked about their favourite bands they were able to extend their descriptive lexicon beyond those conventions in unusual and persuasive ways. Notions of hard rock and metal fandom as a reification of warrior masculinity were challenged in may ways: by descriptions of the music as beautiful, as allowing transcendence and the opening of the mind; by expressions of feelings of companionship between musicians and fans; and via interpretations of musical performances as joyous. Moreover, the pop fandom of some women undermines the rigid boundaries and assumptions that underpin the myth of authenticity. My participants' expressions move our understanding away from a strict notion of the genre as 'masculine' because they highlight how pleasure is also found in aspects of the music that are not associated with masculinity, and some of which are linked to what is considered feminine. This wider consideration of women's pleasure in the music draws attention to the fact that when qualities are ascribed a gender this is a social process: the qualities that are associated with masculinity are not 'essentially' masculine (and similarly those linked to femininity are not 'essentially' feminine). Therefore, when hard rock and metal is thought of as masculine this is the result of constructed understandings of gender, not the cardinal qualities of the music. The importance of considering these elements, therefore, is not just a matter of giving a fuller picture to women's rock and metal pleasure. It is necessary in order to challenge the orthodoxy of the genre as masculine and therefore the naturalised hierarchy that places men upon the stage and/or positioned in the audience as the 'real fan' whilst women are relegated to the subordinate role of the groupie.

References

Ang, Ien. 1985. *Watching Dallas: Soap Opera and the Melodramatic Imagination.* London: Methuen.

Baumgardner, Jennifer. 2005. Aural History: The Politics of Feminist Rock. In *Sleevenotes to Papa, Don't Lay That Shit On Me: The Chicago and New Haven Women's Liberation Rock Band and Le Tigre.* Rounder 82161-4001-2.

Bayton, Mavis. 1997. Women and the Electric Guitar. In *Sexing the Groove: Popular Music and Gender,* ed. Sheila Whiteley, 37–49. London: Routledge.

———. 1998. *Frock Rock: Women Performing Popular Music.* Oxford: Oxford University Press.

Bourdage, Monique. 2010. 'A Young Girl's Dream': Examining the Barriers Facing Female Electric Guitarists. *IASPM@ Journal* 1(1): 1–16.

Churcher, Mel. 2007. What is a Sexy Voice? *Voice and Speech Review* 5(1): 260–262.

Clifford-Napoleone, Amber. 2015b. *Queerness in Heavy Metal Music: Metal Bent*. Abingdon: Routledge.

Coates, Norma. 1997. (R)evolution Now? Rock and the Political Potential of Gender. In *Sexing the Groove: Popular Music and Gender*, ed. Sheila Whiteley, 50–64. Abingdon: Routledge.

European Social Survey. 2013. *Exploring Public Attitudes, Informing Public Policy. Selected Findings from the First Five Rounds*.

Fast, Susan. 1999. Rethinking Issues of Gender and Sexuality in Led Zeppelin: A Woman's View of Pleasure and Power in Hard Rock. *American Music* 17(3): 245–299.

Fetterley, Judith. 1978. *The Resisting Reader: A Feminist Approach to American Fiction*. London: Indiana University Press.

Geraghty, Christine. 1991. *Women and Soap Opera: A Study of Prime Time Soaps*. Cambridge: Polity.

Grant, Judith. 1996. Bring the Noise: Hypermasculinity in Heavy Metal and Rap. *Journal of Social Philosophy* 27(2): 5–30.

Grossberg, Lawrence. 1984. Another Boring Day in Paradise: Rock and Roll and the Empowerment of Everyday Life. *Popular Music* 4: 225–258.

Hebdige, Dick. 1979. *Subculture: The Meaning of Style*. London: Routledge.

Hesmondhalgh, David. 2005. Subcultures, Scenes or Tribes? None of the Above. *Journal of Youth Studies* 8(1): 21–40.

Hill, Rosemary Lucy. 2014b. Representations and Experiences of Women Hard Rock and Metal Fans in the Imaginary Community. Ph.D., Centre for Women's Studies, University of York.

Hunter, Seb. 2004. *Hell Bent for Leather: Confessions of a Heavy Metal Addict*. London: Harper Perennial.

Kahn-Harris, Keith. 2007. *Extreme Metal: Music and Culture on the Edge*. Oxford: Berg.

Kruse, Holly. 2002. Abandoning the Absolute: Transcendence and Gender in Popular Music Discourse. In *Pop Music and the Press*, ed. Steve Jones, 134–155. Philedelphia: Temple University Press.

Leblanc, Lauraine. 1999. *Pretty in Punk: Girls' Gender Resistance in a Boys' Subculture*. New Brunswick, NJ: Rutgers University Press.

McClary, Susan. 1991. *Feminine Endings: Music, Gender, and Sexuality*. Minneapolis: University of Minnesota Press.

McDonnell, Evelyn, and Ann Powers, eds. 1995. *Rock She Wrote: Women Write About Rock, Pop, and Rap*. New York: Delta.

Mynett, Mark. 2013. Humanizing the Machine: Technological Mediation and the Notions of Authenticity, Integrity and Liveness in Contemporary Metal Music. *Heavy Metal and Popular Culture Conference*, Bowling Green, OH, 4–7 April.

Nordström, Susanna, and Marcus Herz. 2013. 'It's a Matter of Eating or Being Eaten.' Gender Positioning and Difference Making in the Heavy Metal Subculture. *European Journal of Cultural Studies* 16(4): 453–467.

Overell, Rosemary. 2010. Brutal Belonging in Melbourne's Grindcore Scene. *Studies in Symbolic Interaction* 35: 79–99.

———. 2012. '[I] Hate Girls and Emo[tion]s: Negotiating Masculinity in Grindcore Music. *Popular Music History* 6(1): 198–223.

———. 2014. *Affective Intensities in Extreme Music Scenes: Cases from Australia and Japan*. Basingstoke: Palgrave Macmillan.

Radway, Janice A. 1984. *Reading the Romance: Women, Patriarchy, and Popular Literature*. Chapel Hill: University of North Carolina Press.

Rat. 2013 [1970]. Cock Rock: Men Always Seem to End Up on Top. In *The Rock History Reader*, ed. Theo Cateforis, 119–124. Abingdon: Routledge.

Riches, Gabrielle. 2011. Embracing the Chaos: Mosh Pits, Extreme Metal Music and Liminality. *Journal for Cultural Research* 15(3): 315–332.

———. 2014. "Throwing the Divide to the Wind": Rethinking Extreme Metal's Masculinity Through Female Metal Fans' Embodied Experiences in Moshpit Practices. *IASPM UK & Ireland Conference*, Cork, Ireland, 12–14 September.

———. 2015. Re-conceptualizing Women's Marginalization in Heavy Metal: A Feminist Post-structuralist Perspective. *Metal Music Studies* 1(2): 263–270.

Riesman, David. 1991 [1950]. Listening to Popular Music. In *On Record: Rock, Pop and the Written Word*, eds. Simon Frith and Andrew Goodwin, 5–13. London: Routledge.

Skeggs, Beverley. 1997. *Formations of Class & Gender: Becoming Respectable*. London: Sage.

Stacey, Jackie. 1994. *Star Gazing: Hollywood Cinema and Female Spectatorship*. London: Routledge.

Vasan, Sonia. 2010. 'Den Mothers and Band Whores': Gender, Sex and Power in the Death Metal Scene. In *Heavy Fundametalisms: Music, Metal and Politics*, eds. Rosemary Lucy Hill, and Karl Spracklen, 69–78. Oxford: Inter-Disciplinary Press.

———. 2011. The Price of Rebellion: Gender Boundaries in the Death Metal Scene. *Journal for Cultural Research* 15(3): 333–349.

Waksman, Steve. 1999. *Instruments of Desire: The Electric Guitar and the Shaping of Musical Experience*. London: Harvard University Press.

Walser, Robert. 1993. *Running with the Devil: Power, Gender, and Madness in Heavy Metal Music*. Hannover, NH: University Press of New England.

Weinstein, Deena. 2000 [1991]. *Heavy Metal: The Music and Its Culture*. Rev. ed. Boulder, CO: Da Capo Press.

Whiteley, Sheila. 2000. *Women and Popular Music: Sexuality, Identity, and Subjectivity*. New York: Routledge.

———. 2006. Popular Music and the Dynamics of Desire. In *Queering the Popular Pitch*, eds. Sheila Whiteley, and Jennifer Rycenga, 249–262. London: Routledge.

Willis, Ellen. 1977. Beginning to See the Light. *Village Voice*.

Wise, Sue. 1984. Sexing Elvis. In *On Record: Rock, Pop, & the Written Word*, eds. Simon Frith, and Andrew Goodwin, 390–398. London: Routledge.

CHAPTER 6

Metal and Sexism

INTRODUCTION

Heavy metal has historically faced serious allegations of sexism, yet despite nearly 30 years of research on the topic, the question—how sexist is hard rock and metal—remains pertinent because academic accounts and fan accounts are at odds on the answer. Historical allegations remain an important part of how metal fans understand the genre and the culture: defensiveness shapes it. The need to defend the genre arose from attacks from the Christian right which were not limited to accusations of sexism (the genre was also charged with inciting paganism, violence, perversion and suicide), but in which feminist ideas were important. In 1980s USA, the Parents Music Resource Center (PMRC) and the Parent Teachers Association (PTA), organisations that were mostly conservative Christian, were deeply concerned that the music and music videos enjoyed by young white men were damaging due to sexist and violent language and imagery. Originally published in 1991, Weinstein's (2000 [1991]) sociological investigation into heavy metal considers the charges against the genre—suicide and aggression, sexual perversion and Satanism—and, with a large dose of ridicule, shows them to be misinformed and lacking in nuanced understanding of lyrical irony. She does not, however, give the charges of misogyny the same space, which allows some of the ridicule levelled at the other charges to accrue also to those of sexism. And yet she asserts that the genre *is* masculinist, chauvinistic and misogynistic. But, she argues,

© The Editor(s) (if applicable) and The Author(s) 2016   133
R.L. Hill, *Gender, Metal and the Media*, Pop Music, Culture
and Identity, DOI 10.1057/978-1-137-55441-3_6

this is alleviated by the 'sense of community' (Weinstein 2000 [1991], 105) because as long as women are prepared to downplay femininity and adhere to the masculine rules there is no problem: sexism is only faced by those who are feminine.

On the other hand, an array of researchers have described the sexism that women face as they participate in hard rock and metal culture. Some of the earliest work on metal is from the field of psychology in the 1980s. This responds to the PMRC and PTA panic, and focusses on the damage associated with hard rock and metal fandom. It finds metal to be sexist—unequivocally so. Rosenbaum's and Prinsky's 1987 article with the promising title '"Leer-ics" or Lyrics: Teenage Impressions of Rock 'n' Roll', concludes that young people do not interpret lyrics in the same ways as adults and that they frequently miss sexual connotations, but it does not look at sexual violence per se. St Lawrence and Joyner (1991) find that listening to heavy metal does correspond to 'higher levels of sex-role stereotyping and negative attitudes towards women' (cited in Mitchell et al. 2001, 29). Hansen and Hansen (1991) conclude that heavy metal fans are more likely to be 'sexist, and higher in machismo' (cited in Mitchell et al. 2001, 30). Mitchell et al. corroborate earlier findings, stating that '[h]eavy metal listeners [...] exhibited more negative attitudes toward women than listeners of other music genres' (2001, 35). These results do not tell us anything about women fans' experiences—or lack thereof—of sexism, but indicate that there is a relationship between preference for hard rock and metal music and sexist attitudes.

More recent work in media and cultural studies and the social sciences confirms metal's sexism, but does so typically through speaking to women about their experiences and examining hard rock and metal texts rather than assessing male fans' attitudes. This work has found sexism that ranges through sexist attitudes and behaviours of peers at hard rock and metal events (Krenske and McKay 2000; Kahn-Harris 2007; Vasan 2011): symbolic violence, such as the violently misogynistic imagery in artwork and lyrics (Kahn-Harris 2007; Overell 2010; Vasan 2010; Barron 2013); women being faced with a barrage of questions to prove the authenticity of their fandom (Nordström and Herz 2013); the dominance of men in bands; and prejudice faced by women musicians (Bayton 1998; Shadrack 2014; Spracklen 2015). And of course there is the myth that all women fans are groupies who are more interested in the musician than the music, a prejudice which underpins differential treatment like that discussed by Nordström and Herz.

The dualities that Nordström and Herz (2013) identify as problematic for women fans participating in metal culture—'whore/goddess', 'acting male'/'looking female', and the 'twilight zone' of being neither masculine enough for metal nor feminine enough for the mainstream—represent a tussle between norms of femininity and metal masculinity and can be characterised as presenting two roles for women fans: groupie or one of the boys. Similar dualities are also discussed by Vasan (2011) as 'band whores' and 'den mothers' and Patterson (2011) as 'chickapoos' and 'chicks-with-dicks'. In all three of these accounts the dualities are shown to present problems for women fans' equal participation. At heart they derive from metal's desire to exscript the feminine so that women must act masculine to fit in, but prejudice about women as essentially feminine inhibits acceptance. Women hard rock and metal fans are seen as extraordinary or unnatural, and therefore need to prove themselves. In short, women hard rock and metal fans are subject to sexism.

Taken together these psychology studies and the more recent works give the distinct impression of a genre that is built upon sexism. However, the women I spoke to did not report high levels of sexism. In fact, they described their experiences as being *less* subject to sexism than in a generalised mainstream. For example Ruby said,

> In my experience I've never had any negativity from guys in metal in terms of being a woman, like that sort of "oh well, you know, shouldn't be in the mosh pit. You're a woman," kind of thing, or them not thinking I should like heavy music cos I'm, you know... You only get that out[side] of the metal scene. (Ruby)

These experiences are reflected in other recent work in the British context. Savigny and Sleight (2015) discuss the contradiction between academic assertions that metal is sexist and assertions to the contrary by the women fans they interviewed at UK metal and rock festivals. The authors argue that the real difference is between the site of production of metal and its consumption by fans. Metal's production is institutionally sexist, and this is apparent in the massive dominance of male musicians in festival line-ups and in sexist album art (life imitating *This Is Spinal Tap* [Reiner 1984]). Women festival goers, however, claim that metal spaces are freer from sexual harassment than mainstream spaces. This is problematic however, as sexual harassment is seen as the primary form of sexism, which Savigny and Sleight declare as 'the equating of an absence of sexual violation with equality is perhaps a damning indictment of our times' (2015, 351). Furthermore, it results in other forms of sexism being not categorised as such. Sexualisation in the form of pressure upon women to show their breasts to cameras recording at festivals is normalised, and it is taken as a matter of personal choice as to whether women want to reveal their chests or not. That they are able to make this choice is a sign that metal is 'empowering' as they can choose whether do so with awareness of sexist pressures—informed decision making! However, this is a neoliberal post-feminist empowerment in which the individual must negotiate her own relationship with capitalist patriarchy rather than form collectives to con-test sexist pressures. Moreover, in spite of metal's empowering potential for fans, sexism remains a barrier should they wish to become performers. Therefore, 'empowerment for women in metal may take place, but only through patriarchally defined spaces' (Savigny and Sleight 2015, 352).

What Savigny and Sleight offer, therefore, is a more nuanced reading of the genre's gender dynamics within a neoliberal and postfeminist context, in which 'empowerment' is seen as an indication that metal can be a site of resistance to patriarchy. However, I am unconvinced that the limited 'empowerment' the authors provide evidence of is enough to make this claim; their evidence suggests a limited sense of being able to choose to participate in sexist practices (showing tits to cameras) or not, and of fewer incidents of harassment than the mainstream. This is not enough to indi-cate that metal provides 'the potential to provide escape from dominant patriarchal structures' (Savigny and Sleight 2015, 354). Rather, it suggests that metal remains a patriarchal site in production and consumption, and that neoliberal postfeminism enables women to make sense of their expe-riences as empowering. As I make this criticism of Savigny and Sleight's argument, I must affirm that they are absolutely right to emphasise the need for a more nuanced reading of hard rock and metal's gender poli-tics. A critique of postfeminism is productive, but it only offers a partial account, however. I am worried that the result is that women's accounts are still being positioned as some form of 'false consciousness'. Of primary concern to me is to listen to women's accounts and to take them seriously. I am not accusing Savigny and Sleight of attributing false consciousness to their interviewees; rather I am saying that their theoretical lens limits the arguments they are able to make. In analysing my interviewees' assertions of a lack of sexism in hard rock and metal I engage with a range of differ-ent feminist literature to try to understand how there can be such a dis-sonance between what scholars say and what women fans say. Questions about the particular interpretations of sexism that my interviewees were making, about the role of the myth of equality, and about the value of thinking through the broader context of women's lives in sexist society need to be asked. What other factors that are not specifically about metal are in play? Is previous work wrong? If metal is less sexist than the mainstream, what does that say about the hypermasculinity of the genre and women's ability to participate?

SEXUAL HARASSMENT

Savigny and Sleight (2015) note that sexual harassment was taken by their interviewees as a key form of sexism, almost to the exclusion of other forms. Seven of my interviewees said that they had never encountered sexual harassment at hard rock and metal events. However, two of these seven also related that they had experienced calls to show men their breasts, incidents they interpreted as 'funny' (Jenny) or not a serious threat (Sally). Only one woman (Bert) described being 'groped' in a hard rock club, and she was enraged about the occurrence. In fact, five women described hard rock and metal clubs as places where they were less likely to experience sexual harassment or be sexually objectified than at mainstream venues, and four of these women accompanied their assertions with specific examples.

Recent research (Phipps and Young 2015) reveals that harassment is an expected and normalised part of the night-time economy. The British young women students they interviewed described groping and other unwanted sexual attention from drunken men and feelings of powerlessness to stop it from occurring. This is particularly a problem that occurs in nightclubs, but not exclusively so. The study investigated campus culture, but due to the importance placed on socialising and alcohol, the culture includes what happens in off-campus social spaces. 'Lad culture'—which is defined as sexism, sexual harassment and the normalisation of sexualisation and pornography, all defended by the argument that this is not sexist, it is irony, jokes and banter (Phipps and Young 2015)—plays a crucial role in creating a sexist and dangerous environment in which women experience myriad problems, including normalised harassment. Hard rock and metal concerts and clubs are part of the social night-time economy. Alcohol plays an enormous role in hard rock and metal culture, with beer and whisky in particular being reified in songs. Therefore, it could reasonably be expected that hard rock and metal events are scenes of harassment, as the NUS report would suggest. However, what is common to nearly all of the accounts given by women, whether they had experienced harassment or not, was that metal events were safer spaces for women. They were less likely to experience unwanted attention than at mainstream events.

Ruby, a lifelong metal fan in her mid-30s, described an incident in a mainstream club in order to emphasise her point about metal events being safer:

> Really, really actually had to ask a bouncer to throw one of them out once because they were trying to touch us up, physically touch us up. And I've *never* experienced anything like that in, you know, in my experience of the metal scene when I was younger or at Download as, as even being older sort of thing. So not in my experience. (Ruby)

Many participants used this idea of the mainstream to make their points about metal as a safer space. This specific incident of harassment in a mainstream club was one of only two particular examples of non-metal harassment (the other related to being shouted at in the street); used in generalised terms, 'the mainstream' was set up as a site of sexism, with metal defined against it as *not sexist*.

Aowyn, a university women's officer in her very early 20s, reasoned that metal clubs were safer because the mindset of male fans is one which eschews objectification:

> People aren't really that interested in your body, or they're interested for who you are, whereas a lot of the time when I've been to places like, you know, like Revolution or I Love Vodka and places like that it's, you tend to get a lot more harassment because people are there to like pick up girls. (Aowyn)

For Aowyn a characteristic of going to metal clubs was a lack of sexual objectification: harassment *could not* take place due to the philosophy of male participants. This may shed some light on one finding mentioned briefly in the NUS report: that some young women would attend 'alternative' (National Union of Students, Phipps, and Young 2012, 47) clubs rather than larger, more mainstream ones because they were less likely to be attended by university sports teams. According to the report, sports teams are major contributors to 'lad culture' found on campuses, and so avoiding them was one way to enjoy a night out without harassment.

A number of the women were quite sure that, when at hard rock and metal events, the focus on the music was the reason that men did not generally subject women to sexual harassment or to unwanted advances:

Honestly, the men are there for the music; they're not there to pick up women and, erm, and it's all business. At a metal gig it's all business. (Jeanette)

I mean they're there to see the band, not get hammered or maybe see the band and get hammered [laughs]. (Jenny)

This squares with the myth of equality in which, as long as one loves the music adequately, acceptance is assured. Underpinning this is the belief that the music is the most important criteria and other visible characteristics (like sex) are irrelevant. This allows women to love the music in peace, free from harassment.

Although the majority of the women had not experienced sexual harassment there were three examples. Two, Jenny and Sally, both in their mid-30s, were somewhat reluctant to tell me about their experiences and classified them as 'fun' rather than harassment. Here's Sally talking about festivals:

[Rosemary] Have you encountered any sexual harassment?

[Sally] [Pause] not seriously.

[Rosemary] What do you mean "not seriously"?

[Sally] You know, you know people say "get your tits out" or stuff like that, but it's all done very light-heartedly, and you know, jokey, so there's no real sexual threat. Erm, I think I would feel much more at risk somewhere like Leeds [festival]. (Sally)

She portrays the harassers as jokers who do not pose a threat: this is not, for her, serious harassment. This resembles the argument that verbal harassment is nothing more than ironic 'banter' and therefore not harmful, although the 'banter' argument has a silencing effect that prevents sexism from being challenged (Mooney 2008). However, Sally did not interpret being told to 'get her tits out' as sexism. Her feelings of inclusion and being part of the group may play a role in her interpretation of the harassment as genuinely comic rather than threatening or exclusionary. Sally's response suggests that her identity within hard rock and metal culture was as one of the boys, able to share in the jokes. However, this did not mean that her womanhood went unconsidered: she felt she would be more likely to feel threatened at a more mainstream rock festival, Leeds. Here mainstream festival attendees are implicitly portrayed in distinction to those who are jokey, light-hearted and happy at metal festivals, their threatening activities thereby fitting in with the stereotype of the 'lad'. Therefore, whilst the verbal utterances may be the same, the architect of the harassment matters. Hard rock and metal fans *cannot* be sexual harassers; this is what the others ('lads') do.

On the other hand, Bert furiously described her experiences at clubs which present a very different picture to that painted by my other participants:

> One room is more like Panic At The Disco, Fall Out Boy, My Chemical Romance, and I love that room, and I've never had any issues. Go into the heavy metal room which is more like Slayer, [and men] like grab me and go like, "yeah how are you doing?" and trying to make out with me, and I'm like, get the hell off me right now. It's like how DARE you. (Bert)

In contrast to Jenny and Sally, Bert did not find the harassment funny—but significantly, this was physical rather than verbal harassment. The phrase that she put into the mouths of her harassers, 'how are you doing?', suggests a laddishness amongst more extreme metal fans—an experience which is at odds with those of my other participants for whom such things never happened. Although Bert does not make a comparison with a mainstream, she does contrast her experiences with those in different rooms in the same venue. What does this mean? I posit that feelings of inclusion play an important part in perceptions of sexism, a point to which I will return.

MEDIA OBJECTIFICATION

The sense of metal as being less likely to objectify women's bodies was also apparent in descriptions of music videos. Three women referred to the mainstream as being more likely to degrade women in music videos or in lyrics. Dolly, in her late 30s, used RnB as her counter to explain metal's less sexist stance:

> The thing with the RnB, all the videos are about women walking round in thongs and bras shaking their booty, and it's so degrading. Whereas, and I can't stand that, can't stand to see sort of women being degraded. But in, when you're listening to metal music they don't degrade women at all; there isn't that side of it. Do you know what I mean? I've not seen that an awful lot. They're not degrading.
>
> [Rosemary] Do you see many women at all though?

[Dolly] No, not an awful lot. See some in some videos. Erm, I mean okay some of the latest ones like Papa Roach singing with "Hollywood Whore", love the song, but the video's quite, she's all dressed up in her gear and all that lot, and the lyrics are quite, what's the word I'm looking for, the lyrics are quite in yer face and tell you how it is, if you like and, erm, but I don't see that as degrading really. Yeah, it's about a Hollywood whore, but there's more of a story to it. Whereas just the videos for the RnB—Kanye West: woman prancing around with her backside out and shaking her hips and I don't know what it is, or the woman with the dog collar round her neck being, I just think, oh just get it off. I can't listen to that, can't watch it and it's just so mundane and dull yeah sorry.

[Rosemary] So there's something quite specifically about metal and the way it treats women, or rather the way it doesn't treat women that really appeals to you?

[Dolly] Yeah it does [...] I mean I'm sure a lot of the songs are about what's happened to them, their experiences with women, but a lot of that you don't get, it doesn't come through. It can just be about, like, itself. They don't degrade women quite so much. I mean you get people like Kid Rock, he does and he does it quite a lot, but the other ones are just, no they don't, they don't. You don't get to see women prancing around with next to nothing on and with dog collars 'round their necks. Well I've not seen it anyway. (Dolly)

Dolly had a feminist idea of how she wanted women to be treated and identified this as being commensurate with a metal portrayal. But there were exceptions in the form of Papa Roach and Kid Rock which she gave as examples of objectifying portrayals in hard rock and metal videos. However, she justified one of these representations with the caveat that the story in the song gave a rationale for the imagery. Dolly was aware of sexism in general and in music videos more broadly, so why was she prepared to exempt some videos from her feminist condemnation?

The weight of examples of objectified women from other genres versus the relative paucity of representations at all in hard rock and metal is an unequal scale when it comes to the perception of sexism here, I posit. Hard rock and metal videos often use live performance footage, and since most bands that are successful enough to make videos are all male, fewer women appear. The lack of women is therefore not a reason to assess hard rock and metal videos as less sexist but is actually sexism in a different form, or symptomatic of another form of sexism (who gets to be in bands). Walser (1993) asserts that heavy metal provides a view of a world without women, and music videos play their part in that. Brown (2009) draws on the work of Gaye Tuchman (1978) to argue that women are symbolically annihilated in metal magazines, and I argue that the same thing is going on in music videos. Objectification, identified by Dolly as sexism, is therefore supplemented by the exscription of women in music videos. Dolly's assertion, however, that when women do appear they are less likely to be objectified than in RnB, is an important reflection and fits in with the other claims of my interviews that hard rock and metal culture is less sexist than other musical forms.

MARGINALISATION

That sexual harassment and objectification are the primary forms of sexism that my interviewees discussed is significant. It suggests that these more publicised sexisms eclipse other forms which are not acknowledged as prejudice. Sexism is so normal and can be so subtle that it is not interpreted as such, as Valentine et al. (2014) discuss in relation to women firefighters. The fire station is another location in which women participate in a male-dominated environment where sexism exists, although in subtle forms. The authors argue that women firefighters are 'less willing or able to identify' (Valentine et al. 2014, 407) sexism. Negative incidents were therefore interpreted as being due to women's 'own personal shortcomings' (Valentine et al. 2014, 407). Similarly, frustrations at hard rock and metal concerts, for instance when women found themselves standing behind a tall man, were not interpreted as forms of sexism, although they are produced by patriarchal power relations.

The difficulty of seeing the band at concerts, due to men being relatively taller, resulted in the necessity of standing at the back or around the sides in order to get a decent line of sight and also to avoid being bumped or barged by more exuberant fans:

> [Jeanette] If it is a thrashy gig, proper proper thrash metal or even anything fast and furious and the pit will automatically form in front of the band where certain, well I would say more energetic and hardcore of the fans will start running around. Now if you choose to go in there you choose, you do not get accidentally involved in that—people will see straight away you don't wanna be there and they will, you know, help you out or basically you will get, you know, excused. But if you choose to go in then people bump into each other they push each other if they fall over they laugh at each other, but that's all part of it, and whoever's chosen to go in there should be treated equally in my opinion. It's not something I do.

[Rosemary] You don't choose to go in there?
[Jeanette] I don't, I don't go in at all, no.
[Rosemary] Is it because of the…
[Jeanette] I don't like to be bumped [laughs], don't like to be bumped!

Typically the exuberant fans moshing will be young men in the pit. The pit is not exclusively used by men, but it so demarcated that when women do mosh this is characterised as transgressive (Riches et al. 2014). The use of space is gendered, but Jeanette's account does not acknowledge this. Young men's privilege and (especially older) women's marginalisation—her own—was accepted as natural and therefore normalised. Practical, personal reasons are given, rather than an interpretation of sexism. Jeanette sums up the pit, stating that that moshing is a matter of personal choice. This resonates with Savigny and Sleight's (2015) argument that the postfeminist narrative of empowerment can be used to explain choices that result in the maintenance of the patriarchal status quo. Jeanette effectively argues that the best viewpoint of the stage remains the preserve of younger men as a matter of choice, not as a tactic to ensure male privilege. The individual choice sounds like an empowered argument in which women can make their lives as they wish. However, as Budgeon (2015) argues, the empowered choice argument does nothing to change the conditions in which the distinctly gendered—sexist—use of space is created. In the 1990s the riot grrrls, a group of feminist punk musicians who carved out their own musical sphere, argued for a reordering of the space at their concerts which directed women to the front. This intervention is a striking contrast to the way in which space is used at metal concerts and highlights that male privilege is at the fore in its ordering.

Kahn-Harris (2007) describes how in his experiences of attending extreme metal gigs he witnessed women being marginalised by their male associates. He would find himself talking to a man but never introduced to female companions so that women were treated as appendages. Most of my interviewees did not describe similar experiences, but Aria did. Notably her visibility and audibility as a death metal guitarist was the key factor in highlighting the marginalisation she experienced:

Generally speaking, I found the guys that we played with, after they'd, it had to be after they'd seen us play, beforehand they didn't even look at me; they looked at me like I was scum. After they saw me play then they would deign to come and talk to me, and I just thought "hmm that's interesting".

However, when I played bass in a couple of bands, nothing. [...] No one talked to me. I wasn't worthy to be talked, to be spoken to. So I actually discovered that the instrument became all pervasive. The fact that I was playing the guitar, which is predominantly a male instrument, because I'd kind of taken it on board and thought "right, well I'm gonna do this myself", they, I suppose after a while they started to gain some respect for me, but it was only after they'd seen what I could do. I had to kind of prove myself. Which was, you know, that's okay, but when it's every single gig you're doing, and you're kind of, you're aware of it the moment you walk into a venue, you're aware of this kind of underlying sexism that was never really spoken about; it was just only ever kind of there hovering in the background. (Aria)

Aria's role as a *guitarist* (not just a musician—bass playing and lead vocals are permitted roles for women in rock music) meant that she gained status as an equal, worthy of being talked to, which threw her experiences as not-guitarist (potentially a girlfriend or groupie) into sharp relief. The differential in the two experiences made her marginalisation as a woman very obvious.

Marginalisation is therefore a generally undiscussed, normalised part of participation in hard rock and metal events for women. In their discussion of women in the architecture, engineering and construction industries, Powell and Sang (2015) argue that some women describe their experiences of sexism as the result of biological differences between men and women, and therefore *justified*. They name this naturalisation of difference as 'misrecognition': sexist social situations are accounted for by the argument of essential differences between women and men. Whilst it is not the case in Aria's depiction of her experiences, for my other interviewees, men's tallness and greater exuberance were naturalised and can therefore be read as misrecognition. This is a problematic argument, however. In the case of Jeanette's decision not to go into the pit, it does not take into account the very real sense of wanting to physically protect herself. It is easy to judge others' decisions as inadequate—why do women hard rock and metal fans not invade the space in front of the stage?—but Jeanette and other interviewees who made similar comments are in a position of fear for their bodily integrity. Hegemony over spaces at the hard rock metal gig therefore relies on women's fear. Riches (2015) argues that the mosh pit and its permission for aggression can be a site of transgression in which women can break barriers of permitted behaviour; however, this is only the case for women who *choose* to participate. That choice is guided by a number of factors, including age (Jeanette was in her mid-30s at the time of the interview), gender and dis/ability. Women must steel themselves to enter the pit, which, as Riches argues, remains a male terrain, even if it does allow space for transgressing expectations of feminine behaviour.

FLIGHT FROM FEMININITY

For all the complicated assessments of sexist or not-sexist incidents and representations, what is very apparent in my interviewees' experiences is their troubled relationships with femininity. This comes in the form of music preference in which pop music is belittled, in clothing choices and in personal relationships.

A couple of my interviewees, Aime and Alexa, spoke of their simultaneous love of metal and pop musicians, but this was exceptional. Most women were frosty towards music they considered manufactured or 'poppy', setting their own musical tastes in opposition to the feminised mainstream. This was very obvious when it came to discussions about lyrics. Lyrics were preferred for their explorative nature, political message or more 'honest' emotional content rather than themes of love or romance. In disparaging mainstream lyrical themes of romance and love in favour of the 'human' themes of the genre, the women were fleeing the mainstream construction of femininity. They were seeking ways to express themselves without being shoehorned into an identity that they felt did not fit them. This was apparent in Hazel's depiction of love and romance as 'frivolous', 'mushy' and 'sentimental'. These are not complimentary terms and certainly indicative of a belief that femininity lacks gravity and authenticity, that it is excessive and a construction (not 'natural'). For Hazel, these qualities are not values she wants to attach to herself: she wants to be taken seriously and for her interests to extend beyond the remit of romantic life. Her sphere goes beyond the private and domestic, and her musical taste reflects this. This is very clearly a flight from the feminine and for Hazel, who was studying gender studies at the time of the interview, is bound up with feminist ideas about the private and public spheres.

Aria went as far as to describe metal as having 'lyrics [that] are always about the human experience, generally speaking' (Aria). This interpretation means that hard rock and metal music can be seen as neutral and definitely not feminine. Yet, as most musicians are men, the lyrical themes will inevitably be about men's experiences. They may well be experiences that both men and women can have, but they will not be about experiences that women have and men do not. Can the genre therefore be said to describe human experiences or only male experiences?

Tori Amos's cover of Slayer's 'Raining Blood' changes the meaning of the song from overthrowing heaven to the experience of menstruation (Hermes 2001). The power of the transformation comes in part from the penetration of women's experiences into a masculine domain. In the gendered binaries of rock/pop (Coates 1997) and subculture/mainstream (Thornton 1995), disparaging pop and the mainstream symbolically aligns those who prefer the music of rock and subcultures with the masculine, enabling gravitas and authenticity to accrue to the speaker. As I have already discussed, the binary is a false one, used to create a sense of superiority, of artistic value, for rock and subcultures by the exclusion of the feminine, which is seen as of no value (Ang 1985; Baym 1999; Mittel 2004).

Clothes were another example of the women's disdain for prescribed notions of femininity. As with Patterson's (2016) discussion of her own experiences, the clothing associated with hard rock and metal provided an opportunity to wear something different. Jess, in her 20s, and Susan, aged 69, both describe their taste in clothes as personal choice, with UK quality clothes chain Marks and Spencer marked as the epitome of feminine convention for older women by Susan:

> I've always been drawn to people who dress unconventionally, although I've never done it myself, although I don't really wear the sort of clothes Marks and Spencer's design for 70 year olds, or I'm assuming that they do. (Susan)

But for Jess clothes choice is specifically bound up with her identity as a 'tomboy'. Clothes and make-up are a key way in which she is able to express this identity:

> Make-up's just not for me: unless it's black make-up, then I don't want anything to do with it! Erm, but I think a lot of the reasons that I do dress sort of tomboy-ish in a sense is to do with the style, cos a lot of it isn't particularly what you'd class as girly, erm, but I just hate girly clothes anyway, so. (Jessica)

Clothing and make-up are closely bound up with femininity and may be a site of struggle with family, peers and societal expectations. Skeggs argues that femininity is displayed 'through appearance *and* conduct' (1997, 102, emphasis in original) and that appearance is used to judge other women's femininity. Wearing hard rock and heavy metal outfits, along with hair, make-up, tattoos and piercings, enables women to sidestep the strictures, or 'structural inconvenience' (Skeggs 1997, 116), of femininity and the work it involves and to find a space in which they are not judged by 'normal' standards. As Patterson recalls, 'I couldn't handle the thought of being judged against some 'standard' of beauty that I knew I could never achieve' (2016, 256–257). Participation in hard rock and metal culture provides a rationale and group identity—safety in numbers—as it announces allegiance to a different ideology in which femininity is not valued. It is a transgressive opportunity for women (as entering the pit is) that provides the tools to *denounce and critique* femininity.

Whilst some of my participants, like Jess, identified their participation as a movement away from femininity, this was not the case for all of my interviewees. However, Aria found the masculinity of hard rock and metal to be the ideal solution that helped her to cope with the particular circumstances of her family life:

> [Aria] When I really got into metal, I think, erm, I was aware that it was a very male-dominated scene. I saw that much more as a challenge than a problem. And I think certainly at that point I identified more with my masculine side than my feminine side because of my personal circumstances up until that point. It was much easier for me to identify with masculinity than I did femininity because I didn't.
>
> [Rosemary] Why was that then?
>
> [Aria] Because I think I would have enormous difficulties at home. I'd been kicked out a number of times, and I was kind of out on my own so in order for me to get on I needed to have a very kind of hard outer casing so that, and I was very angry, so my immediate point of identification was finding some kind of external manifestation of that and for me that was metal.

Clifford-Napoleone (2015b) argues that metal can be seen as a queerscape that allows queer women to perform female masculinities. This helps to explain how Aria found death metal to be a comfortable identity and how my other interviewees found ways to express their identities without recourse to traditional femininity. Building on Clifford-Napoleone's analysis I argue that hard rock and metal represents not only a queerscape in which to perform masculinity, but a scape that allows women to feel a freedom—however temporary—from the constraints of femininity. For the women I spoke to this was not necessarily about asserting queer identities but trying to find a neutral or genderless space. Schippers (2002) argues that women in the alternative rock scene in Chicago in the 1990s developed 'alternative femininities' which did not reproduce the hierarchical relationship between masculinity and femininity. She defines 'alternative' in opposition to the mainstream. But although the women I spoke to objected to mainstream representations of women and the feminised mainstream they did not speak of using hard rock and metal to construct alternative or more fitting femininities. Rather, they rejected mainstream femininities without *necessarily* seeking another or different gendered position.

It is too simplistic to interpret women's metal fandom in terms of moving from one gendered position to another, whether that be an alternative femininity or a female masculinity. The flight from femininity is important as it signifies a recognition of inequality:

> Distancing oneself from stereotypical femininity [...] is a claiming of power. Whether from a feminist standpoint, or through the personal rejection of the feminine declared by tomboy girls (Reay, 2001) and butch women (Halberstam, 1998), to oppose stereotypical or normalized feminine positioning is to reject the disempowerment that comes with it. (Paechter 2006, 257)

In fleeing femininity—stereotypical femininity—the women are rejecting the attendant disempowerment; they may not be consciously attempting to position themselves in a gendered manner at all. Rather, I posit that hard rock and metal culture offers women a way to step outside the strictures of the dominant idea of femininity and to sometimes experience a feeling of 'genderlessness'. Savigny and Sleight assert that metal is a site that can be an 'escape from dominant patriarchal structures' (2015, 354), a position I agree with. But more than that, I argue that the value of equality within metal is what enables women to feel this respite, even though real equality is mythical.

IMAGINARY COMMUNITY AND INTERPRETING SEXISM

Due to the maligning of hard rock and metal music, its audience and its producers as a danger to white boys and women, the women I spoke to could well have been on the defensive about the nature of metal fandom. As members of the imaginary community, they shared in its values (to a greater or lesser degree), including that of the culture's equality.

Their defensiveness of 'their' community would likely have been compounded by defensiveness about the authenticity of their fandom, because as women fans they may have felt the need to prove they were 'real fans' (Nordström and Herz 2013). It was clear during the interviews that metal gave my participants enormous pleasure, and it is this that they wanted to discuss with me. Any problems they faced might have been at the back of their minds, perhaps perceived as inconveniences or only occasional problems, certainly outweighed by the great delight they felt in the music and participation in the community they enjoy. Women's position as a minority group within hard rock and metal is therefore an important consideration in understanding the difference between academic and fan accounts of sexism.

Mills (2003) describes the complex negotiating work that women do in deciding whether something is sexist. She argues that in undertaking this work women need to think about the person who has made the potentially sexist remark/act and measure it against their 'hypothesized feminist community' (Mills 2003, 93) and also against the potential way in which any response might be received. She argues that an accusation of sexism could well be detrimental to relations with the sexist person. In this context, that could mean that the women I spoke to were unwilling to name sexism due to the risk of alienating other hard rock and metal fans. Although my interviewees were happy to talk to me, they may have been reluctant to do anything other than give a glowing portrayal of the imagined community; this may explain the reticence of Jenny and Sally to describe their experiences of sexism as anything other than jokes.

It could be that some of my interviewees strategically ignored sexism in order to maximise their enjoyment. Vasan (2011) argues that her female participants in the Texas death metal scene used a technique of cost reduction: this involved tolerating sexist attitudes from male peers, containing male sexual interest by adopting masculine performance and dress, and excusing or ignoring misogynistic lyrics. Her participants were consciously using these techniques in order to maintain their pleasurable participation in death metal. However, Vasan argues that in adopting these techniques the women show that they accept the 'androcentric codes' (Vasan 2011, 346) of metal and thereby preserve their position as second class fans. Cost reduction techniques enable women to live with the metal status quo rather than challenging it, allowing them to fit in. Whilst Vasan's theory is a tempting one, to my mind it neglects the sense of loyalty or belonging to a community that is an important part of participation in metal for its fans. The myth of equality is evidence that in the metal media a high value is placed on the notion of equality. Whilst the sense of equality is vague and further investigation shows that equality means similarity to the characteristics of young white heterosexual men, it is frequently evoked and used contrastingly with a more sexist mainstream. The myth of equality that is visible in *Kerrang!* also plays a role in creating the mainstream as a 'straw man' against which to measure metal—and in which the mainstream is repeatedly found wanting. In this way, it is easier to configure metal as less sexist. However, it also makes it much harder to challenge sexist incidents or representations when they do occur.

This is a serious problem to those wishing to challenge metal's gender bias. Schippers (2002) discusses similar problems in the alternative rock community of the early 1990s. She argues that both feminist and anti-feminist arguments around equality combine to create an ideology that claims that both women and men are equal and have the strength to reach their potential: to suggest otherwise is to assert that women are victims. The result is that even discussing gender as a barrier is seen to be sexist because women can do whatever men can do. This attitude is mirrored by *Kerrang!*'s myth of equality which is so strong that pronouncements of sexism in metal are construed as misunderstandings and the complainant positioned as an outsider. This problem can be seen in the *Kerrang!* community in letter writers' retorts to the interview responses of Lyn-Z, bassist of art-punk band Mindless Self-Indulgence, whose husband is Gerard Way, previously of My Chemical Romance. Lyn Z's remarks set out a specifically feminist agenda in which she bemoans the lack of female role models amongst rock and metal musicians. She expresses outrage and frustration at becoming known for her famous husband rather than her own musical achievements, saying, 'it's fucked up and totally offensive that my name has totally disappeared and I am now referred to as "Mrs Gerard Way"' (Lyn-Z quoted in Parsons 2008, 30). Published letters dismissed her claims, with one writer arguing that the quality of her bass playing, combined with the greater fame of her husband were all reasons why her arguments could not be called 'feminist':

> Three things really pissed me off about your interview with Lyn-Z (K!1211)... The first, that girls need to see a woman onstage to be able to believe that they could make it as a rock musician. I don't know about any

other female K! readers, but I never looked at Steve Harris, or Tony Iommi, and thought, "damn it, I can never do that because he's a guy and I'm a gal". Clearly the woman believes she's a feminist, but she thinks like a sexist. The second, that if girls do need a good female role model (and they are good to have around) she's the one be it. She admits to being a shitty bass player and yet thinks girls should look up to her just 'cos she's a female and onstage. The third, that she thinks that people calling her Mrs Gerard Way is sexism. It's not. It's because she married GERARD WAY. If she was already famous, or he was less famous, then she would have kept her name, but right now, it's the thing she's most known for. Unfortunate, yes, but not sexism. (Resh Giwa 2008, 4)

This letter was awarded the Letter of the Week title, which gives *Kerrang!* the status of protector of the true nature of feminism, rather than establishing a conversation about the problems faced by women in their quest to be recognised and valued musicians. Combined with the title of the original article in which Lyn-Z was interviewed—'Get Over It!'—a strong and intelligent potential role model for young female fans is ridiculed, just as other strong women of the genre are similarly belittled (for example, Ian Winwood's [2007] interview with Arch Enemy's Angela Gossow focuses upon whether the singer had undergone plastic surgery rather than on the new album she was intending to promote). The myth of equality therefore has a silencing effect so that sexism either does not look like sexism or it is too difficult to talk about because it challenges 'equality' as a highly valued and essential part of the genre's ideology.

The contradiction of an ideal of equality that prohibits challenges to sexism are not exclusive to hard rock and metal. Griffin (2012) describes a similar contradiction within straight edge punk—a relative of hard rock and metal—where musicians might sing an anti-sexist song followed by one asserting that women are bitches. Schippers (2002) describes the Chicago alternative rock scene as underpinned by anti-sexist rhetoric, but it is concurrent with a belief in individual responsibility that disavows the structural problems women face in, for example, removing themselves from abusive relationships. Leblanc (1999) too finds that in the punk subculture there is a claim of egalitarianism but also specific instances of sexism from male punks faced by the punk girls. Hard rock and metal is therefore not unique. Within these three other musical groupings women also found spaces where they could enjoy the music they loved without the same level of harassment they faced outside their community.

Liberation Through Assimilation?

It is important to take what the women said seriously: that in the main they did not experience sexism, particularly sexual harassment. This is a heart-warming message, even though sexism was apparent, yet not always identified as such. The women offered explanations for the genre being less sexist than the mainstream: Aoywn claimed there was a philosophical interest in 'who you are' rather than the body, for example. A number of other women, however, mentioned that the music is the prime concern of men and women at metal events, and this causes them to be 'left alone', as Karen articulated:

> That's the other good thing about rock clubs is you can just get up and dance on your own and no one gives a shite, whereas in like a more trendy club if you're sat on your own, on your own, you got millions of blokes sidling up to you and it's like "go away". (Karen)

Hard rock and metal music and the accompanying sense of community gave my interviewees enormous pleasure which clearly outweighed any unpleasant experiences. Furthermore, their experiences at hard rock and metal events do not occur in isolation from their lives more generally.

Sexism is prevalent in British society, as my interviewees revealed with their references to the mainstream, but there is less sexism in metal spaces, in their experiences. What my interviewees did, then, was something that most researchers on gender and metal do not do: they looked at their experiences within the context of their broader lives, which includes taking account of their non-metal experiences. Sexism is the background noise for *all* their experiences. Patterson (2016), a notable exception amongst metal scholars, highlights that all metal experiences take place within the wider society which forms part of that experience. Therefore, since hard rock and metal exists within sexist society it must be assumed that sexism will appear here. Therefore, examining metal and gender and finding examples of sexism should come as no surprise. What is surprising, however, given metal's hypermasculinity, is that the women interviewed for this study felt that they experienced less sexism in the hard rock and metal context than outside of it. Participation in hard rock and metal culture can actually provide moments that feel ungendered, in which there are no differences between men and women, and in which womanhood can recede into the background.

This means that assumptions and behaviours associated with femininity function as *intrusion*. Intrusion is evident in Riches' (2011) depiction of young women's mosh pit experiences, for whom entering the pit means enjoying the opportunity to transcend gender norms. When men recognise the difference between themselves and women moshers, for example by not pushing women in the mosh pit, it 'works to reinscribe traditional gender expectations' (Riches 2011, 329). Other experiences of sexism, like Bert's experience of sexual harassment in the club, work in the same way. This reinscription functions as a *reminder* of women fans' marked femininity, and gender thereby intrudes upon the temporary feeling of genderlessness.

Whilst the imaginary metal community clearly is not genderless (after all, what is?), it is distinct from the mainstream in that instances of sexism occur less frequently, giving it the appearance of being a more equal community. Problematic ideologies of equality exist in other music cultures too (Brill 2008; Thornton 1995). In her study of goth culture, Brill explores the genre's emphasis on transgressing the gender barrier. This is done with the aid of an ideology of genderlessness that theoretically enables all goths to perform as much masculinity or femininity as they like. However, she argues that the ideology of genderlessness privileges men's ability to perform aspects of femininity whilst simultaneously muting women's ability to perform masculinity. In fact it ends up putting pressure on women to be even more feminine than goth men. In goth, as in broader society, genderlessness is therefore a privilege that only men can really enjoy. At the same time, it limits the ability to speak up about sexism; for example, objectifying images of women are labelled as 'erotica'—expressly so because this is a genderless realm—rather than as objectifying pornography. Genderlessness in goth is therefore nothing of the sort. Whilst in goth the ideology of genderless allows men to transgress masculinity and perform femininity, in hard rock and metal the myth of equality puts masculinity first. In order to experience this kind of equality or genderlessness, 'the masculine code' (Weinstein 2000 [1991], 105) of the genre must be accepted and lived up to. When women are able to do this, as in the case of the young women in the mosh pit discussed by Riches (2011), there is no problem. On these occasions hard rock and metal offers a chance to feel as if there is no difference between women and men, as if gender does not exist. Loving the music first allows my participants to feel as if they are able to transcend their markedness and to be just people rather than 'women'.

However, metal and its 'big topic' lyrical themes, fewer images of sexual objectification, naturalised ideology of equality and the focus upon the music, appears as 'genderless' in the same way that man and masculinity is positioned as the norm and femininity is marked. Using 'gender' here to refer to masculinity and femininity, Monique Wittig argues that masculinity is treated as normal:

> Gender is the linguistic index of political opposition between the sexes. Gender is used here in the singular because indeed there are not two genders. There is only one: the feminine, the "masculine" not being a gender. For the masculine is not the masculine but the general. The result is that there are the general and the feminine, or rather, the general and the mark of the feminine. (1992, 60)

This is exactly why Aria's assertion that metal provides lyrics that are about the 'human' experience is problematic: it treats men's experiences as the general. What hard rock and metal offers in its myth of equality and in its opportunity to feel that gender does not exist, is the opportunity to experience the world as men experience it, that is to be identified as masculine. Hard rock and metal may be a 'space' in which women can slip out of their femininity, but this 'space' is a masculine one. The casting off of difference, therefore, is actually liberation through assimilation: freedom from the constraints of femininity and sexism are only felt when the masculine is acquiesced to. It is only women fans' unwillingness to push against the misogynistic ideology of metal that allows them to experience 'genderlessness': for to challenge the misogyny means being reminded of one's gender and feeling thereby 'marked'.

CONCLUSION

Weinstein argues that 'neither sexist, ageist, nor racist on principle, the metal subculture is exclusivist, insistent on upholding the codes of its core membership' (2000 [1991], 112). She is absolutely right. However, she is not critical of what this means for minority participants such as women, ethnic minority groups and LGBT people. More recent work has identified exactly how this proposition is problematic and how the 'codes of the core membership' impact upon marginalised groups. Sexism, racism, and homophobia have all been identified. However, as Savigny and Sleight (2015) and Riches (2015) argue, when it comes to women's participation in hard rock and metal, it is more complex than a straightforward experience of sexism. Vasan argues that women death metal fans' cost reduction leaves them open to tolerating misogyny, and thus they have much to lose in their metal fandom. In distinction, I argue that women describe their hard rock and metal experiences as less likely to be marred by sexism than when they participate in mainstream culture. Indeed, hard rock and metal fandom allows women a feeling of respite from a traditionally defined, demeaned and sexually exploited femininity through participation in a realm that seems to be genderless. In a society that my participants described as sexist, and a society that is already male dominated and that positions women as sex objects, finding a space that feels free from sexism is significant. In the world of hard rock and metal women can think of themselves as 'people' first without being continually reminded of their womanhood.

Thus the women's stories show that their experience of the mainstream is a more difficult arena to negotiate in terms of sexual harassment and objectification than hard rock and metal culture. This does not mean that hard rock and metal is not sexist—it is part of sexist society so how could it not be?—just that it is *less* sexist. For some of the women I spoke to the appeal of hard rock and metal was specifically down to their perception of the genre as one in which they would not have to experience or grapple with the kinds of sexism they encounter in the mainstream and other parts of their lives.

This does not let men off the hook: when women must play by men's rules they will always be at a disadvantage and, as Nordström and Herz (2013) point out, women fans struggle to find ways to challenge the status quo. The trouble is that the myth of equality is so powerful that to question whether equality really exists acts as a threat to metal culture. But that is exactly what needs to happen if we are to move towards a more respectful cultural experience.

REFERENCES

Ang, Ien. 1985. *Watching Dallas: Soap Opera and the Melodramatic Imagination.* London: Methuen.

Barron, Lee. 2013. Dworkin's Nightmare: Porngrind as the Sound of Feminist Fears. In *Heavy Metal: Controversies and Countercultures,* eds. Titus Hjelm, Keith Kahn-Harris, and Mark Levine, 66–82. Sheffield: Equinox.

Baym, Nancy K. 1999. *Tune in, Log on: Soaps, Fandom, and On-line Community.* Thousand Oaks, CA: Sage Publications.

Bayton, Mavis. 1998. *Frock Rock: Women Performing Popular Music*. Oxford: Oxford University Press.

Brill, Dunja. 2008. *Goth Culture: Gender, Sexuality and Style*. Oxford: Berg.

Brown, Andy R. 2009. 'Girls Like Metal, Too!': Female Reader's Engagement with the Masculinist Ethos of the Tabloid Metal Magazine. *Heavy Metal and Gender International Congress*, Cologne University of Music and Dance, 10 October.

Budgeon, Shelley. 2015. Individualized Femininity and Feminist Politics of Choice. *European Journal of Women's Studies* 22(3): 303–318.

Clifford-Napoleone, Amber. 2015b. *Queerness in Heavy Metal Music: Metal Bent*. Abingdon: Routledge.

Coates, Norma. 1997. (R)evolution Now? Rock and the Political Potential of Gender. In *Sexing the Groove: Popular Music and Gender*, ed. Sheila Whiteley, 50–64. Abingdon: Routledge.

Griffin, Naomi. 2012. Gendered Performance Performing Gender in the DIY Punk and Hardcore Music Scene. *Journal of International Women's Studies* 13(2): 66–81.

Halberstam, Judith. 2012. *Female Masculinity*. London: Duke University Press. Hansen, Christine Hall, and Ranald D. Hansen. 1991. Constructing Personality and Social Reality Through Music: Individual Differences Among Fans of Punk and Heavy Metal Music. *Journal of Broadcasting and Electronic Media* 35(3): 335–350.

Hermes, Will. 2001. Don't Mess with Mother Nature. *Spin Magazine*, October.

Kahn-Harris, Keith. 2007. *Extreme Metal: Music and Culture on the Edge*. Oxford: Berg.

Krenske, Leigh, and Jim McKay. 2000. 'Hard and Heavy': Gender and Power in a Heavy Metal Music Subculture. *Gender, Place & Culture* 7(3): 287–304.

Lawrence, Janet S. St, and Doris J. Joyner. 1991. The Effects of Sexually Violent Rock Music on Males' Acceptance of Violence Against Women. *Psychology of Women Quarterly* 15(1): 49–63.

Leblanc, Lauraine. 1999. *Pretty in Punk: Girls' Gender Resistance in a Boys' Subculture*. New Brunswick, NJ: Rutgers University Press.

Mills, Sara. 2003. Caught Between Sexism, Anti-sexism and 'Political Correctness': Feminist Women's Negotiations with Naming Practices. *Discourse & Society* 14(1): 87–110.

Mittel, Jason. 2004. *Genre and Television: From Cop Shows to Cartoons in American Culture*. London: Routledge.

Mooney, Annabelle. 2008. Boys will be Boys. *Feminist Media Studies* 8(3): 247–265.

National Union of Students, Alison Phipps, and Isabel Young. 2012. That's What She Said: Women Students' Experiences of 'Lad Culture' in Higher Education. Accessed 4 January 2016. http://www.nus.org.uk/Global/Campaigns/That's%20what%20she%20said%20full%20report%20Final%20web.pdf

Nordström, Susanna, and Marcus Herz. 2013. 'It's a Matter of Eating or Being Eaten.' Gender Positioning and Difference Making in the Heavy Metal Subculture. *European Journal of Cultural Studies* 16(4): 453–467.

Overell, Rosemary. 2010. Brutal Belonging in Melbourne's Grindcore Scene. *Studies in Symbolic Interaction* 35: 79–99.

Paechter, Carrie. 2006. Masculine Femininities/Feminine Masculinities: Power, Identities and Gender. *Gender and Education* 18(3): 253–263.

Parsons, Katie. 2008. Get Over It! *Kerrang!*, 24 May, 30–31.

Patterson, Jamie. 2011. When Jane Likes Cannibal Corpse: Empowerment, Resistance, and Identity Construction Among Women in Death Metal. *Home of Metal Conference: Heavy Metal and Place*, Wolverhampton, UK, 1–4 September.

Patterson, Jamie. 2016. 'Getting My Soul Back': Empowerment Narratives and Identities Among Women in Extreme Metal in North Carolina. In *Global Metal Music and Culture: Current Directions in Metal Studies*, edited by Andy R. Brown, Karl Spracklen, Keith Kahn-Harris and Niall W. R. Scott, 245-260. London: Routledge.

Phipps, Alison, and Isabel Young. 2015. Neoliberalisation and 'Lad Cultures' in Higher Education. *Sociology* 49(2): 305–322.

Powell, Abigail, and Katherine J. C. Sang. 2015. Everyday Experiences of Sexism in Male-dominated Professions: A Bourdieusian Perspective. *Sociology* 49(5): 919–936.

Reay, Diane. 2001. 'Spice Girls', 'Nice Girls', 'Girlies', and 'Tomboys': Gender discourses, girls' cultures and femininities in the primary classroom. *Gender and Education* 13 (2):153-166.

Reiner, Rob. 1984. *This is Spinal Tap*. Embassy Pictures.

Resh Giwa. 2008. Letter to the Editor. *Kerrang!*, 7 June.

Riches, Gabrielle. 2011. Embracing the Chaos: Mosh Pits, Extreme Metal Music and Liminality. *Journal for Cultural Research* 15(3): 315–332.

———. 2015. Re-conceptualizing Women's Marginalization in Heavy Metal: A Feminist Post-structuralist Perspective. *Metal Music Studies* 1(2): 263–270.

Riches, Gabrielle, Brett Lashua, and Karl Spracklen. 2014. Female, Mosher, Transgressor: A 'Moshography' of Transgressive Practices within the Leeds Extreme Metal Scene. *IASPM@ Journal* 4(1): 87–100.

Rosenbaum, Jill Leslie, and Lorraine Prinsky. 1991. The presumption of influence: recent responses to popular music subcultures. *Crime and Delinquency* 37 (4):528-535.

Savigny, Heather, and Sam Sleight. 2015. Postfeminism and Heavy Metal in the United Kingdom: Sexy or Sexist? *Metal Music Studies* 1(3): 341–357.

Schippers, Mimi. 2002. *Rockin' Out of the Box: Gender Maneuvering in Alternative Hard Rock*. London: Rutgers University Press.

Shadrack, Jasmine. 2014. Femme-liminale: Corporeal Performativity in Death Metal. *Metal and Marginalisation: Gender, Race, Class and Other Implications for Hard Rock and Metal Symposim*, York, UK, 11 April.

Skeggs, Beverley. 1997. *Formations of Class & Gender: Becoming Respectable.* London: Sage.

Spracklen, Karl. 2015. 'To Holmgard ... and Beyond': Folk Metal Fantasies and Hegemonic White Masculinities. *Metal Music Studies* 1(3): 359–377.

Thornton, Sarah. 1995. *Club Cultures: Music, Media and Subcultural Capital.* Cambridge: Polity.

Tuchman, Gaye. 1978. The Symbolic Annihilation of Women. In *Hearth and Home: Images of Women in the Mass Media,* eds. Gaye Tuchman, Arlene Kaplan Daniels, James Walker Benét, and Foundation National Science, 3–38. New York: Oxford University.

Valentine, Gill, Lucy Jackson, and Lucy Mayblin. 2014. Ways of Seeing: Sexism the Forgotten Prejudice? *Gender, Place & Culture* 21(4): 401–414.

Vasan, Sonia. 2010. 'Den Mothers and Band Whores': Gender, Sex and Power in the Death Metal Scene. In *Heavy Fundametalisms: Music, Metal and Politics,* eds. Rosemary Lucy Hill, and Karl Spracklen, 69–78. Oxford: Inter-Disciplinary Press.

———. 2011. The Price of Rebellion: Gender Boundaries in the Death Metal Scene. *Journal for Cultural Research* 15(3): 333–349.

Walser, Robert. 1993. *Running with the Devil: Power, Gender, and Madness in Heavy Metal Music.* Hannover, NH: University Press of New England.

Weinstein, Deena. 2000 [1991]. *Heavy Metal: The Music and Its Culture.* Rev. ed. Boulder, CO: Da Capo Press.

Winwood, Ian. 2007. Hell Hath No Fury. *Kerrang!,* 29 September, 22–26.

Wittig, Monique. 1992. *The Straight Mind and Other Essays.* Boston: Beacon Press.

CHAPTER 7

The Gendered Experience of Music

Music and participation in music culture is experienced differently by women and men. This is not due to essential differences between the two groups. Rather, the experiences in our lives in sexist society and in associated sexist music cultures, both of which are gendered, contribute to our listenings, understandings and pleasures in music. These are not always felt to be, or experienced as, gendered, but gender nevertheless shapes the experience and therefore plays a part in determining our feelings. This is key in thinking about the role of the media, as the media perform important work in enabling fans to view themselves as part of a community with shared ideals and values. But the experience of reading music magazines differs for women and men: for women it promotes a narrow and limiting self-image that makes them vulnerable to denigration and exploitation. Gender and sexism are also key in considering the private and social experiences of musical engagement.

WOMEN FANS IN THE ROCK MEDIA

Davies (2001) maintains that the rock press represents women fans as groupies and as teenyboppers, but she provides a general overview without examples. My systematic analysis of the rock media's representation of women fans is therefore able to make solid claims about why it is important to consider *women* fans in distinction to more general studies of fans.

© The Editor(s) (if applicable) and The Author(s) 2016   159
R.L. Hill, *Gender, Metal and the Media*, Pop Music, Culture
and Identity, DOI 10.1057/978-1-137-55441-3_7

The mass media are an important part of the experience of musical engagement (although the level to which individuals do engage with the media differs) and therefore play a role in gendering the experience. *Kerrang!*'s letters pages represent women *as* fans, rarely as musicians, and usually in ways that show women as available for touching and potentially fucking. This is the start of a continuum of male sexual entitlement which proceeds to sexual violence (Kelly 1987). Groupie culture inherently makes women vulnerable to exploitation, as Karen Boyle (2015) has argued in relation to the crimes of Jimmy Savile. This book shows, however, that groupie culture and the associated crimes are not 'historical' as implied by the discourse around the UK's Operation Yewtree, which investigated crimes of 'historical' sexual abuse, many perpetrated by media stars from the 1970s and 1980s. No, it remains a fundamental part of the way that hard rock and metal is imagined. The 2013 conviction of Ian Watkins, lead singer of Lostprophets, for sexual offences, some of which involved fans, is a high profile example of this.

WOMEN FANS AND THE MYTH OF THE GROUPIE

The damage done by the representation of women fans as groupies is not restricted to sexual vulnerability, however. It also ignores any passionate engagement with the music (rather than musicians) that women may have, by favouring a one-dimensional assessment of their sexual desires and stereotypical interpretations of the motivations for their fandom. The representation of women's fandom relies upon ideas about women as guided by their bodies and emotions, and unable to make reasoned judgements. This assumption is based upon ideas about women as distinct from men and relies upon the discredited mind/body, man/woman binary. Sam De Boise (2015) also shows how understandings of the link between emotions and music are written upon gendered (and raced and classed) postulations; what I have argued here is that these assumptions have disadvantageous effects for musical engagement (particularly women's).

The characterisation of women as sexual participants, rather than as music lovers, creates a sense of the hard rock and metal genre as exclusively made for and important to men. As Wise argues, this kind of male-generated knowledge about the meanings of rock is only a partial account, but it is presented as 'an objective account of the world as it truly is' (1984, 396). Indeed, Barthes argues that this is how myth works: it applies particular meanings to things and presents them as common sense or natural

(2009 [1957]). Bringing these orthodoxies into dialogue with 'personal and subjective experiences' (Wise 1984, 391) means foregrounding women's experiences in order to question the masculinity of the genre.

None of the women I spoke to viewed themselves as groupies. The dominant representations in music media, therefore, stand in stark contrast to women's experiences of their own fandom. Furthermore, many of them were critical of the way in which the concept of the groupie was read onto female fans, whilst still others attacked the underlying sexism and implicit controlling of women's sexuality that underpinned the concept. Some of the younger women I spoke to sought to redefine the term, but still this was an attempt to rebut the hostility and malevolence that the figure of the groupie has received at the hands of the media. The impact of the myth was apparent in the ways that the women talked about their own fandom and their own sexuality in relation to the music, musicians and other fans. Some took care to stress that engagement with the music is the most precious kind of fandom and in doing so gave their own fandom this quality. Others protected their reputations as fans and *not* groupies: they stated that they would not wish to meet their favourite musicians or bands because they could not trust the performers' reactions. And some settled on a preference for bands who either actively spoke out against rock's sexism, or who were led by a woman. Although the majority of the women I spoke to did not wish to be associated with the figure of the groupie and took steps to avoid such a link, some women did discuss their attractions to musicians and to the warrior aesthetic itself. Furthermore, one woman described her passion for her favoured band in ways that meant her musical pleasure could not be extricated from her sensual desire, and vice versa.

These women did not describe experiences of sexual encounters with musicians. *Kerrang!*'s representation of women fans, therefore, did not reflect their feelings about their own fandom. Yet that did not mean that their fandom was entirely based on intellectual musical appreciation: they also found pleasure in their sexual attractions to musicians. When music fandom is based only on the sound of the songs, a model of fandom that excludes other sensual experiences (and also underplays hearing as a bodily sense) is evoked. This kind of musical pleasure relies upon binary thinking that demeans the body and sensual pleasure, in order to raise up the mind and spiritual pleasures. It is a dichotomy that through association elevates 'male' ways of knowing. This is part of a much broader feminist argument about the inherent problem of dualistic thinking that subordinates women. My interviewees' desire must not be dismissed as the 'wrong' kind of fandom. Women's fandom is multifaceted, it is not *only* a sensual experience; to think of musical pleasure as only intellectual is a limited understanding. By valuing women's erotic musical pleasure as well as their intellectual pleasure this dichotomy can be blurred. Importantly, this helps to rethink men's pleasure too, and to pay attention to more sensual and sexual experiences of musical engagement.

MASCULINITY AND WOMEN'S ROCK FANDOM

Subcultural and scenic accounts of music fans do not fully engage with their participants' musical engagement. When close attention is paid to fan experiences, it is clear that women's understandings of their fandom cannot be reduced to an either/or music/musicians relationship: their self-representations in relation to the figure of the groupie, to meeting musicians and to their erotic and musical sensations are too complex. However, consideration of musical appreciation allows for more nuanced understandings of the music itself, as well as women's position as fans in the imaginary community.

In describing the genre of heavy metal, women use language commonly associated with the genre, and that bears close resemblance to the myths of the warrior and of authenticity (for example, references to electric guitars and musical virtuosity); as Kahn-Harris (2007) argues, this kind of terminology is rooted in the culture of the genre. However, in only considering these elements, ideas about the genre as 'masculine' are reinforced and women's fandom can only be misunderstood as 'false consciousness' (as described by Wise 1984, 394, and Coates 1997, 51). It is in descriptions of love for favourite bands that fresh portrayals of women's fandom appear. My interviewees used language that signified transcendence and transportation, where the music allowed them to feel and to think beyond the limits of their immediate surroundings. They enunciated the ways in which they felt a shared experience with musicians, as though the music was able to transmit emotions to listeners and to communicate something of the musicians directly to them. The language of romance was used to describe listening to music as a fantastical adventure and an erotic moment. The women broke out of the strictures of a rock/pop divide and found their own lexicon of musical pleasure.

These kinds of depictions of hard rock and metal fandom challenge the notion of the genre as one invested in masculinity. This brings the focus to the pleasure that women find in the music they love. It is not restricted

to admiring the masculinity of the warrior myth, or to defending the stul-
tifying myth of authenticity. Whilst some significant thrill may be gained
from those mythical aspects, they are not the only aspects of women's hard
rock and metal fandom. Alongside the discussions of women's desire for
musicians, these other understandings of pleasure allow us to think about
musical appreciation in a more holistic sense, as it engages the intellect,
the body and the imagination.

Fast writes that

> It is much easier always to begin from the premise that the music and images
> are sexist and macho because not only is it a comforting notion that this
> kind of semiotic stability might exist, but it simultaneously locks out the
> dangerous possibility of woman as sexual and powerful. (1999, 294)

This partly explains why women's fandom is reduced to a singular concern—sex with musicians—and why the figure of the groupie is maligned
rather than celebrated for sexual autonomy. When Des Barres (2007)
argues that she was doing exactly what she wanted in her groupie activities, and that those actions were informed by her passion for the music *as
well as* the musicians, she is asserting a formidable active presence. The
women I spoke to were not interested in pursuing sex with band members (although the idea of the sex itself was appealing to some), but nor
were their engagements with the music limited to appreciations of intellectual pleasures. Indeed, what they gained from the music had more to
do with giving them a sense of freedom, of companionship and of fantasy
or romance.

RETHINKING GENDER IN HARD ROCK AND METAL

My interviewees *did* use language that is embedded in the myths communicated by *Kerrang!*. This language reinforces the myths and so plays
a part in shoring up understandings of the genre as 'naturally' masculine.
However, the women also expressed themselves in ways that went beyond
the ideologically expected terminology, and that exposed the inadequacy of
understandings of the genre as masculine: there is much more to women's
musical pleasure than those elements culturally coded as masculine. This
new consideration highlights how calling the genre 'masculine' is meaningless and misjudged because it relies on strict ideas of about the nature of
masculinity and femininity: gender is socially ascribed. The community's

male dominance and denigration of the feminine are maintained when gendered meanings are ascribed to musical qualities, instruments and ways of enjoying. Furthermore, the music has many meanings which go beyond those that have been called 'masculine', including some which are labelled 'feminine'. When the 'masculine' qualities alone are considered, women are not imagined as full participants in the community, nor are they seen as engaging with the music in ways worthy of being taken seriously. Their fandom can only be read as existing against the grain, as breaking boundaries by listening to 'men's' music. They are always to be considered exceptional and their presence questionable. In this sense, women can never be perceived as hard rock and metal fans in the same ways as men because they are always only transgressive and listening in spite of their gender. Understanding women's pleasure in rock music means rethinking the orthodoxy that 'hears' the genre as masculine. It means accepting the messy ambiguities in musical engagement—both women's and men's.

Rethinking understandings of hard rock and metal as a masculine genre enables a more sophisticated understanding of women's fandom and of the genre itself. It is not quintessentially masculine: it is much more interesting than that. Hesmondhalgh argues that in order to give a 'richer account of the role of culture in people's lives' (2012, 366) understanding the emotional experience of music is vital. Feminist metal scholars are increasingly working to understand the pleasures and emotions associated with metal fandom and paying particular attention to gender (e.g., Patterson 2011; Overell 2014; Riches 2014). This book is part of that endeavour and indicates that there is yet much to learn about emotional engagement with music. However, what Hesmondhalgh does not consider is the ways in which music appreciation is not limited to an aural experience but can also include other sensual and imaginative encounters. And importantly, music is always experienced in a social context, and this differs across the gender divide and is not immune to sexism.

WOMEN AND MALE-DOMINATED CULTURE

Hard rock and metal may be experienced as less sexist than the mainstream, and it may provide moments that feel genderless; however, it remains a sexist environment but is increasingly being challenged by the genre's participants. Understandings of women's cultural engagement tend to focus on engagement with media forms marked as 'feminine' (e.g., Radway 1984; Ang 1985; Baym 1999; Franiuk and Scherr 2012; Burwell

2014). This habilitation of women's culture as valuable of study, and as more complex than typical derogatory assertions of such media forms as 'rubbish', is extremely important (Gill 2007). It enables feminists to challenge sexist essentialist assumptions about women's interests and intellectual capacities and to move towards an understanding of how patriarchal ideology works through pleasure. Understandings of women's cultural engagement with male-dominated media forms are less well developed. A great deal of research into women's experiences in male-dominated workplaces and professions, and to a lesser extent sport, has been undertaken. But the neglect of this area of culture is perhaps symptomatic of the focus on the reappraisal of women's culture.

In popular music studies, work tends to focus on the experiences of women as musical participants, that is as women making music in male-dominated scenes (Cohen 1997; Leonard 2007 and others). With regards non-music making participants, Leblanc's (1999) account of the experiences of women as non-musical participants in male-dominated music environments stands out. However, Leblanc's use of subcultural theory, as I discussed earlier, limits her account to only thinking about participation as a form of resistance to constrictive normative femininity for young women. This is an exciting conclusion prompting a tantalising vision in the reader: if femininity is getting you down, just be a punk! Of course, as this book shows, participation in male-dominated music groups is not as straightforward as that. Nor is it simply a matter of feeling oppressed within the music group (though this may be the case for some women) or of straightforwardly accepting the cultural norms and media representations—the ideology—of hard rock and metal. My interviewees actively negotiated the representations both of women fans and of the music itself in order to ensure that their experiences of participation in the imaginary community were safe and, most importantly, pleasurable. Their experiences at hard rock and metal events occurred in the context of their non-metal lives, and they made sense of the sexisms they experienced—or didn't experience—in light of this.

This says something about women's participation in men's culture more broadly, enabling new perspectives on why women become involved, how they negotiate any prejudice that they may encounter and why they remain. Even if it is less frequent than elsewhere in their lives, sexism does impact upon women as they engage in hard rock and metal culture, and the ideology which celebrates masculinity and disparages femininity is damaging. Vasan's (2011) theory of cost reduction highlights some of the work that women do to minimise the impact of metal misogyny, but my interviewees spoke of freeing moments in which they could forget their gender in their own, and the surrounding men's, pleasure in the music. *Pace* Vasan, hard rock and metal is not all work for women. Some of the women I spoke to did not accept the ideological position of hard rock and metal culture and some confronted it overtly. Others raised a challenge through their practices of meaning making in the music they listened to and in their choices of music. Although these may be only small resistances to the juggernaut of rock's supposed masculinity they are nevertheless important. On the other hand, some of the practices by which sexism was resisted were not confrontational or challenging; they could be interpreted as ultimately supporting hard rock and metal's masculinity-valorising ideology, as Vasan's work suggests. Yet such a position does not take into account the difficulties that women face when they do encounter negative behaviour from their peers—and interpret it as such. When music is a leisure pursuit, and attending events done for the purpose of fun, who wants to get into an argument when it is easier—because it is normal—to brush off the offence? When your physical safety is at risk from the gendered use of space, who is prepared to mount a solo assault on the pit? When society describes angry interpretations of 'banter' as overreacting, what language is there to challenge this? When women are already in the minority, how can women feel comfortable and accepted if they set out to challenge the misogyny they see around them? Understanding some of the complexity of women's participation in male-dominated hard rock and metal is therefore helpful in suggesting the kinds of questions that need to be asked about other engagements with culture.

What Next for Hard Rock and Metal?

As I write 'metalgate' rumbles on (Clifford-Napoleone 2015a). Discussion of sexism and racism is now happening in the genre's mainstream. Journalists, bloggers and academics argue that metal needs to consider its white male privilege; others contest this point. A great deal of anger is evident on both sides of the argument. Accusations of discrimination are viewed as false by (mostly) white men who pinpoint various women in bands to prove their point. Women and other men angrily describe their own and their friends' experiences of being harassed at gigs. The debate is taken very seriously and there are fears of women becoming more involved and metal therefore losing its status as a safe space in which men can do 'dumb shit' (Corey Taylor quoted in Wise et al. 2005), and of femininity permeating and 'diluting' (Gruzelier 2007) the aesthetic qualities. But metal exists in sexist, racist society and it is not immune to the ideological prejudices of the parent culture (Brown 2009). To argue that metal is not sexist or racist is to argue that metal is a utopian arena that has somehow magically overcome those problems without actively trying to. Brill (2008) argues that in goth the ideology of genderlessness masks sexist practices. Within metal, the myth of equality does similar work, allowing sexism to prevail and inhibiting challenges or resistance to it.

Identifying metal's sexism is crucial if the genre is ever to move towards the mythical realm of equality that it is already thought to inhabit. The next step—striving to achieve equality—is much harder. Haraway (1991) posits that the figure of the cyborg and science fiction writing are a route out of the morass of dualisms that control our lives. Hard rock and metal's historical and continued interest in technology, futures, science fiction, monsters and cyborgs offers a cultural opportunity to provide new visions of what a cyborg future might be like, one that embraces visions of worlds without gender.

In order to begin to build these new cultural visions, lovers of hard rock and metal must face up to the ways in which the genre continues to maintain gender as a divisory organising concept; then it can address its sexisms. My recommendations here are given with love and a sense that with many metal participants' interest in science fiction, envisaging a new future can be a welcome endeavour.

1. Metal needs to move away from its reification of masculinity and its link with authenticity. This could be done through a rethinking of metal's masculinity: it is drag, it is absurd (in the best possible way) and it is to be played for laughs. Clifford-Napoleone's book (2015b) argues that masculinity in metal is a mirage: an acceptance of this (lovingly sketched) position would do wonders for the genre.

2. By accepting masculinity as a performance, and one which is therefore not attached to male bodies, hard rock and metal musicians can find a way to create music and imagery that retains a strong, powerful sound, without relying on the exscription of the feminine in either absence or misogynistic lyrics or artwork. There are musicians who are already doing this, and the rise of new gender identities that disavow the gender binary offer some hope that the social and cultural understanding exists more generally.

3. Women need to be accepted as musicians. This would require broader musical changes, and these are happening, albeit slowly. Women need to be seen more in the metal mainstream and to be taking more diverse musical roles. They need to be allowed to be mediocre and to make mistakes, just as men are, without this being read as (for example) 'women can't play guitar'. And they need to be able to wear and do what they want without being read as sexually available.

4. Representation of women fans should focus less on relationships with men, acknowledging their active roles and their musical appreciation. A move away from photographs of young women fans with older men musicians' arms around them would be a good start— perhaps through the use of in-gig photographs rather than pre- or post-gig.

5. Those men who support inclusivity should actively campaign towards making it a reality. A Metal Hates Sexism festival or tour might be one way of doing this.

6. A feminist metal movement that uses the snarls and violent aesthetic of metal to shout its demands should emerge. Some bands already exist. They need to be connected, to be heard more widely, to be higher profile and to be actively supported by more well-known bands.

Already some of these things are happening and are to be celebrated. Nevertheless, the mainstream media need to play a greater role in highlighting these exciting changes and in supporting women's endeavours to become full participants.

And what of the structural problems that underpin some of the equalities women face in music participation? Well, metal fans have always liked to see themselves as oppositional; in actively working towards a more inclusive culture, hard rock and metal can be presented as different and forward-thinking.

REFERENCES

Ang, Ien. 1985. *Watching Dallas: Soap Opera and the Melodramatic Imagination*. London: Methuen.

Barthes, Roland. 2009 [1957]. *Mythologies*. Translated by Annette Lavers. London: Vintage.

Baym, Nancy K. 1999. *Tune in, Log on: Soaps, Fandom, and On-line Community*. Thousand Oaks, CA: Sage Publications.

Boyle, Karen. 2015. Hiding in Plain Sight: Sexism as Disguise in the Jimmy Savile Case. *FWSA Biennial Conference*, Leeds, 9–11 September.

Brill, Dunja. 2008. *Goth Culture: Gender, Sexuality and Style*. Oxford: Berg.

Brown, Andy R. 2009. 'Girls Like Metal, Too!': Female Reader's Engagement with the Masculinist Ethos of the Tabloid Metal Magazine. *Heavy Metal and Gender International Congress*, Cologne University of Music and Dance, 10 October.

Burwell, Catherine. 2014. You Know You Love Me. *Feminist Media Studies* 15(2): 306–323.

Clifford-Napoleone, Amber. 2015a. Living in the Margins: Metal's Self-in-reflection. *Metal Music Studies* 1(3): 379–384.

———. 2015b. *Queerness in Heavy Metal Music: Metal Bent*. Abingdon: Routledge.

Coates, Norma. 1997. (R)evolution Now? Rock and the Political Potential of Gender. In *Sexing the Groove: Popular Music and Gender*, ed. Sheila Whiteley, 50–64. Abingdon: Routledge.

Cohen, Sara. 1997. Men Making a Scene: Rock Music and the Production of Gender. In *Sexing the Groove: Popular Music and Gender*, ed. Sheila Whiteley, 17–36. Abingdon: Routledge.

Davies, Helen. 2001. All Rock and Roll is Homosocial: The Representation of Women in the British Rock Music Press. *Popular Music* 20(3): 301–319.

De Boise, Sam. 2015. *Men, Masculinity, Music and Emotions*. New York: Palgrave Macmillan.

Des Barres, Pamela, ed. 2007. *Let's Spend the Night Together: Backstage Secrets of Rock Muses and Supergroupies*. London: Helter Skelter Publishing.

Fast, Susan. 1999. Rethinking Issues of Gender and Sexuality in Led Zeppelin: A Woman's View of Pleasure and Power in Hard Rock. *American Music* 17(3): 245–299.

Franiuk, Renae, and Samantha Scherr. 2012. 'The Lion Fell in Love with the Lamb'. *Feminist Media Studies* 13(1): 14–28.

Gill, Rosalind. 2007. *Gender and the Media*. Cambridge: Polity.

Gruzelier, Jonathan. 2007. Moshpit Menace and Masculine Mayhem. In *Oh Boy! Masculinities and Popular Music*, ed. Freya Jarman-Ivens, 59–75. New York: Routledge.

Haraway, Donna Jeanne. 1991. A Cyborg Manifesto: Science, Technology, and Socialist-feminism in the Late Twentieth Century. In *Simians, Cyborgs, and Women: The Reinvention of Nature*, 149–182. New York: Routledge.

Hesmondhalgh, David. 2012. Towards a Political Aesthetics of Music. In *The Cultural Study of Music: A Critical Introduction*, eds. Martin Clayton, Trevor Herbert, and Richard Middleton, 364–374. New York and Abingdon: Routledge.

Kahn-Harris, Keith. 2007. *Extreme Metal: Music and Culture on the Edge*. Oxford: Berg.

Kelly, Liz. 1987. The Continuum of Sexual Violence. In *Women, Violence and Social Control*, eds. Jalna Hanmer, and Mary Maynard, 46–60. Basingstoke: Macmillan.

Leblanc, Lauraine. 1999. *Pretty in Punk: Girls' Gender Resistance in a Boys' Subculture*. New Brunswick, NJ: Rutgers University Press.

Leonard, Marion. 2007. *Gender in the Music Industry: Rock, Discourse and Girl Power*. Aldershot: Ashgate.

Overell, Rosemary. 2014. *Affective Intensities in Extreme Music Scenes: Cases from Australia and Japan*. Basingstoke: Palgrave Macmillan.

Patterson, Jamie. 2011. When Jane Likes Cannibal Corpse: Empowerment, Resistance, and Identity Construction Among Women in Death Metal. *Home of Metal Conference: Heavy Metal and Place*, Wolverhampton, UK, 1–4 September.

Radway, Janice A. 1984. *Reading the Romance: Women, Patriarchy, and Popular Literature*. Chapel Hill: University of North Carolina Press.

Riches, Gabrielle. 2014. "Throwing the Divide to the Wind": Rethinking Extreme Metal's Masculinity Through Female Metal Fans' Embodied Experiences in Moshpit Practices. *IASPM UK & Ireland Conference*, Cork, Ireland, 12–14 September.

Vasan, Sonia. 2011. The Price of Rebellion: Gender Boundaries in the Death Metal Scene. *Journal for Cultural Research* 15(3): 333–349.

Wise, Jessica Joy, Sam Dunn, and Scot McFadyen. 2005. *Metal: A Headbanger's Journey*. Seville Pictures; Warner Home Video.

Wise, Sue. 1984. Sexing Elvis. In *On Record: Rock, Pop, & the Written Word*, eds. Simon Frith, and Andrew Goodwin, 390–398. London: Routledge.

Appendix: Biographies of Participants

Aime*

Aime, aged 16, was my youngest interviewee. She is the younger sister of Gwen and Bert, and we met at a Yorkshire comic shop café. She described herself as white, English and upper middle class. She declared herself to be an atheist who believed in science. Like her sisters she lived in a Yorkshire city and was currently unemployed. On the day of the interview, Aime was trialling the wearing of high heel shoes. Aime's passion was for Avenged Sevenfold, and she also liked Britney Spears, My Chemical Romance and Green Day. She said she was 'definitely' a metal fan and that,

> I always have been—I never kind of knew it, but when I was younger I kind of grew up with a girl called Allanna. She was all—she was a fan of it and she kind of almost made me a fan of it and it's just stuck. (Aime)

Alexa

Alexa was a 20-year old psychology student from a large Yorkshire town. She described herself as white and atheist and said she had no class identity. She was a *Kerrang!* reader and named her current favourite band as Leftover Crack, and she also discussed Taking Back Sunday, Black Flag and Adam Lambert. She had played keyboards when at school and wanted

© The Editor(s) (if applicable) and The Author(s) 2016
R.L. Hill, *Gender, Metal and the Media*, Pop Music, Culture and Identity, DOI 10.1057/978-1-137-55441-3

to take up drums. Her parents instead bought her a guitar, but this was not a success.

ARIA

My interview with Aria was spontaneous, and so I did not have an interview schedule with me. Nevertheless we covered most of the topics on the schedule. Aria was a death metal guitarist who had performed across the country, and her band had had a recording contract. In this she was different to my other interviewees whose primary link to metal was through fandom: Aria's was through fandom and musicianship. Aria was aged 35, lived in the Midlands and was a University lecturer about to embark on a PhD in gender studies.

BERT

Bert is the elder sister of Aime and was aged 22 at the time of the interview. She is white, British and atheist, and called herself middle class. She worked as a telephone helpdesk operator. The main band she talked about was Avenged Sevenfold, and she also mentioned My Chemical Romance and Fall Out Boy. The interview took place in the same café of the comic shop as the interview with Aime. Bert confessed herself shy and brought her sister and friends to the interview for support, although they sat separately so that the interview could be conducted privately. Luckily, she felt at her ease during the interview so her shyness did not manifest as taciturnity.

CAROL

Carol was 54 at the time of the interview, had no religion and was a working class accountant. She discussed High On Fire, but she had been a fan of rock and heavy metal since her teenage years, having been introduced to the genre by a friend who took her to see Ten Years After, Blodwyn Pig and Stone The Crows in concert. She was a frequent and affectionate contributor to an online stoner rock forum and used the site to make new friends. Carol was particularly embedded in the community, having donated money to help others attend festivals and, now unemployed, being helped in return.

DOLLY

Dolly and I sat outside a bar in a small town on the outskirts of a major Yorkshire city. She was on her lunch break from her job as a university administrator. At the time of the interview she was 38 and had two teen-age sons. She is white, English, working class and agnostic. Her favourite band was LostProphets, and she also talked about Metallica and Foo Fighters. She was 'definitely' a metal fan, although she had been an indie fan. She had become disillusioned with indie:

> I started off, kind of, I was an indie fan. And then I realised that that wasn't enough and it became, there were too many bands like The Hoosiers who thought that they were indie, and it was too 'oh for goodness sake here we go singing pathetic songs', and then I moved on to things like your Foo Fighters, and I quite liked emo music, that sort of thing. (Dolly)

She was keen to make new friends to attend gigs with; in the meantime her main gigging companions were her teenage son and her brother-in-law.

ÉOWYN

Éowyn was 19 at the time of the interview and originally from a large town in the home counties. A psychology student at the time, she is white and British, and described herself as a Christian, working class to middle class, and a 'soft metal' fan. She did not have a favourite band but was just starting to listen to Rise Against, and so we discussed them. She also liked the music of Avenged Sevenfold and Within Temptation. Éowyn had played guitar in a band with her school friends, playing 'wizard rock'—a genre based on Harry Potter.

GWEN

Gwen, the eldest sister of Bert and Aime, was a 28-year old white, British bank mediator at the time of the interview who described herself as having no class identity, but class pride due to her 'ridiculously working class background'. She was 'staunchly atheist', believed in science and was spiritually Wiccan. The band she discussed with me was Panic! At The Disco, but she also discussed Avenged Sevenfold, My Chemical Romance and Fall Out

Boy. She said that the names of bands or songs were never something that particularly interested her, and this had caused her to be snubbed by a fellow student and metal fan in her friendship group at university. This fellow student was the only other woman in her friendship group. The interview location was in the café of a Yorkshire city comic shop.

HAZEL

Hazel was 26 at the time of the interview and studying for an MA in gender studies. She lived in a city in the North East, although the interview was conducted in a Yorkshire city. Hazel was white. Unfortunately, the interview was conducted under difficult circumstances in a noisy environment and with time pressures that meant I was unable to gather class, nationality, or religious data. The band she discussed was Tura Satana, although she also loved the Manic Street Preachers and named them as her favourites.

JEANETTE

I interviewed Jeanette and Carol together in a quiet pub in a city in the South of England, where they both lived. Parts of the interview needed to be re-done due to a malfunctioning recording device. I interviewed them separately and then together. Jeanette was 36 at the time of the interview. She is white and had recently received her British citizenship, having been born and raised in South Africa. She described herself as a working class atheist and named her favourite band as Red Sparowes. However, she discussed a large number of other bands, some of which were Tool, Black Sabbath and Cult of Luna. Jeanette had used a stoner rock forum to find a friend to accompany her on a road trip in the US, and she had later married this person.

JENNY

Jenny lived in a town in the South of England and was part of the same group of music-fan friends as Jeanette and Carol. She was, at the time of the interview, 35, and we met in a small park in a city in the South. She is a white, British, atheist, a lab manager who described herself as middle to working class. Jenny tended to give short answers and was not particularly garrulous. The band she wanted to discuss was Slabdragger, and we also talked about Grand Magus, Deep Purple and Kylesa, amongst other bands.

JESSICA

Jessica, at the time of the interview, was 19 and a psychology student. She too is white and British, and she called herself working class and atheist. Her hometown is a market town in Lincolnshire. She positioned herself as a metal fan but saw that this was not straightforward:
[Rosemary] Would you call yourself a metal fan?

[Jessica] I would yeah, some people would consider me one of the rock fans, […] I think it's, they're sort of intertwined and they sort of, there is a lot of overlap in the two, whereas like, I did like Meat Loaf and things like that, but I'd consider that more rock than metal, but I listen to both really. (Jessica)

The main band she discussed with me was Avenged Sevenfold, and she also mentioned Within Temptation and My Chemical Romance. Jessica was a singer and guitarist, and was thinking about joining a new band.

KAREN

Karen was a 36 year old Rammstein fan. She is a white, middle class, British, market analyst, who described herself as atheist. The interview was conducted in a side room at a Yorkshire university where she had been employed. Her enthusiasm for Rammstein was so contagious that I subsequently booked tickets to see them on their tour, something I would not have done had I not met Karen. I was not disappointed. She also professed a love for Metallica and Nine Inch Nails and frequented a local goth nightclub.

KIMBERLEY

Kimberley was 30 at the time of the interview and lived in a city in the North West of England, where I interviewed her in her home. She defined herself as middle class, white, atheist and European. She worked as an administrator. The band she enthused about was Young Guns, but this was one band amongst many: she also talked about Lostprophets, Fall

Out Boy and Green Day as current favourites, and Pantera and Slayer as older favourites. The Wildhearts were her all-time favourite, and she also loved Metallica and Guns N' Roses. She had a best friend in another city, and together they would go to as many gigs as possible, often staying overnight in other cities.

LAURA

Laura was 29. A white Finnish national, she lived in a Yorkshire city and had recently completed a PhD in English Literature. She was seeking work as a lecturer in the UK. The band she discussed with me was My Chemical Romance (her favourite), and she also professed a liking for U2 and Queen. Her introduction to My Chemical Romance was through the slash fiction culture around bands (bandom) such as My Chemical Romance and Fall Out Boy. Laura did not call herself a metal fan, but described some of what she liked as heavy metal:

[Rosemary] So you wouldn't call yourself a heavy metal fan then?

[Laura] No.
[Rosemary] Rock music?

[Laura] Yeah, and heavy metal would be a part of that, but the particular bands that I listen to I wouldn't call heavy metal. I think with My Chemical Romance that [...] the guitarist plays like he's in a heavy metal band regardless of what anyone else is doing. (Laura)

The interview took place in hotel bar on a busy shopping day before Christmas, meaning that the recording was not clear in places.

PATTI

Patti is white and British and was 29 at the time of the interview. She was a special needs teacher in a Yorkshire city who described herself as middle class and atheist. Her favourite band that featured in *Kerrang!* was a progressive rock/metal band named Coheed and Cambria, but she also declared a preference for Neil Young. Despite enjoying the music of a number of metal bands (Led Zeppelin, Tenacious D, Rammstein) she did not call herself a metal fan:

I would describe myself as a fan of some classic rock that errs towards metal. [...] I would consider myself to be a fan of many different kinds of music. (Patti)

The interview took place in my home, and Patti seemed at first to feel somewhat uncomfortable and shy about being recorded, although this eased towards the end of the interview.

RUBY

Ruby and I met in a Yorkshire city's convent's café, so the interview was conducted over a background of singing nuns. Ruby, a white, British civil servant, was 35 at the time of the interview and described herself as agnostic. She did not know what her class identity was. The band she discussed with me was Killswitch Engage. She had first started listening to metal as a teenager, to bands such as Skid Row and Guns N' Roses. Indeed, she and her friend had seen Guns N' Roses in their heyday, had met guitarist Slash's brother and been invited to party backstage with the band. They refused as Ruby had to sit a GCSE exam the following day.

SALLY

Sally was the friend with whom Ruby saw Guns N' Roses. She lived in a town in the Midlands, but the interview was conducted in a café in a Yorkshire city, as Sally was en route to a music festival in the North York Moors. She is white, British and Christian, and employed at the time as a charity manager. She described herself as between working and middle class. She did not have a favourite band so we discussed those bands that she had been listening to recently: Limp Bizkit, Skindred, Metallica.

SUSAN

I met Susan, a white, British retiree, at her home in a Yorkshire city. She was 69 at the time and felt that in her life she had moved from working to middle class. She described herself as an atheist or humanist. We discussed Led Zeppelin and Pink Floyd (her favourite band), and also a number of other bands such as Deep Purple, Black Sabbath and Rush. She did not consider herself a 'proper fan':

Erm, what is a proper fan? I think proper fans, well if they've got more musical knowledge than I have, will talk about particular riffs and particular tones of drums and which particular drums are being played, erm, and how one artist supports another, and I tend not to hear it like that. (Susan)

*All names have been changed.

Index[1]

---

[1] Note: Page numbers with "n" denote notes.

© The Editor(s) (if applicable) and The Author(s) 2016
R.L. Hill, *Gender, Metal and the Media*, Pop Music, Culture
and Identity, DOI 10.1057/978-1-137-55441-3

Printed by Printforce, the Netherlands